ALVIN EICOFF

Direct Marketing Through Broadcast Media

TV, Radio, Cable, Infomercials, Home Shopping, and More

Printed on recyclable paper

658.872
EICOFF
c.1

NTC Business Books

a division of *NTC Publishing Group* • Lincolnwood, Illinois USA

Library of Congress Cataloging-in-Publication Data

Eicoff, Alvin
    Direct marketing through broadcast media : TV, radio, cable,
infomercials, home shopping & more / Alvin Eicoff.
        p.   cm.
    Includes bibliographical references and index.
    ISBN 0-8442-3518-0
    1. Direct marketing.   2. Broadcast advertising.   3. Advertising
media planning.   I. Title.
HF5415. 126.E33   1995
658.8'72—dc20   94–39786
                                                                             CIP

Published by NTC Business Books, a division of NTC Publishing Group
4255 West Touhy Avenue
Lincolnwood (Chicago), Illinois 60646-1975, U.S.A.
© 1995, 1988 by NTC Publishing Group.
All rights reserved. No part of this book may be reproduced, stored
in a retrieval system, or transmitted in any form or by any means,
electronic, mechanical, photocopying, recording or otherwise, without
the prior permission of NTC Publishing Group.
Manufactured in the United States of America.

5 6 7 8 9 BC 9 8 7 6 5 4 3 2 1

Contents

CHAPTER 5

Creating Dynamic Radio Commercials   97

CHAPTER 6

A Look to the Future of Broadcast Direct Marketing: Cable TV and Interactive Technologies   115

CHAPTER 7

Support Advertising and Trade Support Marketing   132

CHAPTER 8

Test Marketing   153

CHAPTER 9

After the Test Campaign: Handling Customer Response   162

CHAPTER 10

The Magic Number Concept: The Mathematics of Broadcast Direct Marketing   172

CHAPTER 11

Record Keeping   194

Preface

As the world enters the early phases of the Communication Revolution, it presents the greatest opportunity for the entrepreneur to make a fortune with one good creative idea and a minimum of capital. The guidelines for the essential characteristics and the various methods available for launching a product or service with a minimal capital investment are clearly outlined in this book and are being successfully used every day.

Many products and services are cyclical and one can often become successful looking into the archives of previous winners. This is being done by those who have re-introduced auto polish and spot removing products, record packages, memory courses, kitchen gadgets; all of which were previously successfully aired in almost the same format. The major difference usually is only in the price increase. As set forth in the subsequent pages of this book, the only characteristic of a product that is absolutely essential is the mark-up or profit margin. If the spread between cost and selling is not sufficient, then even the greatest ideas and presentations will fall.

As more television and cable channels enter the air, and new methods of electronic communications the opportunity for the small investor to become a Horatio Alger, but in a much shorter period, becomes easier and faster. It is essential to understand that in the early days of all electronic media, it was the small direct marketing entrepreneur that kept the new media afloat until it was recognized and accepted as a viable advertising medium by the general advertising and marketing community. For example, the large advertisers refused to recognize cable until it had about 80% penetration of the designated areas in which they claimed coverage. Of course, spotty national coverage was of no value to either the local or regional advertiser, so the direct marketer, who was not concerned with ratings or penetration, but only with ability of the media to produce results, sustained cable in its infancy. The same will be true as more and more new interactive marketing concepts enter the "super highway" race.

What does this mean to the direct marketer? It opens a new world of opportunity to present inspirational ideas for products and services either at minimal rates or on a guarantee or PI basis which completely eliminates the capital investment risks for media purchases.

In the next 200 pages, you will be given the history of electronic mail order; taken step-by-step through the product or service evaluation process; explained the various ways and means of negotiating media terms and rates; explained the logistics or order processing; shown the basic forms that are needed for each step and given case histories of successful entrepreneur who have risen from a basic idea to millions in less than a year.

The ingredient most important to your success is *motivation.* Nothing will ever happen until you decide that there is a future in electronic direct marketing for you! ■

CHAPTER ONE

The Basics of Broadcast Direct Marketing

This book is about a specialized area of marketing: broadcast direct marketing. Before examining this area, let's first look at broadcast direct marketing within a marketing context. How does it fit into the marketing picture?

WHAT DOES BROADCAST DIRECT MARKETING INVOLVE?

Every year, a corporation formulates a marketing plan. That plan contains overall corporate marketing objectives: sales, market share, profits, and so on. To achieve these objectives, a corporation creates strategies within the plan. These strategies can range from universal distribution to franchising to direct marketing.

Direct marketing is the strategy that is critically important to readers of this book. In a nutshell, direct marketing is the direct sale of a product or service to consumers or businesses. As differentiated from many other forms of marketing, direct marketing demands immediate, measurable results.

Direct marketing techniques include direct mail, matchbooks, telemarketing, door-to-door selling, party plans/seminars, take-ones/handouts, and package inserts. Broadcast direct marketing is also an integral technique. As the name implies, broadcast direct marketing requires the use of television or radio. Throughout this book, references to *direct marketing* are to be taken as meaning broadcast direct marketing and not the general category of direct marketing. Exhibit 1–1 clearly illustrates broadcast direct marketing's place in an overall marketing framework.

In recent years, broadcast direct marketing has become an important element in many corporations' marketing mix. A major misconception about this direct marketing strategy is that it's used only by small, entrepreneurial companies. Nothing could be further from the truth.

Today, broadcast direct marketing is used by a cross section of *Fortune* 500 corporations to achieve a wide variety of objectives. To give you an understanding of its flexibility and broad-based appeal, let's review a sampling of broadcast direct marketers.

American Express uses television direct response commercials to generate leads for its travel division's vacation packages. These commercials have been enormously successful, creating thousands of new leads each time a flight of commercials airs.

Most large magazines employ 2-minute direct response commercials to solicit new subscribers, frequently featuring a premium in the commercial as an incentive for subscribing. *Time, TV Guide, Wall Street Journal, Playboy, Psychology Today,* and *Sports Illustrated* are just some of the magazines using this strategy.

Companies offering financial services—from commodities brokers to investment houses—use broadcast direct marketing as a lead-generation vehicle. Direct marketers include Smith Barney, Merrill Lynch, and Bache.

Many catalogers have recently tested television as a method of getting their catalogs into the hands of the buying public, and they have had excellent results. Spiegel is one of the most well-known catalog companies in this category. Pepperidge Farm is a packaged goods company that has used broadcast direct marketing for its catalog. Some direct marketers offer their catalogs free to callers, and others charge a nominal price to qualify respondents.

Other major broadcast direct marketers include such phone companies at MCI, AT&T, and Sprint and such record clubs as RCA and Columbia. Insurance companies are another major industry that has made a strong commitment to broadcast direct marketing. Insurance marketers, such as National Liberty, Allstate, Mutual of Omaha, and CNA have created highly effective television offers targeting specific groups: insurance of senior citizens and home-replacement insurance for homeowners. Still other broadcast direct marketers include hotels and motels (Hyatt, MGM Grand, Hilton, Holiday Inn) and motor clubs (Shell, Sears, AAA). Finally, a number of companies have found broadcast direct marketing to be an important recruiting tool. Avon, for instance, uses direct response television commercials to recruit salespeople.

EXHIBIT 1-1
Broadcast Direct Marketing's Role in the Marketing Plan

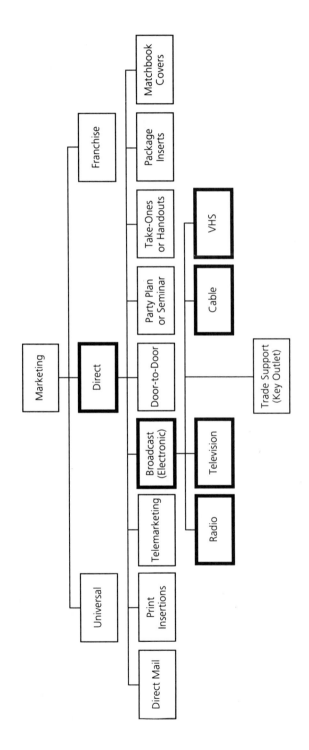

CUSTOMERS, DIRECT MARKETERS, AND AGENCIES

Regardless of the type of direct marketing in which one becomes involved, it is essential to understand the basic characteristics of the key players in the field: the mail order buyer, the direct marketer, and the direct marketing advertising agency.

The Direct Marketing Customer

Mail order buyers are divided into two categories: the true mail order buyer and the pseudo mail order buyer.

The True Mail Order Buyer	**The Pseudo Mail Order Buyer**
1. Enjoys buying products through the mail.	1. Emphatically denies being a mail order buyer.
2. Respects other mail order buyers.	2. Has little regard for anyone who buys through the mail.
3. Looks forward to receiving daily mail.	3. Believes anything in the mailbox other than bills and personal mail is junk.
4. Is convinced that most direct marketers offer unique products, good values, and a convenient shopping method.	4. Believes most direct marketers are dishonest and unrealiable and overprice their merchandise.
5. Desires detailed, descriptive mail order copy presented in a clear, complete, and straightforward manner.	5. Refuses to read detailed and long copy and is convinced that lengthy letters, long commercials, and copy-filled ads are written by idiots.
6. Will buy almost anything by mail if the presentation is motivating.	6. Avoids buying anything by mail, no matter how convincing the copy or how desirable product.
7. Classifies anything delivered by mail, UPS, or Federal Express as a mail order purchase.	7. Classifies subscription purchases, catalog orders from prestigious merchants, book club memberships, applications for credit cards, etc., as *non–mail order purchases.*

8. Often refuses to buy by mail when the information on the product is not sufficiently or clearly presented.

8. Can sometimes be motivated to buy by mail (as in the case of book and recipe clubs) when the presentation allows for a non–mail order purchase rationale.

The Direct Marketer

The fact that an advertiser asks for some type of mail or phone reply does not necessarily make that advertiser a true direct marketer. Many advertisers merely include a mailing address or phone number with little or no expectation about the ratio of replies to the advertising expenditure. Direct marketers are divided into two categories: the true direct marketer and the pseudo direct marketer.

The Direct Marketer

1. Has an open-ended advertising budget limited only by the ability of the advertising to produce results at a profitable level or by product availability.

2. Sets forth a maximum advertising allowable per sale that allows for a reasonable profit.

3. Will not renew any advertising media that does not deliver sales within the predefined advertising allowable.

4. Works with a sophisticated program that tracks every customer and every order.

5. Demands a continuous program of post-analysis.

6. Uses customer names and histories as a database for increasing profits; often adds to profits by marketing the data-base information.

The Pseudo Direct Marketer

1. Appropriates a set budget for the program period.

2. Most often arrives at the advertising cost per sale after the advertising campaign is concluded.

3. Continues to run advertising schedules without regard to the allowable.

4. Has a hit-or-miss follow-up and tracking program, if any.

5. Analyzes schedules at the end of each advertising campaign, long after adjustments can be made.

6. Does not have a database system for customers; is often not aware of the value of the name lists.

7. Sets primary goal at achieving sales within the advertising allowable, keeping corporate image as a secondary consideration.

7. Makes corporate image a priority over achieving orders within the advertising allowable.

The Direct Marketing Advertising Agency

It is important to understand who implements broadcast direct marketing strategies. Some companies handle implementation in-house, but most use outside agencies—direct response advertising agencies. Unlike general agencies, direct response agencies specialize in direct response advertising. Some agencies create both print and broadcast direct response advertising, some do only print, and a few (such as A. Eicoff & Company) focus only on broadcast.

The entire advertising agency community has recognized the great profit potential that lies in direct marketing. Established, highly successful, mainstream agencies have opened or acquired subsidiaries around the world designated as "direct marketing specialists." Advertising entrepreneurs are also spawning new direct advertising agencies in all parts of the world. (See sidebar.) Direct marketing advertising agencies are divided into two categories: the direct marketing agency and the pseudo direct marketing agency.

The Direct Marketing Agency

1. Evaluates the long-range profit potential of a direct marketer client to evaluate the feasibility of accepting the account.

2. Keeps media testing to a minimum; carefully limits the budget and time exposure in determining the profitability of the offer.

3. Evaluates incoming data on a day-by-day, medium-by-medium, exposure-by-exposure basis in relationship to the advertising allowable.

The Pseudo Direct Marketing Agency

1. Determines a fee for handling a direct marketer account based on the income the agency needs to make a profit.

2. Uses mainstream advertising agency budget techniques, often recommending higher levels of media and continuity than are needed to get readable test results.

3. Does a post-analysis of the advertising campaign.

4. Recommends expansion of the advertising campaign on a conservation basis, being well aware of the pitfalls that direct marketers can encounter on campaign expansions.

5. Assumes the responsibility for the mail and phone logistics.

6. Guides direct marketer in all aspects of advertising, merchandising, and fulfillment functions.

7. Organizes the agency to allow for the most efficient communication between agency and direct marketer.

8. Provides direct marketer with regular reports on all aspects of the ongoing campaign.

4. Often expands successful tests too quickly, resulting in high levels of losses for the direct marketer.

5. Leaves all mail and phone logistic functions to the direct marketer.

6. Believes the advertising agency's functions should be confined to creative and media.

7. Uses normal agency organization methods with account supervisor and account executive obstructions.

8. Provides reports on request.

RESTRUCTURING THE DIRECT MARKETING ADVERTISING AGENCY

Many advertising agencies are structured for maximum waste and minimum effectiveness. Too often, they do everything except what they are supposed to do: sell the client's product. The problem begins with the typical relationship between client and agency. Often, the agency worships at the client's feet, devoting their energies and talents to keeping the client happy, rather than honestly evaluating and implementing the best possible advertising for the client.

Ideally, account executives should be trouble-shooters for the agency and participate in bringing in new business. In reality, however, they rarely have time or talent for either of these goals. Account executives are infrequently hired for their sales ability or even their knowledge of advertising and marketing. Those who do have selling skills often are promoted to a level where their main function is administrative, rather than selling.

The complete elimination of the position of account executive would greatly facilitate the day-to-day operation of advertising agencies. By eliminating the account executive, the client and the people who "dig the ditches" for the agency would be forced to deal with each other directly, no longer relying on the intermediary, the messenger, the "host." Clients could talk directly to the media buyers, working with those who plan the most effective media-buying strategy. They could talk directly to the writers who create the ads, ensuring that they are operating on the same wavelength.

The responsibilities of the account executive (although most never fulfill those responsibilities) could easily be disseminated to others within an agency. Those responsible for selling a campaign to a client or for getting new business should be drawn from teams of highly trained, top-level executives within the agency, men and women with the experience and ability to sell. They should have first gained their experience on the client side so they have a dual perspective to bring to their accounts. They should also have spent time in the field so they understand the nuts-and-bolts aspects of marketing a product.

In structuring an agency, it is essential that media buyers be chosen for their ability to sell, because it is their job to sell the media on giving them the best exposure for the client expenditure. Many large agencies make the mistake of promoting superior media buyers into supervisory capacities. This leaves media-buying departments barren of talent. To help good media buyers remain media buyers, agencies should provide them with the increased responsibility, security, and salaries they are entitled to. If this is done, an agency can not only establish solid working relationships with the media representatives, but also involve them in the end objective: moving merchandise for the client.

Creative departments at many large agencies have talented people working in their creative departments, but that talent never blossoms because it is choked off by a chain of command that dictates concept. Too often, the writers and artists become robots of the bureaucratic hierarchy. Once again, direct contact between artist, writer, and the client could facilitate communication and result in advertising that reflects the client's main objective: to sell the product.

Creative departments should be streamlined for maximum effectiveness. To create effective broadcast advertising, all writers should be producers, and all producers should be writers. If the writer produces his or her own creation, then the end result will be exactly what the writer intended, free from the aesthetic standards a producer imposed. The writer/producer should deal directly with the client, presenting the ad concept. After all, who can better explain a campaign than the person who wrote it?

Writer/producers should not be isolated from the selling/marketing process. Too often, agencies isolate their creative people, letting them dwell in the realm of ideas instead of the world of profit and loss. They should be encouraged to learn everything there is to know about the product they write about: where it is distributed, how it is manufactured, who the audience is. Only then will they be able to sell product rather than win awards.

Finally, there are research departments. I have found that the only research with credibility is post-analytical research, which tells you what has happened, not what might happen. This theoretical research is a defense mechanism, providing clients with justification for their decisions and the agency, for its marketing strategy. To eliminate this dependence on research would save the client a great deal of time and money. In fact, common sense often can be profitably substituted for research.

The structure of many advertising agencies has not changed with the times. With few exceptions, they are organized the same way they were 40 years ago. A new agency organizational chart could easily be designed and implemented, using what I call the team approach.

A client should be assigned a creative team, a media team, and a marketing team. The members of each team would be responsible for planning and executing work for the client and would meet directly with the client. If the client and team cannot work out a problem (this would be rare), an agency trouble-shooter would be called in to solve it. This team approach would facilitate communications between client and agency, eliminating scores of intermediaries and administrators.

In the ideal team structure, the separate teams would coordinate their work. The marketing strategy for a client would fit the creative strategy like a glove. Because these teams would have the responsibility for making important decisions, they would have a greater incentive to ensure that those decisions were the right ones. Thus, the team approach would result in greater agency efficiency and diligence. ■

THE LANGUAGE OF BROADCAST DIRECT MARKETING

Broadcast direct response advertising, like any specialized field, has its own terminology. This section will give you the basic vocabulary necessary to enhance your understanding and appreciation of the subject matter.

Advertising is the essence of direct marketing sales, so it is important to understand the definitions of advertising. Albert Lasker, the patriarch of the advertising industry, defines *advertising* as "salesmanship in print." This definition is still accepted by modern advertising authorities, despite the development of numerous new media, including radio and television. In pursuit of direct marketing sales, however, it is important to understand an entirely different definition of advertising.

The broad definition of *direct marketing advertising* involves a wide range of strategies, including the immediate sale of a product or service, generating leads for salespeople, recruiting personnel, selling franchises, recruiting for club membership, fund raising, etc. Direct marketing, unlike other forms of advertising, attempts to reach an audience that will respond directly to the medium with a phone call or letter.

Direct response advertising can use virtually any medium to accomplish its goals. Media options include direct mail pieces, newspapers, magazines, radio, cable, videotex, store-to-home computer, take-ones, transportation cards, and matchbooks.

What differentiates direct marketing from other marketing strategies is that it cannot be implemented without a "Magic Number," also referred to as an "allowable." Essentially, a Magic Number is the amount an advertiser can afford to spend on advertising per unit sold and still earn a satisfactory profit. If the final sale is not made within the limits of the Magic Number, the medium should not be renewed under the same conditions.

Following are other useful terms in broadcast direct marketing:

Access channels   Channels set aside by the cable operator for use by the public, educational institutions, municipal government, or for lease on a nondiscriminatory basis.

Area of dominant influence (ADI)   In television or radio, the ADI of a station is those counties where the station reaches at least 50 percent of the viewers at least once a week.

Advertising   An attempt by a seller to implant a suggestion in the conscious or subconscious minds of potential customers that will motivate immediate or subsequent buying reactions.

Affiliate   The cable system or TV station through which a satellite or network transmits its programming.

Amplifier   A device that boosts the strength of an electronic signal. Amplifiers are spaced at regular intervals throughout a cable system to keep signals picture perfect no matter where you live.

Aural cable   The origination of radio programming on an FM channel leased from an existing cable system, available to cable subscribers only.

Basic cable   Service offered by a cable system that usually includes over-the-air broadcast signals imported by the operator.

Bi-directional   Interactive or two-way cable communications.

Bird   Colloquial for any communications satellite.

Broadband communications system   Frequently used as a synonym for cable TV. It can describe any technology capable of delivering multiple channels and services.

Business-to-business direct marketing   A business contacting another business through some advertising medium in an attempt to make a sale. Generally, the preferred direct marketing media for business-to-business are direct mail, magazines, newspapers, and telemarketing. The business-to-business advertiser often has to pay too much for waste circulation in a mass medium to make it viable within the advertising allowable. Both television and radio, however, have been successfully used for the sale of business computers and office copy machines.

Buzz words   Such motivating words as "new," "amazing," "revolution-ary," "sensational," "one-in-a-lifetime," or "never before."

Cable   Any type of attachment to a television set that delivers a better quality or different picture than one would have without the attachment. Viewers perceive cable as "television" and not another medium. It is best to think of cable as another logistic means of bringing a picture to a television tube.

Cablite   Combining a direct transmission from a satellite or a videotex transmission from a regular TV station with a direct-to-computer return through the existing phone system.

Cash library   An inventory of direct marketing commercials retained by radio and television stations that may be scheduled in any open time periods. Advertisers pay for these spots on a per-sale or per-inquiry basis. Stations benefit by turning unsold time into net profit.

Chromo-rhythm   The physical changes that an individual goes through in the course of a day that influence his or her lifestyle and buying behavior.

Coaxial cable   The pairs of lines of transmission for carrying TV signals. Its principal conductor is either a pure copper or copper-coated wire, surrounded by insulation and then encased in aluminum and rubber or plastic.

Comsat (Communications Satellite Corporation)   A privately owned common carrier operating under a Congressional mandate to provide commercial communications satellite services.

Continuous shipment   A direct marketing concept that allows a company to sell a series of products over a designated period. The seller automatically ships merchandise to the buyer, and the buyer has the right to return any undesired product and/or instruct the seller to discontinue further shipments.

Converter   A device that sits on top of a television that can increase the channel load of the TV set to accommodate the multiplicity of channels offered by cable TV.

Cost per thousand (CPM)   The cost of the advertising medium to reach 1,000 demographically defined prospects.

Cume   The total audience reached by a media. This total is usually expressed in a percentage of the audience within the circulation area reached by a given amount of advertising, supplemented with the average number of times (frequency) that segment of audience has been exposed to the advertising message. For example, a 400 GRP schedule might cume 72 percent of the total potential audience 5.6 times.

Dead beat factor   The percentage of direct marketing buyers who do not fulfill their commitments or obligations.

Demographics   A profile of the audience of a medium, including sex, age, income, ethnic background, etc. *See* Target audience.

Descrambler   A decoder that restores a scrambled video signal to its standard form.

Direct broadcast satellite (DBC)   A system in which signals are transmitted directly from a satellite to a home receiving dish.

Direct marketing   A marketing method that calls for the sale of a product or service directly to the consumer without intermediaries.

Direct response An action carried out by the consumer in response to a direct marketing advertisement.

Dish *See* Earth station.

Earth station A structure used for receiving and transmitting electromagnetic signals coming from satellites. *Also* Dish.

Fiber Optics A very thin, pliable tube of glass or plastic that carries a wide band of transmission in both directions.

Focus group A panel of consumers (6–10 per group) who are exposed to various test concepts for an evaluation of their reactions. This method is frequently used to measure how effectively different creative concepts communicate the desired message. Focus groups are used for small-scale, exploratory research. As such, they are not statistically projectable to the entire population or target groups by themselves.

Gross rating points (GRP) The total number of rating points achieved, usually stated on a per-week or per-schedule basis. Rating point levels can be translated into broadcast circulation, reach, and frequency. *See* Rating point, Reach.

High definition TV The enhancement of a television picture to film projection quality by increasing picture imagery to 1,170 lines per screen from the normal 610.

Holder The promise of a future action or reward at the start of a commercial or in the headline of an ad designed to gain audience attention (e.g., "In just a minute, I'll tell you how you can win a free trip to Europe, but first . . .") and hold the audience.

Homes passed The total number of homes with the potential for being hooked up to a cable system.

Infomercial A program-length commercial, not limited in length to traditional commercial breaks but to the length of time necessary to sell the product or service.

Interactive A sophisticated, two-way system capable of connecting two points or more. A method of communication between originator and viewer using cable, fiber optics, or horizontal blanking areas of FM radio or TV.

Investment spending Advertising expenditures based on expected future results. Investment spending may continue for months before there are any measurable sales results. Direct marketing, on the other hand, requires an immediate, profitable response.

Isolation factor The selling effectiveness of an advertising exposure when isolated (not exposed in a cluster of commercials, amid a series of print ads, or included in a mailing piece composed of multiple direct marketing ads).

Key outlet marketing *See* Trade support marketing.

Magic number The maximum advertising allowable per-unit sale that allows for an acceptable return on investment for the advertiser. Often referred to as a profitable advertising-to-sales ratio.

Media guarantee A promise by the medium to deliver a minimum number of orders or inquiries to a direct marketer in exchange for a regular media buy contract at certain predetermined rates.

Microwave A way of interconnecting cable systems with a series of high-frequency receiving antenna transmitters mounted on towers spaced up to 50 miles apart.

Multipoint distribution service (MDS) A private service utilizing a very high frequency to transmit one TV signal. Its most common function is to bring pay TV to hotels, but it can, in some cases, be beamed to private homes.

Multiplex programs Programs shown at different times on multiple channels.

Narrowcasting The delivery of programming that addresses a specific need or audience.

Negative option A method of selling a number of products to the consumer by automatically shipping subsequent products unless the consumer specifically cancels an individual shipment in advance. The seller contacts the buyer by mail shortly before shipping each additional unit of product. The buyer must send back a reply device refusing the product or automatically receive it and be responsible for payment. For many years, record and book clubs used the negative option program, but such methods have been disavowed by reputable firms and are no longer used by responsible companies.

Negative recall An advertisement or commercial that has a negative impact on the potential customer. The consumer remembers the advertising but dislikes its message. Commercials that receive the highest recall scores often do not help and sometimes deter product sales. *See* Positive recall.

Pay per view Cable programming for which subscribers pay on a one-time basis, as in prize fights, Broadway shows, and movie premieres.

Positioning A creative strategy used to produce a distinct perception of a product or service. For example, aspirin could be positioned as a headache remedy, a painkiller, an arthritis treatment, etc.

Positive recall Advertising that establishes a favorable image for a product, service, or company and that motivates a potential buyer to purchase that product. *See* Negative recall.

Profit center A product or service that can be isolated and the profit or loss individually determined; an individual market that can be isolated for specific products where the profitability can be determined; a specific division of a company that can be isolated and the profit or loss determined; or a television or radio station that can be isolated for a direct marketing offer and the profit or loss for that specific station determined.

QUBE An advanced cable system, first used in Columbus, Ohio, that allows two-way communications between the subscriber and the cable company. Subscribers could use cable returns for answering polls and surveys, banking, and shopping.

Rating point One percent of the total television homes in the surveyed area.

Reach The total number of unduplicated homes reached by a designated advertising program, expressed either in percentages of the total homes in the area or in specific numbers of homes.

Run of paper (ROP) A purchase of newspaper or magazine advertising that allows the publication to run the ad in any section they choose.

Run of station (ROS) A purchase of broadcast time that allows the station to run the commercials in any period that is open and any day within the schedule's parameter. ROS flexibility allows the station to offer the time at a lower rate than normal.

Sales resistance theory The concept that there are times of the day and days of the week which people become more resistant to advertising messages.

Satellite A device located in stationary orbit above the earth that receives transmissions from separate points and retransmits them to cable systems over a wide area.

Shop-at-home Any program allowing subscribers to view products or services and allowing viewers to order them by cable or phone. Larger specialized home shopping operations include Home Shopping Network and QVC I and II.

Spot   A commercial on radio or TV.

Subscription TV (STV)   Pay TV programs delivered by MDS or over the air. Signals are scrambled, then decoded in the subscriber's set by a special receiver. *See* Multiple distribution service.

Support advertising   The use of one advertising medium to call attention to an advertising exposure delivered by a second medium. Normally, support refers to a television or radio commercial that directs the viewer to a mailing piece or print advertisement.

Take-ones   An advertising piece, usually found at high-traffic locations, that asks for a direct response, either by coupon or phone.

Target audience   The designated audience most desirable for the sale of a product or service, usually determined by sales experience or research and expressed in demographic terms for media buying. For creative purposes, this may also include attitudinal factors (e.g., nurturing parents, snobs, feminists).

Telemarketing   A direct marketing program that uses the telephone as the medium of sale. There are both inbound and outbound telemarketing.

Television time divisions   In the Eastern Standard and Mountain Standard time zones, TV time is divided as follows:

Late Night	Early Time	Daytime	Early Fringe	Prime Access	Prime	Late Access
12M 1A 2A 3A	4A 5A 6A 7A	8A 9A 10A 11A 12N 1P	2P 3P 4P	5P 6P 7P	8P 9P 10P	11P 12P

In Central Standard and Pacific Standard time zones, the designation falls one hour earlier.

Tiered programming   A series of programmed cable offered to a subscriber at a charge in addition to the basic cable service.

Trade support marketing (TSM)   Advertising that directs the consumer to specific retail stores where the advertised product is sold. In TSM advertising, expenditures are controlled by the relationship of sales to the advertising allowable, and each market becomes an individual profit center. *Also* Key outlet marketing.

Turn   That moment in a television or radio commercial when the commercial stops giving information about the product or service and asks the consumer to place an order.

Two-step process   A direct marketing selling method that requires the consumer to respond to the advertisement with an inquiry rather than an order. The seller answers the inquiry with a direct mail selling piece or personal sales call. This method is most often used for items priced over $50. The two-step process is also used when a signature is necessary (as in the case of insurance); whenever the product needs more explanation than can be given in a commercial; and whenever the purchaser must sign a commitment to purchase more products under the introductory offer (as is the case with book and record clubs).

Two-way cable   A system in which the viewer can communicate directly with the advertiser or cable company, using the cable not only as a communication system, but also as a home computer.

Unique selling proposition (USP)   A benefit or feature that differentiates one product from other, competitive products. USP can be achieved with a unique product characteristic, higher or lower pricing, unique packaging, a new positioning for an old product, or a new advertising approach.

Videotex   A computer graphic picture delivered to a TV set that uses the vertical blanking area of a television station to send many different signals that can be selected for the screen of a home TV set. When Videotex achieves the capabilities of synchronizing the sound and picture, it will become an effective new advertising medium.

---

* Additional cable definitions taken from the 1992 edition of the National Cable Television Association's *Glossary of Cable Television Terms.*

CHAPTER TWO

Selecting a Product or Service

Direct marketing is effective for tangible products, such as books, compact discs, real estate, magazine subscriptions, and unique, mass-market merchandise offered in catalogs. It can also be used to sell such services as correspondence schools; franchises like rug cleaning, fast food, and key-making machinery; and many other types of products. It can be used to achieve inquiries to be followed up by a door-to-door salesperson. Or it can be used to attract potential customers to seminars where companies attempt to solicit fees for revealing privileged information (e.g., "How to Make Money in Real Estate").

This chapter will discuss qualities of a product or service that make it suitable for broadcast direct marketing.

UNIQUENESS

The most desirable qualification for a successful direct marketing offer or campaign is uniqueness—of product, price, packaging, positioning, or advertising. The chances of success are enhanced when the offer contains at least one of these unique components.

Product

If a product or service is readily available at a local store, it is far more difficult to convince a prospective customer to order it by mail. If a product is unique and not readily available—or its ready availability is a well-kept secret—then it is far easier to motivate a direct marketing sale. Following are some examples of unique products for which broadcast direct marketing was very effective.

The Dexter Sewing Machine was the first hand-operated, portable sewing machine. It allowed you to hem a skirt while you were wearing it or mend a drape while it was still hanging. The Handi-Screen was a tennis-racquet-shaped aluminum screen used to cover frying pans. It allowed you to see what was happening in the pan while it kept the grease from splattering. It also allowed for the addition of liquids without removing the Handi-Screen lid. d-CON Rat & Mouse Killer was another unique product. Certainly there were other rat poisons on the market, but d-CON was unique because it took several days to become lethal. The rats never knew which of their foods were poisoned, thus no "bait shyness" developed. Vegamatic, a multi-use vegetable processor, was unique because it did in one operation what normally required several steps. For example, a Vegamatic could cut potatoes for french fries or slice an entire tomato with a single action, as opposed to the other slicers, which required several steps to do the same thing. The Robot Gardener was a plastic chamber that fit between the end of a hose and the nozzle of a sprinkler. This plastic chamber could be filled with fertilizer, insect killer, or weed killer, which was then spread over the lawn and garden through the normal watering process.

Uniqueness can also be accomplished by adding an ingredient or function to an otherwise ordinary product, as was done with the electric knife and the electric toothbrush. The mere addition of a vibrating motor made both of these everyday products perform better and easier. The Blitzhocker was an ordinary manual food chopper that was made unique because the blade rotated. This turned an old product into a new one with a unique selling factor.

Most books are unique in that there are no other books exactly like the one being offered. Although there are how-to books available on almost all subjects, the mere rewriting of an old book gives it uniqueness.

All franchises assert that they offer the public something desirable and at the same time offer the franchisee a unique opportunity to become financially successful. Thus, the offering of a franchise is accomplished by adding the unique ingredients necessary for success.

An extra ingredient in an education process can add a unique and desirable factor. One such ingredient is a numbered keyboard for learning to play the piano or guitar. This allows the direct marketer to state, "If you can read numbers, you can play the piano." Or "If you can distinguish colors, you will be playing the guitar after one lesson."

In most cases, products or services that are made unique by adding an ingredient are short-lived. As soon as the marketing success of any new "unique" product is proven, there is an immediate army of "knock-off" manufacturers who wish to cash in on someone else's success. (See sidebar.) It is extremely important in direct marketing, therefore, to expand marketing exposure as rapidly as production and finances allow after a product's success becomes apparent.

A WORD ABOUT THE KNOCK-OFF SYNDROME

What happened to the electric toothbrush, the Shower Massage, the electric knife, the Crock Pot, the Moon Stone, the Hula Hoop? Were they merely fads, products that enjoyed a brief moment in the spotlight and then vanished from view because they exhausted their market? These products were victims of the "knock-off syndrome."

It begins when a new product is introduced to the marketplace. Its extensive advertising campaign—which educates the public and heralds its uniqueness and consumer benefits—is responsible for the product's success. Of course, merchandising and advertising a new product require markup. As soon as sales start to soar, however, numerous manufacturers jump on the bandwagon and rush to bring out their parade of clones. In some instances, the products are legitimate—well made and fairly priced. But often, these copies are of lower quality and are lower priced than the original product and only claim to do what the original product actually does.

When these knock-offs start appearing, they do a brisk business. Many buyers shun the high-priced originator for the lower-priced copy. Sales of the original product begin to drop off. The originator's advertising, which was instrumental in fostering awareness of the unique new product, is cut back. Soon, all advertising for the category stops. In a short time, both the original and the knock-off products stop selling.

The plagiarists stop manufacturing and withdraw from the market, but the game is over. The originator is afraid to go back to an intensive advertising campaign, because the competitors are waiting in the wings for the advertising to begin again so they can dump their inventory.

There are many variations on this knock-off syndrome. Consider what happened when General Electric introduced the original electric knife at $24.95. For two years, their advertising worked overtime to educate the public about the need for and uses of their new product. Gradually, the idea took hold in consumers' minds, and GE found itself with a highly successful product. In less than a year, however, no less than 65 companies flooded the market with electric knives ranging in price from $4.95 to $19.95.

Greedy chains and department stores put all products side by side in their newly established "electric knife department." Because GE couldn't afford the advertising to move these competitive products, they cut back their advertising. The entire category dropped 86 percent in sales in less than one year. The chains, experiencing only one fleeting moment of success, had killed the goose that laid the golden egg.

The electric toothbrush suffered a similar fate. Shortly after its introduction, more than 500 imitations flooded the market. And again, within a year, a multimillion-dollar product category dropped by 75 percent. Other victims of the knock-off syndrome include the tabletop rotisserie, the electric frying pan, the Crock Pot, the deep fryer, Shower Massage, the automobile sun visor, food chopper, and even the yo-yo.

What is so shameful about the pretenders is that they can be thwarted. Retailers merely have to understand that knock-offs are detrimental to their profits in the long run and refuse to stock them. The unusual aspect of the knock-off syndrome is that after all the smoke clears away, few manufacturers of synthetics have made any profit, and the only product left on the shelf is the high-priced originator and one or two clones that competed for quality, not for the price.

I do not condemn copies because they represent competition. I am a strong advocate of competition—the kind of competition that benefits the manufacturer, the product, and the consumer. In its ideal form, competition forces manufacturers and ad agencies to create an informative, motivating commercial, and it forces the public to evaluate a product and act on that evaluation.

When one of my clients decides to clone a product, I always advise them to price it higher than the original, rather than lower. This provides the markup to make a top-quality product and necessary funds to properly advertise and merchandise it. And I always emphasize that when the smoke clears away, only the higher-priced products will be left in the market. ■

Price

An old product can often be made unique merely by moving it out of the mainstream of competitive price. For example, a 19-inch color TV set for $99.95 would be unique because of its low price. Direct marketing ads often offer such items as army surplus, pure-silk parachutes for $9.95. The buyer would most likely buy the parachute only to use the silk to make other items. Such offers as "books up to $50 in value, now just $2 each"; "14k gold chain and matching bracelet for only $14.95"; "100 double-edged razor blades, guaranteed to be of top quality, just $1"; "Nationally advertised Longine, Bulova, and Elgin watches at 50 percent off retail list" are all examples of the use of low prices to motivate buyers.

On the other hand, greatly overpricing a product or service can also make it unique and highly desirable. There are numerous examples of pricing a product in excess of its worth, ranging from Rolls-Royces and $250-an-ounce perfumes to designer jeans and smoker's toothpastes. These products are all non–direct marketed products, but the principle is the same.

Direct marketed products using this technique include d-CON Rat Killer, which was sold by mail for $2.98 when all others were selling for less than $1. The Hair Wiz sold for $2.98 when similar products were selling for under $1. Vita-Mix was priced at nearly $300 when other products in the category were selling for under $100. The Hydro-Jet Whirlpool sold for $249 when similar products were sold for $9 to $98.

The American public perceives a direct relationship between quality and price. Very often, the public refuses to buy a product for $1 but jumps at the opportunity to buy the same product at a higher price. One of the best examples of high-priced uniqueness is Tarn-X Silver Cleaner. People would not risk their sterling silver family heirlooms by using an inexpensive silver cleaner. They are more comfortable using a $3 silver cleaner than one offered for 49¢.

Packaging

Often the same "old" product can be made unique by a change in packaging. Most direct marketed record offers are successful because the marketer has taken musical hits from old releases and repackaged them in a new album that offers the "Top Hits of the '60," "The Greatest Rock & Roll Hits of the Decade," or "The Best of the Big Bands." Many people do not realize that virtually all record packages are merely repackaged, previously released recordings.

Other products can find uniqueness in repackaging, too. For example, when the first aerosol shaving cream was introduced, its uniqueness came from packaging in an aerosol can (although the same ingredients were used).

Putting 300 pieces together in a unique tool set or fishing kit is making a new product from a number of old parts. One of the most effective direct marketing offers in history was one made by Bell & Howell that combined a movie camera, a projector, a screen, a film editor, and film into a single package.

Sometimes packaging uniqueness can be achieved by merely changing numbers: putting books in sets or series, jewelry in sets, and recipes on cards instead of in books. All are examples of repackaged old products.

Positioning

Uniqueness can be achieved by using the same old product, at the same old price, in the same old package, and focusing on a different positioning for the product. By packaging chlorine in a spray bottle and positioning it as a mildew remover, a company found a new, unique niche for chlorine. Taking a product that removes calcium and lime and packaging it as a stain remover for the rust-stained lime on sidewalks and buildings positions the product for an entirely new market. Repositioning baking soda as a "deodorant" for refrigerators gave Arm & Hammer Baking Soda new life. Repositioning electronic teaching cassettes as a game is one of many ways of achieving uniqueness.

Advertising

Sometimes it is possible to take the same old product, in the same old package, at the same old price, and sell it for the same old use. The twist is to create a new advertising "look" to make it unique.

There are many products that repair and fill flat tires, but people are not aware of them. Thus, demonstrating the danger of a breakdown on a lonely road and showing how the repair kit works can stimulate direct marketing orders.

CLR, a calcium, lime, and rust remover, was repositioned from a bathroom tile cleanser to a profitable direct marketing product. A strong demonstration showed how quickly CLR changed tile from rusty to clean. Sona, a cosmetic concealer that blends lines and wrinkles, is another example of an old product in an old package at an old price that motivated immediate sales with a before-and-after commercial. This same before-and-after approach helped Donatelli Honey and Egg Cream Facial and Caswella's many weight-reducing products become exceptionally strong direct marketing products, even though their marketing mix (product, package, price, position) wasn't unique.

OTHER CONSIDERATIONS

While it is true that a direct marketing offer should be unique in some way, other factors should be considered. The product should appeal to the broadest possible market; its benefits should be demonstrable; and it should provide the direct marketer with a sufficiently high markup to allow for a profit.

Universality

One should always try to market a product that has the widest possible demographic potential. It's easier to sell a headache remedy than an arthritis painkiller or a drug that will ease the aches of a broken bone. All three painkillers can be positioned to encompass a relatively large, definitive market.

When you are looking at a product, question its ability to solve a real existing problem or problems; then evaluate the range of the problems. The more universal the problem, the greater the market potential for the product.

If you are attempting to invent or create a product or service, first find a problem that needs a solution—or a better solution—and then develop the service or product that will solve the problem. Keep in mind that there is always a relationship between the need for solving a problem and the cost. If the problem is cancer, probably no price is too high to ask for the sure solution. However, if the problem is a flat tire, then the repair solution cannot exceed the cost of a new tire.

In examining the potential of a product, too often the marketer becomes so engrossed in making the solution work that the ultimate solution becomes too costly for the problem. For example, a toothbrush sterilizer that would cost $40 or antislide pads for pots that would retail for $20 could not possibly be successful because of the high price.

In evaluating a product for universality, always ask yourself, "Does it solve a problem? How universal is the scope of the problem? Can the product be marketed within a price range that would make the product a worthwhile buy for the consumer?"

Demonstrability

A product that can convey its benefits through demonstration facilitates the creation of a highly motivational TV commercial. If a product or service cannot be demonstrated—as is the case with books, unique plants, and money-saving devices—the radio or TV commercial must bring the product to life. The commercial must portray the subject matter in such a way as to conjure up a mental image of desirability for the potential customer.

For example, a commercial for plant fertilizer could use animated drawings or time-lapse photography to demonstrate effectiveness. A product such as Tarn-X silver cleaner could show tarnish instantly being removed. This credible, realistic demonstration is what's needed to motivate the viewer to make a positive buying decision.

Although radio is not a visual medium, a good writer can paint a mental picture of product capabilities that often is comparable to a live demonstration. Examples of how to bring products to life on TV and radio will be more fully discussed in Chapter 6.

Markup

Although all of the aforementioned ingredients should be part of a successful direct marketing offer, none is as essential as profit markup. The ultimate measure of business success is profit, and if the proper atmosphere for profit does not exist, then all direct marketing efforts become futile.

The rule of thumb in the direct marketing business dictates that a direct marketer should work with a minimum of 3½ times (350 percent) markup from the actual cost of the product packaged and ready to ship to the final selling price. However, as the selling price rises, the essential markup can decrease. A $100 product may need only a 2½ times (250 percent) markup, and a $500 product could be successful with a 1½ (150 percent) markup. In figuring the cost of product, all costs of materials, labor, and packaging should be included, but not tools and dies or general overhead. These costs, as well as the cost of advertising, become part of the profit formula explained in Chapter 10 on the mathematics of direct marketing.

It is important to remember that tools and dies and commercial production costs are one-time fees that must be paid out of initial profits but should not be figured as costs in arriving at an advertising allowable.

CHAPTER 3

Strategic Broadcast Media Buying

One could write thousands of pages on the technique of buying radio and television time. There are literally dozens of different ways to purchase broadcast time. It is important to understand that rates are determined not only by supply and demand, but also by rating points, buyer-seller relationships, and, most importantly, negotiation. Today, broadcast media buying is a highly skilled art.

In this chapter we will cover the tools of media buying, the various techniques, the importance of media relations, and the various theories and concepts that apply to buying direct marketing broadcast time.

MASTERING THE TOOLS OF THE TRADE

A knowledge of accounting practices is critical to any advertising specialist and even more important to the direct marketer. Because direct marketing is really a numbers game, anyone who anticipates a successful career in the field must be able to read and evaluate all types of statistical, research and financial data.

Standard Rate and Data (SRDS)—TV and Cable Service

This publication, organized into nine sections by designated marketing areas (DMA), defines the geographic boundaries of the stations' areas of dominant influence (ADI) and offers detailed profile of the demographics of the DMA. It indexes the stations by market ranking and actual expendable income and sets the limitations on cost per rating point in various time segments. (See Exhibits 3–1 to 3–3.)

EXHIBIT 3-1
Standard Rate and Data Service: TV Market Map

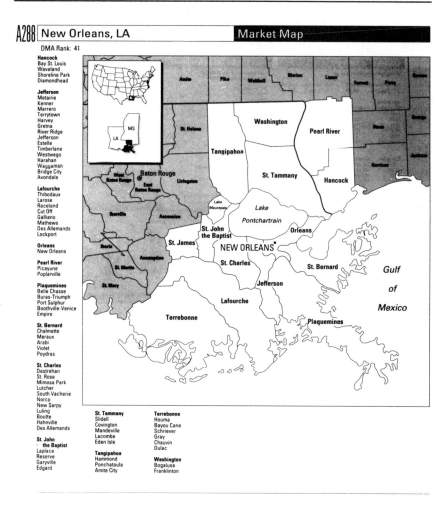

EXHIBIT 3-2
Standard Rate and Data Service: Market Profile

Market Profile	New Orleans, LA A289

DMA Rank: 41

DEMOGRAPHIC PROFILE

Demographics Base Index US = 100

Current Total HH:	617,300	Total Adult Pop.:	1,212,600
5-Yr. Projected:	638,500	5-Yr. Projected:	1,241,762

Age of Head of Household	Households	Race/Ethnicity	Population
Under 25	29,600	White	835,700
25-34	125,200	Black	348,000
35-44	148,600	Other	11,400
45-54	106,900	Hispanic	44,200
55-64	82,400	Asian/Pacific	17,500
65 and Older	124,600		

	Male		Female	
Age by Sex	Current	5 Yr.	Current	5 Yr.
< 25	333,300	334,733	328,000	329,203
25-34	131,100	125,660	138,800	130,929
35-44	130,600	138,654	139,500	147,749
45-54	91,500	107,040	99,200	115,498
55-64	62,100	66,337	71,300	75,349
65 +	72,600	72,285	109,900	107,063

Household Income	Households
$10,000-$19,999	104,651
$20,000-$34,999	136,792
$35,000-$49,999	103,774
$50,000-$74,999	101,210
$75,000-$99,999	37,845
$100,000-$124,999	12,081
$125,000-$149,999	5,403
$150,000 and Over	8,847

Top 15 Industries	Total Employment	Total Establishments
Health Services	48,076	2,880
Eating & Drinking Places	44,382	2,447
Business Services	32,821	1,690
Food Stores	24,201	1,418
Wholesale - Durable Goods	19,121	1,898
Transportation Equipment	18,195	103
Educational Services	18,003	318
Water Transportation	16,395	581
Wholesale - Nondurable Goods	16,389	1,037
General Merchandise Stores	16,050	251
Miscellaneous Retail	14,092	2,014
Special Trade Contractors	13,573	1,510
Hotels & Other Lodging Places	13,526	205
Engineering & Management	13,482	1,184
Banking	12,418	460

Unemployment Rate: 6.6

Occupational Categories	
White Collar Total:	385,887
Blue Collar Total:	148,809
Service Occupations	131,503
Clerical Workers	129,243
Marketing and Sales	80,269
Engineers	8,408
Lawyers	3,735
Computer Specialists	6,081
Management/Administrative Occupations	59,724
Physicians	2,528
Teachers, Librarians, Counselors	46,973
Communication Equipment Operators	1,889
Food Preparation and Service Occupations	54,960

© Market Statistics, producers of The Survey of Buying Power, 1994

SALES RANKINGS BY MERCHANDISE

Total Retail Sales: 14,088,906,000
Buying Power Index: 0.6224

Merchandise Line	Sales ($000)	Rank
Alcoholic Drinks	168,417	35
Audio Equipment	134,504	38
Cars, Trucks & Powered Vehicles	1,753,123	44
Cigars, Cigarettes & Tobacco	254,171	31
Computer Hardware & Software	46,439	36
Drugs, Health Aids & Beauty Aids	802,113	31
Footwear	238,208	29
Furniture	269,386	40
Groceries & Other Foods	2,333,014	33
Kitchenware & Home Furnishings	192,036	39
Major Household Appliances	209,774	29
Meals & Snacks	1,428,011	36
Men's & Boys' Wear	347,532	42
Soap, Detergents, Household Cleaners	107,484	27
Sporting Goods	175,926	42
Television, Video Recorders & Tapes	111,611	40
Women's & Girls' Wear	738,455	39

© Market Statistics, producers of The Survey of Buying Power, 1994

COST PER POINT LEVELS - HOUSEHOLDS

Daypart	Average	Low	High
Day	26	23	29
Early News	51	44	55
Prime Access	55	51	62
Prime	73	67	81
Late News	71	62	78
Combined Fringe	34	30	38

© Spot Quotations and Data Inc., 2nd Quarter, 1994

DAILY NEWSPAPERS AND COMMUNITY NEWSPAPER GROUPS

Times-Picayune Houma/Thibodaux Combo	Hammond Daily Star	USSPI Newspaper Network Suburban-New Orleans

Compiled by SRDS

RADIO STATIONS BY METRO MARKET

Jefferson, LA		St. Charles, LA	St. Tammany, LA
Gretna, LA	WRNO FM	WNOE FM	
KGLA AM	WBYU AM	WQUE AM	Norco, LA	Covington, LA
KKNO AM	WSHO AM	WADU AM	WASO AM
Jefferson Davis, LA	WEZB FM	WYLD AM	St. John the	Slidell, LA
Jennings, LA	WSMB AM	WQUE FM	Baptist, LA	WLTS FM
KJEF AM	WLMG FM	WYLD FM	Garyville, LA	WSLA AM
KJEF FM	WTIX AM	Plaquemines, LA	WCKW AM	Terrebonne, LA
Orleans, LA	WMXZ FM	Belle Chasse, LA	Laplace, LA	Houma, LA
New Orleans, LA	WVOG AM	KMEZ FM	WCKW FM	KHOM FM
WBOK AM	WNOE AM	Port Sulphur, LA	Reserve, LA	
	WWL AM	KQLD FM	WADU FM	

Compiled by SRDS

EXHIBIT 3-3
Standard Rate and Data Service: Television Stations

| Television Stations | New Orleans, LA | 187 |

Nashville, TN—Continued

WXMT-TV ch 30
PHONE: 615-256-3030 | FAX: 615-244-7442
300 Peabody St.
Nashville, TN 37210
TVB

Mailing Address
Same as above.

Affiliation
Independent

Personnel
Britton, Jerry — Gen Mgr
Friedenberg, Michele — Gen Sales Mgr
Stravos, Tracey — Prog Dir
Davidson, Teresa — Mktg Dir
Lewis, Lisa — Traffic Mgr

Corporate Ownership
MT Communications

Representatives
Not Applicable

Facilities
Video 5,000,000w; Audio 50,000w
Operating schedule: 20 hours daily
Time zone: Central
Airdate: February 18, 1984

Special Features
Mono
Billboards: 10 sec
Infomercials: 30min
Dayparts available: Various

Production Specifications
3/4in. U-Matic
1in. Reel
Mfd 088315-000

WZTV-TV ch 17
PHONE: 615-244-1717 | FAX: 615-259-3962
631 Main Stream Dr.
Nashville, TN 37228
TVB

Mailing Address
Same as above.

Affiliation
Fox

Personnel
Jay, Bob — Gen Mgr
Bankston, Jim — Gen Sales Mgr
Bankston, Jim — Natl Sales Mgr

Corporate Ownership
Act III Broadcasting of Nashville, Inc.

Representatives
Seltel

Facilities
Video 2,340,000w; Audio 234,000w
Antenna Height: 1,062 ft. above avg. terrain
Operating schedule: 24 hours daily
Time zone: Central
Airdate: March 1976

Special Features
Stereo
Billboards: 5 sec, 10 sec
Infomercials: 30min
Dayparts available: Daytime, Weekend

Production Specifications
3/4in. SP
1in. Reel

Programming
MON-FRI
7:00-8:00a Bonkers/Mighty Morphin Power Rangers
8:00-9:00a Merrie Melodies/Talespin
9:00-10:00a Bewitched/Kenneth Copeland
10:00-11:30a Informational Programming
11:30-12:30p Ricki Lake
12:30-1:30p The Montel Williams Show
1:30-2:00p Andy Griffith
2:00-3:00p Bullwinkle/The Flintstones
3:00-4:00p Tom & Jerry/Tiny Toon Adventures
4:00-5:00p Animaniac/Batman Animated
5:00-6:00p Mama's Family/Married w/Children
6:00-6:30p Cheers
10:00-10:30p Married w/Children
10:30-11:30p Star Trek
11:30-12:30a Arsenio Hall Show
MON PRIME
7:00-9:00p FOX Night At The Movies
9:00-10:00p Star Trek: The Next Generation
TUE
7:00-8:00p Monty/Roc
8:00-9:00p Front Page
9:00-10:00p Star Trek: The Next Generation
WED
7:00-8:00p Beverly Hills 90210
8:00-9:00p Melrose Place
9:00-10:00p Star Trek: The Next Generation
THUR
7:00-8:00p The Simpsons/Sinbad
8:00-9:00p In Living Color/Herman's Head
9:00-10:00p Star Trek: The Next Generation
FRI
7:00-8:00p Adventures of Brisco County Jr.
8:00-9:00p The X-Files
9:00-10:00p Star Trek: The Next Generation
SAT
7:00-8:00p Cops (2x)
8:00-9:00p America's Most Wanted
SUN
6:00-7:00p Code 3 (2x)
7:00-8:00p Martin/Living Single
8:00-9:00p Married w/Children/George Carlin
Mfd 086404-000

New Orleans, LA

WDSU-TV ch 6
PHONE: 504-527-0666
520 Royal St.
New Orleans, LA 70130

Mailing Address
Same as above.

Affiliation
NBC

Personnel
Barnett, Wayne — Gen Mgr
Carpenter, John — Gen Sales Mgr
Mitchell, Blaine — Local Sales Mgr
Barnett, Wayne — Prog Dir
Chastain, Scott — Adv/Promotion Dir
Freeman, Pat — Traffic Mgr

Corporate Ownership
Pulitzer Broadcasting, Inc.

Representatives
Katz Television Group, American

Facilities
Video 100,000w; Audio 20,000w
Antenna Height: 930 ft. above avg. terrain
Operating schedule: 24 hours daily
Time zone: Central

Production Specifications
1in. Reel
Mfd 086461-000

WGNO-TV ch 26
PHONE: 504-581-2600 | FAX: 504-942-9246
2 Canal St.
New Orleans, LA 70017

TRIBUNE BROADCASTING Company

Mailing Address
Same as above.

Affiliation
Independent

Personnel
Ross, William C — Gen Mgr
LaBonia, Michael — Gen Sales Mgr
Zickmund, Mike — Natl Sales Mgr
Quinn, Kath — Prog Dir
Clemons, Jeff — Adv/Promotion Dir
Peer, Pat — Traffic Mgr
Goodlad, Jim — Local Sales Mgr

Corporate Ownership
Tribune Broadcasting

Representatives
TeleRep

Facilities
Mono
Antenna Height: 1,049 ft. above avg. terrain
Operating schedule: 24 hours daily
Time zone: Central
Airdate: October 25, 1967

Special Features
Mono
Billboards: 5 sec, 10 sec

Production Specifications
3/4in. U-Matic
1in. Reel

Sports Programming
WGNO Sportspage
Saints Sideline
Friday Night Football
WGNO Metro Track & Field Championship
High School Football Kickball Classic
Saints Draft Specials
Mfd 087698-000

WNOL-TV ch 38
PHONE: 504-525-3838 | FAX: 504-569-0908
1661 Canal St.
New Orleans, LA 70112

Mailing Address
Same as above.

Affiliation
Fox

Personnel
Bonnot, Madelyn — VP/Gen Mgr
Scollard, Steve — Dir Sales
Foshee, Dale — Local Sales Mgr

Corporate Ownership
Quincy Jones Broadcasting

Representatives
Seltel, Inc.

Facilities
Video 5,000,000w; Audio 500,000w
Antenna Height: 1,049 ft. above avg. terrain
Operating schedule: 24 hours daily
Time zone: Central
Airdate: March 25, 1984

Special Features
Stereo
Billboards: 10 sec
Infomercials: 30min, 60min
Dayparts available: Various

Production Specifications
Beta SP
3/4in. SP
1in. Reel

Programming
MON-FRI
7:00-8:00a Sonic The Hedgehog/Mighty Morphin Power Rangers
8:00-9:00a Merrie Melodies/Dennis The Menace
9:00-10:00a I Dream of Jeannie/Bewitched
10:00-11:00a Star Trek
11:00-12:00n I Love Lucy (2x)
12:00-1:00p Jerry Springer
1:00-2:00p Ricki
2:00-2:30p People's Court (M-W, F)
2:30-3:00p Woody Woodpecker
3:00-4:00p Tom & Jerry Kids/Tiny Toon Adventures
4:00-5:00p Animaniacs/Batman
5:00-6:00p Ricki Lake
6:00-7:00p Different World/Hard Copy
10:00-10:30p Real Stories of The Highway Patrol
10:30-11:30p Arsenio Hall
MON PRIME
7:00-9:00p FOX Night At The Movies
9:00-10:00p Babylon 5
TUE
7:00-8:00p South Central/Roc
8:00-9:00p Front Page
9:00-10:00p Star Trek: The Next Generation
WED
7:00-8:00p Beverly Hills 90210
8:00-9:00p Melrose Place
9:00-10:00p Star Trek: The Next Generation

WZTV
Airdate:
March 1976
NASHVILLE

FOX 17

SELTEL

Location ID: 6 TLST TN
Act III Broadcasting of Nashville, Inc.
631 Mainstream Drive
Nashville, TN 37228
Phone: 615-244-1717
Fax: 615-259-3962
PERSONNEL
VP/General Manager - Bob Jay
Gen. Sales Mgr. - Jim Bankston
Natl. Sales Mgr. - Jim Bankston
REPRESENTATIVES
Seltel, Inc.

FACILITIES
Video 3,266,000w., audio 326,000w.; Ch. 17,
stereo. Antenna ht.: 1,161 ft. above average terrain.
Operating schedule: 24 hours daily. CST. Satellite
capabilities, downlink.
AGENCY COMMISSION
15% to recognized agencies on time; no cash discount.
Rate Protection: 10k, 11k, 12k, 13k, 14f, 15, 17
Contracts: 20b, 21, 25, 26, 28, 31a, 31b, 32a, 32c,
32d, 33, 34
Basic Rates: 40a, 41b, 41c, 41d, 42, 43b, 45a, 47,
60, 62

Comb., Cont. Discounts: 60a, 60d
Cancellation: 70b, 70k, 71, 72, 73a, 73b
Prod. Services: 80, 82, 83, 84, 85, 86, 87a
Affiliated with Fox Broadcasting Company.
Member of INTV.
TIME RATES
Rates not submitted.
SPECIAL FEATURES
COLOR: Schedules network color, film, slides,
tape and live.

The network section of *SRDS* provides the location and personnel directory with job responsibilities for both domestic and foreign networks providing feeds to local stations. (See Exhibit 3–4.)

The *SRDS*—Cable section provides the various cable operators covering the DMA, along with interconnect information. The location of each cable operator as well as key personnel listings are covered in this section. (See Exhibit 3–5.)

Standard Rate and Data (SRDS)—Spot Radio

Published monthly to keep all information current, this publication indexes the call letters of all AM and FM stations alphabetically, clearly designates the Class A and Class B coverage areas of each station, defines the area of dominant influence (ADI) as well as the designated marketing area (DMA). A specific section defines the network affiliations and programming formats. The statistics on each DMA includes radio households and purchasing power. The publication also sets fourth detailed demographic information. Radio *SRDS* also lists the dial position and power of each station as well as the location and key personnel with their designated jobs. It sometimes publishes the stations current rate card. (See Exhibits 3–6 to 3–9.)

TV Datatrak

This relative newcomer publishes current data on TV and cable that offers basic station statistics by alphabetical call letters. For each TV station, it includes station location, personnel, and job designations. The section on cable not only includes the address, personnel, and job designation of each cable operator, but also interconnects affiliations. (See Exhibits 3–10 and 3–11.)

Factbooks

The *Television, Radio, and Cable Factbooks* offer much more information about each station. These books give you the exact geographical location of the transmitter, an up-to-date listing of the operating personnel, the type of equipment available at the station, the base rates, and, more important, the coverage map of the station detailing "A" and "B" signal strength and detailed information on the program format for radio stations. (See Exhibit 3–12.)

EXHIBIT 3-4
Standard Rate and Data Service: Television Networks

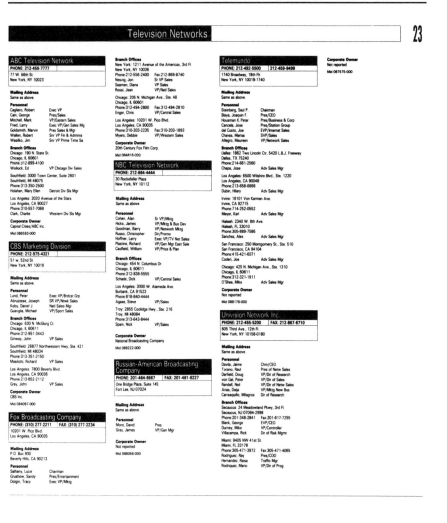

EXHIBIT 3-5
Standard Rate and Data Service: Interconnects of Cable Systems

538 | Nashville, TN | Interconnects & Cable Systems

Nashville, TN—Continued

TMC OF LOGAN COUNTY—cont

Personnel
Richardson, Dave — System Mgr
Benner, Bill — Dir

Corporate Ownership
Tele-Media Corp.

Mid 087990-000

United Artists Cable of Tennessee
PHONE: 615-898-1810

340 New Salem Highway
Murfreesboro, TN 37129

Mailing Address
Same as above.

Personnel
Butler, Greg — System Mgr
Roberts, Doug — Adv Sales Mgr
Cunningham, Mindy — Traffic Mgr

Corporate Ownership
TCI

Representatives
None

Interconnect
Nashville-Tennessee

System Background
Channel capacity:38, Channels utilized:38

Coverage

City	County	Zipcode
Gallatin	Sumner	
Winchester	Franklin	
Iaclard	Franklin	
Cowan	Franklin	
Estill Springs	Franklin	
Manchester	Bedford	
Shelbyville	Bedford	
Mt. Juliet	Wilson	
Woodbury	Cannon	

Programming

Service	Ad Insertion Avails
A&E	Yes
BET	No
CNBC	No
CNN	Yes
Discovery	No
ESPN	Yes
Family Channel	No
Lifetime	No
MTV	Yes
Nickelodeon	No
Nick-At-Nite	No
SportsChannel	Yes
TNN	Yes
TNT	Yes
USA	Yes
VH-1	No
Weather Channel	Yes
FNN	No

Broadcast Networks Carried
ABC
CBS
FOX
NBC

Production Specifications
3/4in. U-Matic

Subscriber Data
Basic 45,000
Pay 0
Total 45,000

Mid 085476-000

Viacom Cablevision of Nashville
PHONE: 615-244-9615 | FAX: 615-255-6628

660 Mainstream Drive
Nashville, TN 37228

Mailing Address
Same as above.

Personnel
Smith, Stan — System Mgr
Walser, John — Adv Sales Mgr
Brandon, Janice — Adv/Promotion Dir
Dunning, Margaret — Traffic Mgr

Corporate Ownership
Viacom

Representatives
CNI

Interconnect
Nashville Cable Interconnect

System Background
Turn on: June 1, 1980
Franchise expires: 1994
Channel capacity:39, Channels utilized:39
Homes in franchise area:243,257
Homes passed:236,651

Programming

Service	Ad Insertion Avails
A&E	Yes
BET	No
CNBC	No
CNN	Yes
Discovery	Yes
ESPN	Yes
Family Channel	Yes
Headline News	Yes
Lifetime	Yes
MTV	Yes
Nickelodeon	No
Nick-At-Nite	No
Sci-Fi Channel	Yes
SportsChannel	No
TNN	Yes
TNT	Yes
USA	Yes
VH-1	Yes
Weather Channel	No
CMT	Yes

Broadcast Networks Carried
ABC
CBS
FOX
NBC
Telemundo
Univision

Production Specifications
3/4in. U-Matic

Special Features
Stereo

Subscriber Data
Basic 125,978
Pay 39,644
Total 165,622

Mid 084700-000

New Orleans, LA

Interconnects

New Orleans Interconnect
PHONE: 504-733-5812 | FAX: 504-733-7910

338 Edwards Ave.
Harahan, LA 70123

Mailing Address
Same as above.

Personnel
Salgado, Michael C. — Gen Mgr
Cathey, Sonny — Adv Sales Mgr
Manuel, Kirtrell — Traffic Mgr

Representatives
NCA

DMA(s) Served
New Orleans, LA

Service Areas
Arabi	Gretna
Harahan	Harvey
Kenner	Marrero
Metairie	Westwego

Subscriber Data
Market Name	Total Subscribers
New Orleans, LA	228,000

Mid 087433-000

Cable Systems

Cablevision Industries of Jennings
PHONE: 318-824-2981 | FAX: 318-824-0907

910 N. Main St.
Jennings, LA 70546

Mailing Address
P.O. Box 100
Jennings, LA 70546

Personnel
Matte, J.R. — System Mgr

Corporate Ownership
Cablevision Industries Inc.

Representatives
None

Interconnect
None

System Background
Not reported

Programming
Not reported

Broadcast Networks Carried
ABC
CBS
FOX
NBC

Production Specifications
Not reported

Special Features
Not reported

Subscriber Data
Not reported

Mid 085972-000

Cablevision Industries of LaFourche Parish
PHONE: 504-446-9444 | FAX: 504-446-9849

1306 Ridgefield
Thibodaux, LA 70301

Mailing Address
Same as above.

Personnel
Angelette, Andrew — System Mgr
Yelder, George — Adv Sales Mgr

Corporate Ownership
Cable Vision Industries

Representatives
HTV

Interconnect
None

System Background
Turn on: April 1, 1970
Franchise expires: 2001
Channels utilized:43
Homes in franchise area:24,300
Homes passed:23,960

Broadcast Networks Carried
ABC
CBS
FOX
NBC

Production Specifications
Not reported

Subscriber Data
Not reported

Mid 085901-000

Callais Cablevision, Inc.
PHONE: 504-475-5711 | FAX 504-475-6390

315 Callais St
Golden Meadow, LA 70357

Mailing Address
P.O. Box 788
Golden Meadow, LA 70357

Personnel
Callais, Corey — System Mgr
MArtinez, Angel — Adv Sales Mgr
Callais, Tina — Prog Dir
Martinez, Angel — Traffic Mgr
Callais, Tina — Adv/Promotion Dir

Corporate Ownership
Harold J Callais

Representatives
None

Interconnect
None

System Background
Turn on: April 1, 1968
Channel capacity:41, Channels utilized:41

Headends
Golden Meadow, LA

Programming
Not reported

Broadcast Networks Carried
ABC
CBS
FOX
NBC

Production Specifications
3/4in. U-Matic

Special Features
Stereo

EXHIBIT 3-6
Spot Radio Rates and Data: Call Letter Index

Call Letter Index to AM/FM Stations
*Denotes listing in an MSA.

CANADIAN STATIONS:
*CIMX (FM)—Detroit, MI

MEXICAN STATIONS:
*XEAS—Laredo, TX
*XEAZ—San Diego, CA
*XEMO—San Diego, CA
*XENU—Laredo, TX
*XERKS—Brownsville-Harlingen, TX
*XEROK—El Paso, TX
*XERT—Brownsville-Harlingen, TX
*XEWG—El Paso, TX
*XEWL—Laredo, TX
*XEXX—San Diego, CA
*XHFG-FM—San Diego, CA
*XTRA—San Diego, CA
*XTRA-FM—San Diego, CA

UNITED STATES STATIONS:
*KAAA—Kingman, AZ
*KAAB—Batesville, AR
*KAAK (FM)—Great Falls, MT
*KAAM—Dallas, TX
*KAAN—Bethany, MO
*KAAN-FM—Bethany, MO
KAAQ (FM)—Alliance, NE
*KAAR (FM)—Spokane, WA
KAAT (FM)—Oakhurst, CA
*KAAY—Little Rock-North Little Rock, AR
*KABC—Los Angeles Long Beach, CA
KABI—Abilene, KS
KABL (FM)—Oakland, CA
*KABL FM—San Francisco, CA
KABQ—Albuquerque, NM
*KABX (FM)—Merced, CA
*KACE (FM)—Los Angeles-Long Beach, CA
KACH—Preston, ID
KACI—The Dalles, OR
KACI-FM—The Dalles, OR
KACT—Andrews, TX
*KACT—Andrews, TX
*KACY—Lafayette, LA
KADA—Ada, OK
KADA-FM—Ada, OK
KADQ (FM)—Rexburg, ID
KADR—Elkader, IA
KADS—Elk City, OK
*KAFE (FM)—Bellingham, WA
KAFF—Flagstaff, AZ
KAFF-FM—Flagstaff, AZ
KAFM (FM)—Red Lodge, MT
KAFX—Diboll, TX
KAFX-FM—Diboll, TX
*KAFY—Bakersfield, CA
*KAGC—Bryan-College Station, TX
*KAGE—Winona, MN
KAGE-FM—Winona, MN
KAGI (FM)—Madisonville, TX
KAGH—Crossett, AR
KAGH-FM—Crossett, AR
KAGI—Grants Pass, OR
KAGO—Klamath Falls, OR
KAGO-FM—Klamath Falls, OR
KAGY—Port Sulphur, LA
*KAHI—Sacramento, CA
KAHM (FM)—Prescott, AZ
KAHR (FM)—Poplar Bluff, MO
*KAHU—Hilo, HI
*KAIM—Honolulu, HI
KAIM-FM—Honolulu, HI
KAIN—Vidalia, LA
*KAJA (FM)—San Antonio, TX
KAJN-FM—Crowley, LA
KAJO—Grants Pass, OR
*KAJZ (FM)—Los Angeles-Long Beach, CA
*KAKC—Tulsa, OK
*KAKI (FM)—Little Rock-North Little Rock, AR
*KAKS—Amarillo, TX
KAKS (FM)—Amarillo, TX
*KALB—Alexandria, LA
*KALE—Richland-Kennewick-Pasco, WA
KALF (FM)—Red Bluff, CA
*KALL—Los Angeles-Long Beach, CA
KALK—Mount Pleasant, TX
*KALL—Salt Lake City-Ogden, UT
*KALL-FM—Salt Lake City-Ogden, UT
KALM—Thayer, MO
KALN—Iola, KS
*KALO—Beaumont-Port Arthur, TX
KALP (FM)—Alpine, TX
KALQ (FM)—Alamosa, CO
KALS (FM)—Kalispell, MT
KALT—Atlanta, TX

KALV—Alva, OK
*KALY—Albuquerque, NM
*KAMA—El Paso, TX
*KAMA-FM—El Paso, TX
*KAMB (FM)—Merced, CA
KAMD—Camden, AR
*KAMG—Victoria, TX
KAMI—Cozad, NE
KAMI-FM—Cozad, NE
KAML—Kenedy-Karnes City, TX
KAML (FM)—Gillette, WY
KAMO—Rogers, AR
KAMO-FM—Rogers, AR
KAMP—El Centro, CA
KAMQ—Carlsbad, NM
KAMS (FM)—Mammoth Spring, AR
KAMV-FM—Victoria, TX
*KAMX—Albuquerque, NM
*KAMZ (FM)—El Paso, TX
KAND—Corsicana, TX
KAND-FM—Corsicana, TX
KANE—New Iberia, LA
KAN—Wharton, TX
*KANN—Salt Lake City-Ogden, UT
KANR—Nampa, ID
KANS—Larned, KS
KAOI—Kihei, HI
KAOI-FM—Wailuku, HI
*KAOK—Lake Charles, LA
KAOL—Carrollton, MO
KAOY (FM)—Kealakekua-Kona, HI
KAPA—Raymond, WA
KAPB—Marksville, LA
KAPB-FM—Marksville, LA
KAPE—Cape Girardeau, MO
*KAPL—Riverside-San Bernardino, CA
KAPP—Douglas, AZ
KAPS—Mount Vernon, WA
*KAPX—San Francisco, CA
KAPY—Port Angeles, WA
*KAPZ—Bald Knob, AR
*KAQQ—Spokane, WA
KAQU (FM)—Huntington, TX
*KARA (FM)—San Jose, CA
KARB (FM)—Price, UT
*KARI—Bellingham, WA
*KARN—Little Rock-North Little Rock, AR
KARQ (FM)—Columbia, MO
KARQ (FM)—Ashdown, AR
KARS—Belen, NM
KARS-FM—Belen, NM
KARV—Russellville, AR
KARV—Longview-Marshall, TX
*KARX (FM)—Amarillo, TX
*KARY—Richland-Kennewick-Pasco, WA
*KARY-FM—Richland-Kennewick-Pasco, WA
KASA (FM)—Redding, CA
*KASA—Phoenix, AZ
*KASE (FM)—Austin, TX
*KASH-FM—Anchorage, AK
*KASI—Ames, IA
*KASK (FM)—Las Cruces, NM
KASL—Newcastle, WY
KASM—Albany, MN
KASO—Minden, LA
KASO-FM—Minden, LA
*KASP—St. Louis, MO
KAST—Astoria, OR
KAST-FM—Astoria, OR
*KASY (FM)—Albuquerque, NM
KATA—Arcata, CA
KATE—Albert Lea, MN
*KATF (FM)—Dubuque, IA
KATI (FM)—Douglas, WY
*KATI—Casper, WY
*KATJ (FM)—Riverside-San Bernardino, CA
KATK—Carlsbad, NM
KATK-FM—Carlsbad, NM
KATL—Miles City, MT
KATO—Safford, AZ
KATP (FM)—Amarillo, TX
KATQ—Plentywood, MT
KATQ-FM—Plentywood, MT
KATS (FM)—Yakima, WA
*KATT-FM—Oklahoma City, OK
KATW (FM)—Lewiston, ID
KATX (FM)—Plainview, TX
*KATY (FM)—Riverside-San Bernardino, CA
KATZ—St. Louis, MO
*KATZ-FM—St. Louis, MO
KAUB (FM)—Auburn, NE
KAUM (FM)—Colorado City, TX
KAUS—Austin, MN
KAUS-FM—Austin, MN
KAVC (FM)—Bakersfield, CA
*KAVE-FM—Eugene-Springfield, OR
KAVI—Rocky Ford, CO

KAVI-FM—Rocky Ford, CO
KBIC (FM)—Alice, TX
*KBIF—Fresno, CA
*KBIG (FM)—Los Angeles-Long Beach, CA
*KBIL—San Angelo, TX
KBIM—San Angelo, TX
KBIM-FM—Roswell, NM
KBIM-FM—Roswell, NM
*KBIS—Little Rock-North Little Rock, AR
*KBIU (FM)—Lake Charles, LA
KBIV—Muskogee, OK
KBIZ—Ottumwa, IA
KBJM (FM)—Marshall, MN
KBJM—Lemmon, SD
KBJT—Fordyce, AR
*KBJZ (FM)—Anaheim-Santa Ana, CA
KAVV (FM)—Benson, AZ
KAWL—York, NE
KAWS—Hemphill, TX
KAWW—Heber Springs, AR
KAWW-FM—Heber Springs, AR
*KAXM-FM—Albuquerque, NM
*KAXX (FM)—Oxnard-Ventura, CA
*KAYC—Beaumont-Port Arthur, TX
*KAYD (FM)—Beaumont-Port Arthur, TX
KAYE (FM)—Muskogee, OK
KAYL—San Angelo, TX
KAYL-FM—Storm Lake, IA
KAYN (FM)—Nogales, AZ
KAYO-FM—Aberdeen, WA
KAYO-FM—Aberdeen, WA
*KAYS—Fort Smith, AR
KAYS—Hays, KS
KAYY (FM)—Fairbanks, AK
KAYZ (FM)—El Dorado, AR
*KAZA—San Jose, CA
*KAZN—Sedona, AZ
*KAZN—Los Angeles-Long Beach, CA
KAZO (FM)—Soldotna, AK
KAZR—Denver, CO
*KAZZ (FM)—Spokane, WA
KBAA (FM)—Ortonville, MN
KBAI—Morro Bay, CA
KBAK (FM)—Longview, WA
KBAR—Burley, ID
KBAS—Bullhead City, AZ
*KBAT (FM)—Midland, TX
*KBAU (FM)—Houma-Thibodaux, LA
KBAZ—San Diego, CA
*KBAY (FM)—San José, CA
KBBC (FM)—Lake Havasu City, AZ
KBBF (FM)—McPherson, KS
KBBK—Rupert, ID
KBBM (FM)—Winterset, IA
KBBN (FM)—Broken Bow, NE
KBBO—Yakima, WA
KBBQ (FM)—Fort Smith, AR
KBBS—North Bend, OR
KBBS—Buffalo, WY
*KBBT—Portland, OR
KBBU—Riverside-San Bernardino, CA
*KBBW—Waco, TX
*KBBX—Salt Lake City-Ogden, UT
KBBY (FM)—Oxnard-Ventura, CA
KBBZ (FM)—Kalispell, MT
KBCQ (FM)—Imperial, CA
*KBCE (FM)—Alexandria, LA
KBCH—Lincoln City, OR
*KBCK (FM)—Salt Lake City-Ogden, UT
*KBCL—Shreveport, LA
KBCO (FM)—Boulder-Longmont, CO
*KBCO-FM—Boulder-Longmont, CO
KBCQ (FM)—Roswell, NM
KBCR—Steamboat Springs, CO
KBCV (FM)—Bentonville, AR
*KBCW—Minneapolis-St. Paul, MN
*KBCY (FM)—Abilene, TX
*KBEA—Kansas City, MO
KBEB—Tulare, CA
*KBEE-FM—Modesto, CA
KBEL (FM)—Idabel, OK
KBEN—Carrizo Springs, TX
KBEQ (FM)—Kansas City, MO
KBEP (FM)—Spanish Fork, UT
*KBET—Los Angeles-Long Beach, CA
KBEV (FM)—Fayetteville-Springdale, AR
KBEV-FM—Millbrae, CA
KBEW—Blue Earth, MN
KBEY (FM)—Garberville, CA
KBEZ (FM)—Tulsa, OK
KBFC (FM)—Forrest City, AR
KBFG—Bonners Ferry, ID
KBFL (FM)—Buffalo, MO
*KBFM—McAllen-Edinburg-Mission, TX
KBFS—Belle Fourche, SD
*KBFW—Bellingham, WA
KBFX (FM)—Anchorage, AK
KBGA—Caldwell, ID
KBHB—Sturgis, SD
KBHC (FM)—Nashville, AR
KBHL (FM)—Osaka, MN
KBHM (FM)—Paris, AR
KBHS—Hot Springs, AR
KBHT (FM)—Crockett, TX
KBHW (FM)—International Falls, MN

*KBUY (FM)—Amarillo, TX
*KBUZ (FM)—Wichita, KS
KBWD—Brownwood, TX
KBWJ (FM)—Roosevelt, UT
KBWS (FM)—Sisseton, SD
KBXB (FM)—Canton, MO
KBXL (FM)—Caldwell, ID
KBXS (FM)—Ely, NV
*KBXX (FM)—Houston, TX
*KBYE—Oklahoma City, OK
KBYO—Tallulah, LA
*KBYR—Tallulah, LA
*KBYR—Anchorage, AK
*KBYZ (FM)—Bismarck, ND
KBKB—Fort Madison, IA
KBKB-FM—Fort Madison, IA
KBKG (FM)—Corning, AR
KBKR—Baker City, OR
*KBLA—Los Angeles-Long Beach, CA
*KBLE—Seattle, WA
KBLF—Red Bluff, CA
KBLG—Billings, MT
KBLI—Blackfoot, ID
KBLJ (FM)—La Junta, CO
KBLL—Helena, MT
KBLL-FM—Helena, MT
KBLP (FM)—Lindsay, OK
KBLQ-FM—Logan, UT
KBLT (FM)—El Dorado, AR
KBLU—Yuma, AZ
*KBLV—Oakland, CA
*KBLX-FM—Oakland, CA
KBMB (FM)—Hot Springs, AR
KBMG (FM)—Hamilton, MT
KBMI (FM)—Roma, TX
KBMN—Bozeman, MT
*KBMR—Bismarck, ND
*KBMX (FM)—Vancouver, WA
KBMV—Birch Tree, MO
KBMV-FM—Birch Tree, MO
KBMW—Breckenridge, MN
KBMX (FM)—Osage Beach, MO
*KBNA—El Paso, TX
*KBNA-FM—El Paso, TX
KBND—Bend, OR
*KBNO—Denver, CO
*KBNP—Portland, OR
KBOA—Kennett, MO
*KBOB (FM)—Los Angeles-Long Beach, CA
KBOE—Oskaloosa, IA
KBOE (FM)—Oskaloosa, IA
*KBOI—Boise City, ID
KBOK—Malvern, AR
*KBOL—Boulder-Longmont, CO
*KBOM (FM)—Santa Fe, NM
KBON—Pleasanton, TX
KBOP-FM—Pleasanton, TX
*KBOQ (FM)—Salinas-Seaside-Monterey, CA
*KBOR—Brownsville-Harlingen, TX
*KBOS (FM)—Visalia-Tulare-Porterville, CA
KBOV—Bishop, CA
KBOW—Butte, MT
*KBOX (FM)—Santa Barbara-Santa Maria-Lompoc, CA
*KBOY (FM)—Medford, OR
KBOZ—Bozeman, MT
KBOZ-FM—Bozeman, MT
*KBPI-FM—Denver, CO
KBQQ (FM)—Minot, ND
*KBQN—Boise City, ID
KBRB—Ainsworth, NE
KBRB-FM—Ainsworth, NE
*KBRD—Mount Vernon, WA
KBRE (FM)—Cedar City, UT
KBRE-FM—Cedar City, UT
KBRF—Fergus Falls, MN
KBRF-FM—Fergus Falls, MN
KBRI—Brinkley, AR
*KBRJ (FM)—Anchorage, AK
KBRK—Brookings, SD
KBRL—McCook, NE
KBRN—Boerne, TX
KBRO—Bremerton, WA
KBRQ (FM)—Fort Morgan, CO
KBRS—Spearfish, SD
KBRX—O'Neill, NE
KBRX-FM—O'Neill, NE
KBRZ—Brazoria, TX
KBSF—Springhill, LA
*KBSG—Tacoma, WA
KBSG-FM—Tacoma, WA
*KBSN—Moses Lake, WA
KBSR—Billings, MT
KBST—Big Spring, TX
*KBST-FM—Big Spring, TX
*KBSY (FM)—Fort Smith, AR
KBTA—Batesville, AR
KBTO—Houston, MO
KBTM—Jonesboro, AR
KBTN—Joplin, MO
KBTO (FM)—Bottineau, ND
KBTR (FM)—Oracle, AZ
KBUF—Garden City, KS
KBUK (FM)—La Grange, TX
KBUL (FM)—Carson City, NV
KBUN—Bemidji, MN
*KBUN—Burlington, IA
*KBUQ (FM)—Tempe, AZ
KBUX (FM)—Quartzsite, AZ
KBUY—Ruidoso, NM

KCLK—Clarkston, WA
KCLK-FM—Lewiston, ID
*KCLN-FM—Clinton, IA
KCLR—Ralls, TX
KCLS (FM)—Boonville, MO
KCLT (FM)—West Helena, AR
KCLV—Clovis, NM
KCLV-FM—Clovis, NM
KCLW (FM)—Hamilton, TX
KCLX—Colfax, WA
*KCLX-FM—San Diego, CA
KCLY (FM)—Clay Center, KS
*KCMA (FM)—Tulsa, OK
KCMB (FM)—Baker City, OR
*KCMC—Texarkana (TX)-Texarkana (AR), TX
KCMG—Mountain Grove, MO
KCMG-FM—Mountain Grove, MO
KCMI (FM)—Terrytown, NE
*KCMJ—Riverside-San Bernardino, CA
*KCMJ-FM—Riverside-San Bernardino, CA
*KCMN—Colorado Springs, CO
*KCMN—Kansas City, MO
KCMN-FM—Kansas City, MO
*KCMQ (FM)—Columbia, MO
*KCMS (FM)—Seattle, WA
KCMT (FM)—Chester, CA
KCMX—Medford, OR
*KCMX-FM—Medford, OR
*KCMZ—Dallas, TX
KCNA (FM)—Cave Junction, OR
KCNE (FM)—Chadron, NE
*KCNI—Broken Bow, NE
KCNN—Sapan, MR
KCNN—East Grand Forks, MN
*KCNQ (FM)—Bakersfield, CA
*KCNR—Salt Lake City-Ogden, UT
*KCNW—Kansas City, MO
KCNY—Moab, UT
KCOB—Newton, IA
*KCOG—Centerville, IA
*KCOH—Houston, TX
KCOQ (FM)—Fort Collins-Loveland, CO
*KCOR—San Antonio, TX
*KCOS—Salem, OR
*KCON—Little Rock-North Little Rock, AR
KCON—Comanche, TX
KCON—Abilene, KS
KCDA (FM)—Coeur d'Alene, ID
KCON—Monahans, TX
*KCOU (FM)—Fort Worth-Arlington, TX
KCOY (FM)—Carlsbad, NM
KCDZ (FM)—Riverside-San Bernardino, CA
*KCEE—Tucson, AZ
*KCEG—San Diego, CA
KCEP (FM)—Eufaula, OK
KCEZ (FM)—Corning, CA
*KCFI—Waterloo-Cedar Falls, IA
*KCFM (FM)—Kansas City, MO
KCFO—Tulsa, OK
*KCFX (FM)—Kansas City, MO
KCGB-FM—Hood River, OR
KCGM (FM)—Scobey, MT
*KCGQ (FM)—Ortonville, MN
KCGQ (FM)—Gordonville, MO
*KCGR (FM)—Corpus Christi, TX
KCGS—Marshall, AR
KCGY (FM)—Laramie, WY
*KCHA—Charles City, IA
KCHA-FM—Charles City, IA
*KCHE—Cherokee, IA
KCHE-FM—Cherokee, IA
*KCHG—San Antonio, TX
*KCHH (FM)—Chico, CA
*KCHI—Chillicothe, MO
KCHI-FM—Chillicothe, MO
*KCHK—Minneapolis-St. Paul, MN
*KCHL—San Antonio, TX
KCHM—Charleston, MO
*KCHN—Truth or Consequences, NM
*KCHT (FM)—Bakersfield, CA
*KCHT-FM—Yellville, AR
*KCHU—Childress, TX
*KCHX (FM)—Monahans, TX
KCHY—Salinas-Seaside-Monterey, CA
*KCUB—Tucson, AZ
*KCUE—Red Wing, MN
*KCUL—Longview-Marshall, TX
*KCUL-FM—Longview-Marshall, TX
KCUV—Denver, CO
KCUZ—Clifton, AZ
KCVL—Colville, WA
*KCVN—Stockton, CA
KCVS (FM)—Salina, KS
KCWD (FM)—Harrison, AR
*KCWR—Bakersfield, CA
*KCWW—Phoenix, AZ
KCXY (FM)—Camden, AR
KCYL—Lampasas, TX
KCYN (FM)—Pocahontas, AR
*KCYY (FM)—San Antonio, TX
KCZQ (FM)—Cresco, IA
KCZY (FM)—Osage, IA
KDAC—Fort Bragg, CA
*KDAE—Corpus Christi, TX
*KDAF—Carrington, ND
*KDAL—Duluth, MN
*KDAL-FM—Duluth, MN
KDAM (FM)—Monroe City, MO
*KDAO—Marshalltown, IA
*KDAP—Douglas, AZ
KDAP-FM—Douglas, AZ

EXHIBIT 3-7
Market Statistics: Designated Market Areas

DESIGNATED MARKET AREAS

DMA TITLES As defined by Nielsen 1992 (Ranked Largest to Smallest)	TV HH	% OF U.S.	RANKING BY TV HH	($000) TOTAL	MEDIAN	$10,000 TO $19,999	$20,000 TO $34,999	$35,000 TO $49,999	$50,000 TO $74,999	$75,000 TO $99,999	$100,000 TO $124,999	$125,000+	BUYING POWER INDEX
NEW YORK	6,733,920	7.24%	1	374,744,554	43,610	11.64%	18.03%	16.92%	21.79%	11.09%	4.93%	5.21%	8.3726
LOS ANGELES	4,965,780	5.34%	2	255,547,248	40,201	12.94%	21.05%	18.80%	21.41%	9.34%	3.64%	3.77%	5.7080
CHICAGO	3,028,500	3.25%	3	154,283,377	41,464	11.89%	19.93%	19.35%	22.67%	9.39%	3.53%	3.69%	3.6669
PHILADELPHIA	2,658,130	2.86%	4	129,841,862	40,003	12.74%	20.89%	19.69%	22.08%	8.84%	3.22%	3.05%	3.0783
SAN FRANCISCO - OAKLAND - SAN JOSE	2,246,220	2.41%	5	121,484,244	44,878	10.96%	19.05%	18.77%	23.74%	11.39%	4.43%	4.17%	2.8005
BOSTON	2,109,390	2.27%	6	107,658,351	42,975	11.74%	18.96%	19.11%	23.86%	10.31%	3.85%	3.19%	2.6379
WASHINGTON, D.C.	1,851,480	1.99%	7	101,950,557	45,927	9.26%	19.53%	19.81%	24.51%	11.71%	4.62%	3.94%	2.2931
DALLAS - FT. WORTH	1,803,680	1.94%	8	83,886,766	36,752	13.96%	23.13%	19.09%	19.61%	7.84%	2.84%	3.07%	1.2200
DETROIT	1,729,460	1.85%	9	77,842,294	37,918	13.54%	20.45%	19.21%	21.46%	8.19%	2.65%	2.37%	1.9224
ATLANTA	1,475,590	1.59%	10	63,629,899	35,491	13.90%	24.27%	20.38%	19.68%	6.43%	2.04%	2.19%	1.6065
HOUSTON	1,455,000	1.56%	11	68,740,480	36,558	13.96%	22.26%	18.20%	19.27%	8.15%	3.10%	3.35%	1.6813
CLEVELAND	1,442,370	1.55%	12	57,084,603	32,640	16.22%	25.16%	20.34%	17.60%	5.05%	1.54%	1.63%	1.4622
SEATTLE - TACOMA	1,389,810	1.49%	13	64,378,103	37,564	13.85%	23.53%	20.97%	20.80%	7.30%	2.42%	2.39%	1.5733
TAMPA - ST. PETERSBURG, SARASOTA	1,374,310	1.48%	14	49,525,761	28,043	20.65%	28.91%	18.22%	12.87%	3.75%	1.29%	1.59%	1.3191
MINNEAPOLIS - ST. PAUL	1,368,670	1.47%	15	58,374,436	35,884	14.80%	24.46%	21.82%	20.26%	5.74%	1.76%	1.80%	1.5182
MIAMI - FT. LAUDERDALE	1,291,940	1.39%	16	53,616,938	31,223	17.12%	24.35%	17.71%	16.16%	5.73%	2.11%	2.68%	1.4181
PITTSBURGH	1,126,760	1.21%	17	42,495,619	29,698	18.95%	25.40%	18.59%	15.32%	4.63%	1.49%	1.62%	1.0550
ST. LOUIS	1,102,600	1.18%	18	46,517,535	35,009	15.35%	23.48%	20.38%	19.67%	6.14%	1.95%	1.87%	1.1543
SACRAMENTO - STOCKTON - MODESTO	1,082,200	1.16%	19	49,458,816	35,420	15.79%	24.10%	20.26%	20.31%	6.45%	1.93%	1.67%	1.2308
PHOENIX	1,068,050	1.15%	20	40,859,256	30,437	18.20%	27.14%	19.48%	15.51%	4.49%	1.39%	1.55%	1.0895
DENVER	1,034,000	1.11%	21	45,826,233	35,994	14.86%	23.85%	19.82%	20.01%	7.00%	2.40%	2.21%	1.1324
BALTIMORE	966,110	1.04%	22	43,455,525	37,984	12.84%	22.53%	20.88%	21.57%	7.83%	2.22%	2.10%	1.0564
ORLANDO - DAYTONA BEACH - MELBOURNE	947,330	1.02%	23	36,477,952	30,712	18.24%	28.07%	19.56%	15.58%	4.53%	1.42%	1.57%	.9749
HARTFORD & NEW HAVEN	930,870	1.00%	24	47,888,774	43,563	11.03%	19.50%	18.96%	24.85%	10.10%	3.51%	3.11%	1.1011
SAN DIEGO	910,990	.98%	25	43,417,917	37,549	14.15%	23.83%	20.09%	20.75%	7.85%	2.59%	2.61%	1.0596
INDIANAPOLIS	895,790	.96%	26	35,661,179	32,815	16.67%	25.79%	20.30%	18.07%	5.18%	1.42%	1.46%	.9295
PORTLAND, OREG	867,780	.93%	27	35,256,141	33,278	16.37%	26.29%	21.01%	18.05%	4.99%	1.52%	1.52%	.9202
MILWAUKEE	771,520	.83%	28	33,015,775	36,658	14.96%	23.54%	21.60%	21.45%	6.03%	1.71%	1.70%	.8212
KANSAS CITY	760,020	.82%	29	32,362,814	34,771	15.27%	24.21%	20.04%	19.21%	6.38%	2.02%	1.99%	.8054
CHARLOTTE	758,710	.82%	30	28,708,873	31,514	16.93%	26.91%	20.55%	16.44%	4.47%	1.27%	1.26%	.7437
CINCINNATI	756,230	.81%	31	31,460,235	34,235	15.30%	23.68%	19.85%	19.01%	6.15%	1.88%	1.93%	.7922
RALEIGH - DURHAM	728,290	.78%	32	27,856,979	30,891	17.19%	28.03%	19.33%	16.54%	4.70%	1.42%	1.34%	.7189
NASHVILLE	727,150	.78%	33	27,453,469	29,811	17.75%	25.97%	18.78%	15.38%	4.46%	1.36%	1.59%	.7135
COLUMBUS, OHIO	678,420	.73%	34	27,537,279	33,533	15.67%	25.25%	20.37%	18.33%	5.59%	1.70%	1.63%	.7045
GREENVILLE - SPARTANBURG - ASHEVILLE	656,130	.71%	35	22,599,562	28,412	19.35%	27.28%	19.40%	13.88%	3.45%	.92%	.93%	.6104
GRAND RAPIDS - KALAMAZOO - BATTLE CREEK	634,720	.68%	36	25,226,733	33,602	16.26%	25.32%	21.56%	18.61%	4.76%	1.39%	1.36%	.6565
BUFFALO	628,780	.68%	37	22,294,596	29,564	18.82%	26.31%	19.83%	15.47%	3.61%	.99%	.93%	.5882
NORFOLK - PORTSMOUTH - NEWPORT NEWS	614,640	.66%	38	24,036,581	32,216	15.74%	27.58%	21.09%	17.21%	4.43%	1.25%	1.11%	.6265
SAN ANTONIO	605,200	.65%	39	22,258,838	28,146	18.96%	25.83%	17.65%	14.14%	4.30%	1.42%	1.59%	.6202
NEW ORLEANS	600,770	.65%	40	22,842,084	29,190	17.56%	23.07%	16.83%	15.80%	5.37%	1.76%	1.99%	.6256
SALT LAKE CITY	600,230	.65%	41	24,230,746	34,160	15.62%	26.62%	22.22%	18.79%	4.84%	1.36%	1.30%	.6438
MEMPHIS	590,100	.63%	42	20,885,190	27,055	18.96%	24.20%	16.84%	14.06%	4.10%	1.40%	1.59%	.5540
PROVIDENCE - NEW BEDFORD	567,110	.61%	43	22,978,636	34,327	16.03%	22.92%	20.55%	19.29%	5.96%	1.86%	1.51%	.5880
HARRISBURG - LANCASTER - LEBANON - YORK	564,990	.61%	44	24,530,877	36,559	14.03%	25.46%	23.11%	20.65%	5.68%	1.68%	1.54%	.6169
OKLAHOMA CITY	562,920	.60%	45	19,109,890	26,990	20.53%	27.36%	17.89%	13.17%	3.14%	.95%	1.07%	.5194
WEST PALM BEACH - FT. PIERCE	559,670	.60%	46	25,989,725	33,649	16.13%	25.54%	19.17%	16.54%	5.96%	2.42%	3.72%	.6276
WILKES-BARRE - SCRANTON	546,050	.59%	47	19,341,410	28,879	20.21%	26.91%	19.74%	14.36%	3.37%	1.00%	1.07%	.5101
GREENSBORO - HIGH POINT - WINSTON-SALEM	530,140	.57%	48	19,411,127	30,069	18.17%	27.47%	20.14%	15.06%	3.71%	1.21%	1.33%	.5114
ALBUQUERQUE - SANTA FE	521,930	.56%	49	18,976,646	27,715	19.58%	26.02%	17.54%	13.95%	4.07%	1.36%	1.28%	.5105
LOUISVILLE	518,830	.56%	50	19,512,546	30,358	17.74%	24.59%	18.78%	15.78%	4.51%	1.25%	1.40%	.5126
BIRMINGHAM	514,640	.55%	51	18,416,009	29,000	18.99%	24.94%	17.30%	14.60%	4.27%	1.35%	1.55%	.4836
ALBANY - SCHENECTADY - TROY	507,360	.55%	52	21,018,450	34,729	15.88%	24.75%	20.87%	19.49%	6.01%	1.78%	1.42%	.5388
DAYTON	503,440	.54%	53	20,113,750	33,998	15.53%	24.94%	21.16%	19.01%	5.48%	1.44%	1.28%	.5112
RICHMOND - PETERSBURG	478,850	.51%	54	19,376,643	33,654	15.52%	25.48%	20.93%	18.51%	5.29%	1.51%	1.53%	.4849
JACKSONVILLE	473,030	.51%	55	18,039,491	30,357	17.67%	26.82%	19.72%	15.38%	4.35%	1.27%	1.49%	.4920
CHARLESTON - HUNTINGTON	465,250	.50%	56	14,113,946	23,212	22.51%	24.45%	15.76%	11.65%	2.66%	.74%	.84%	.3941
FRESNO - VISALIA	463,760	.50%	57	17,642,337	29,257	20.25%	26.26%	18.26%	15.01%	4.58%	1.48%	1.54%	.4688
LITTLE ROCK - PINE BLUFF	455,320	.49%	58	15,581,819	26,893	20.12%	26.72%	17.15%	13.48%	3.48%	1.08%	1.18%	.4275
TULSA	444,690	.48%	59	14,855,485	26,058	21.25%	27.06%	17.13%	12.53%	3.06%	.96%	1.23%	.4029
FLINT - SAGINAW - BAY CITY	444,100	.48%	60	16,411,786	31,029	18.14%	23.34%	19.20%	17.64%	5.33%	1.23%	.90%	.4387
WICHITA - HUTCHINSON, PLUS	418,280	.45%	61	15,784,054	30,870	17.85%	27.21%	20.37%	16.00%	4.20%	1.20%	1.25%	.4094
MOBILE - PENSACOLA	412,770	.44%	62	14,506,465	27,911	19.04%	26.68%	17.96%	14.28%	3.73%	1.02%	1.20%	.3895
KNOXVILLE	406,670	.44%	63	12,648,692	25,673	20.88%	25.79%	16.23%	12.78%	3.52%	1.11%	1.24%	.3759
TOLEDO	405,800	.44%	64	15,369,863	32,149	16.50%	25.77%	21.26%	17.32%	4.23%	1.15%	1.29%	.4067
ROANOKE - LYNCHBURG	382,110	.41%	65	12,582,305	26,740	20.81%	28.19%	16.50%	12.52%	2.70%	.77%	.79%	.3437
SYRACUSE	380,010	.41%	66	13,425,620	32,996	16.81%	25.24%	20.57%	18.57%	4.97%	1.46%	1.14%	.3477
AUSTIN, TEX.	373,670	.40%	67	15,779,880	32,401	16.44%	23.87%	18.16%	17.08%	6.39%	2.33%	2.24%	.3992
GREEN BAY - APPLETON	371,470	.40%	68	14,049,440	32,642	17.50%	26.93%	22.82%	17.05%	3.65%	.99%	1.12%	.3675
SHREVEPORT	368,700	.40%	69	12,195,880	25,359	20.31%	24.19%	16.14%	13.23%	3.55%	1.05%	1.15%	.3354
HONOLULU	362,380	.36%	70	20,362,903	45,539	9.99%	19.98%	18.94%	24.13%	11.99%	4.69%	3.77%	.5373
LEXINGTON	356,890	.38%	71	12,758,799	25,965	20.01%	24.47%	16.58%	13.14%	3.89%	1.39%	1.25%	.3350
ROCHESTER, N.Y	358,570	.39%	72	15,512,257	37,242	14.23%	22.78%	21.11%	21.74%	6.97%	2.03%	1.49%	.3983
DES MOINES - AMES	354,710	.38%	73	13,906,532	32,537	16.99%	26.67%	20.88%	17.26%	4.82%	1.37%	1.39%	.3589
PORTLAND - AUBURN	346,020	.37%	74	13,732,008	33,521	16.21%	26.09%	21.63%	18.32%	4.51%	1.41%	1.40%	.3724
OMAHA	344,780	.37%	75	12,616,308	33,653	15.97%	26.16%	20.68%	18.37%	5.44%	1.65%	1.62%	.3542
PADUCAH - CAPE GIRARDEAU - HARRISBURG	343,280	.37%	76	10,550,497	23,595	22.72%	24.91%	16.00%	11.57%	2.69%	.72%	.79%	.2969
CHAMPAIGN & SPRINGFIELD - DECATUR	340,050	.37%	77	13,398,945	32,305	17.38%	25.08%	20.16%	17.95%	4.94%	1.38%	1.35%	.3465
LAS VEGAS	333,050	.36%	78	13,772,598	33,227	16.21%	24.79%	20.37%	17.33%	5.24%	1.62%	1.96%	.3426
SPOKANE	324,870	.35%	79	11,567,077	28,130	20.08%	27.27%	18.58%	13.96%	3.59%	1.06%	1.12%	.3113
SPRINGFIELD, MO	320,400	.34%	80	10,001,903	24,338	23.19%	29.44%	16.11%	9.81%	2.36%	.79%	1.02%	.2795

EXHIBIT 3-8
Spot Radio Rates and Data: Market Map

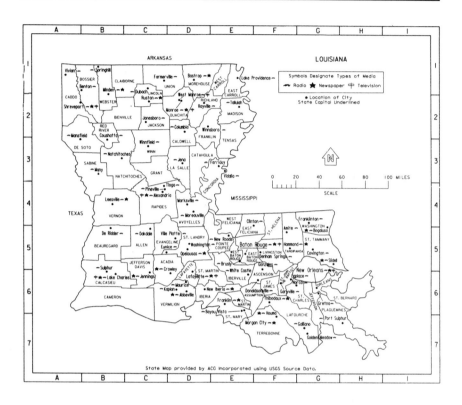

State Map provided by ACG Incorporated using USGS Source Data.

EXHIBIT 3-9
Spot Radio Rates and Data: Market Profile

Markets 41-62

Table 5

Rank Order   **STATION AFFILIATION BY MARKET**

Market / DMA Rank	ABC	CBS	NBC	FOX	Independents
New Orleans, LA / 41	WVUE 8	WWL 4	WDSU 6	WNOL 38	WGNO 26
Memphis, TN / 42	WHBQ 13	WREG 3	WMC 5	WPTY 24	WLMT 30
Oklahoma City, OK / 43	KOCO 5	KWTV 9	KFOR 4	KOKH 25	KOCB 34
Harrisburg-Lancaster-Lebanon-York, PA / 44	WHTM 27	WLYH 15 WHP 21	WGAL 8	WPMT 43	WGCB 49
West Palm Beach-Ft. Pierce, FL / 45	WPBF 25	WPEC 12	WPTV 5	WFLX 29	W19AQ 19, WTVX 34
Providence-New Bedford, RI-MA / 46	WPRI 12	WLNE 6	WJAR 10	WNAC 64	WOST 69
Wilkes Barre-Scranton, PA / 47	WNEP 16	WYOU 22	WBRE 28	WOLF 38	
Greensboro-High Point-Winston Salem, NC / 48	WGHP 8	WFMY 2	WXII 12	WNRW 45	WAAP 16, WEJC 20
Louisville, KY / 49	WHAS 11	WLKY 32	WAVE 3	WDRB 41	WBNA 21
Albuquerque-Santa Fe, NM / 50	KOAT 7	KRQE 13	KOB 4	KASA 2	KCHF 11, KHFT 29, KLUZ 41, K59DB 59, K63CD 63
Birmingham, AL / 51	WBRC 6	WBMG 42	WVTM 13	WTTO 21	WACN 55, WABM 68
Albany-Schenectady-Troy, NY / 52	WTEN 10	WRGB 6	WNYT 13	WXXA 23	
Dayton, OH / 53	WDTN 2	WHIO 7	WKEF 22	WRGT 45	WTJC 26, WKOI 43
Jacksonville-Brunswick, FL-GA / 54	WJKS 17	WJXT 4	WTLV 12	WAWS 30	WBSG 21, WNFT 47
Richmond-Petersburg, VA / 55	WRIC 8	WTVR 6	WWBT 12	WRLH 35	WZXK 65
Charleston-Huntington, WV / 56	WCHS 8	WOWK 13	WSAZ 3	WVAH 11	WTSF 61
Fresno-Visalia, CA / 57	KFSN 30	KJEO 47	KSEE 24	KMPH 26	KFTV 21, KAIL 53, KMSG 59
Little Rock-Pine Bluff, AR / 58	KATV 7	KTHV 11	KARK 4	KLRT 16	KVTN 25, KASN 38
Tulsa, OK / 59	KTUL 8	KOTV 6	KJRH 2	KOKI 23	KTFO 41, KWHB 47
Flint-Saginaw-Bay City, MI / 60	WJRT 12	WEYI 25	WNEM 5	WSMH 66	WAQP 49
Wichita-Hutchinson, KS / 61	KAKE 10	KWCH 12	KSNW 3	KSAS 24	
Mobile-Pensacola, AL-FL / 62	WEAR 3	WKRG 5	WALA 10	WPMI 15	WHBR 33, WFGX 35, WJTC 44

EXHIBIT 3-10
TV Datatrack: Station Affiliation by Market

WDAY-WEAR

WDAY-TV Ch 6 (A) Fargo-Valley City, ND

301 S. 8th St.
Fargo, ND 58103
TM: Sue Eider
Ph: 701-241-5346
FAX: 701-241-5368
Tapes: 1", Stereo & Mono

WDBB Ch 17 (F) Tuscaloosa, AL

5455 Jug Factory Rd.
Tuscaloosa, AL 35405
TM: Brenda Thomas
Ph: 205-345-1117 ext. 9
FAX: 205-345-1173
Tapes: 3/4", Mono

WDBD Ch 40 (F) Jackson, MS

7440 Channel 16 Way
Jackson, MS 39209
TM: Cindy Fendlason
Ph: 601-922-1234
FAX: 601-922-6752
Tapes: 1", Mono

WDBJ Ch 7 (C) Roanoke-Lynchburg, VA

2001 Colonial Ave., SW
Roanoke, VA 24015
TM: Ellen Bishop
Ph: 703-344-7000 ext. 220
FAX: 703-344-5097
Tapes: 1", Stereo & Mono

WDCA-TV Ch 20 (I) Washington, DC

5202 River Rd.
Bethesda, MD 20816
TM: Charmaine Marie
Ph: 301-986-9322
FAX: 301-654-5209
Tapes: 1", Stereo

WDEF-TV Ch 12 (C) Chattanooga, TN

3300 Broad St.
Chattanooga, TN 37408
TM: Tonetta Jones
Ph: 615-785-1206
FAX: 615-785-1271
Tapes: 1", Stereo & Mono

WDHN Ch 18 (A) Dothan, AL

Hwy. 52 E.
Webb, AL 36376
TM: Sandra Goodman
Ph: 205-793-1818 ext. 126
FAX: 205-793-2623
Tapes: 3/4", Mono

WDIO-TV Ch 10 (A) Duluth-Superior, MN-WI

10 Observation Rd.
Duluth, MN 55811
TM: Diane Sargent
Ph: 218-727-6864 ext. 22
FAX: 218-727-4415
Tapes: 3/4", 2", Mono

WDIV Ch 4 (N) Detroit, MI

550 W. Lafayette Blvd.
Attn: R. Calloway
Detroit, MI 48231
TM: Sue Ayala
Ph: 313-222-0433
FAX: 313-222-0471
Tapes: 1", Stereo & Mono

WDJT-TV Ch 58 (I) Milwaukee, WI

509 W. Wisconsin Ave. Suite 2500
Milwaukee, WI 53203
TM: Tom Erwin
Ph: 414-271-5800 ext. 135
FAX: 414-272-1368
Tapes: 3/4", Stereo & Mono

WDKY-TV Ch 56 (F) Lexington, KY

434 Interstate Ave.
Lexington, KY 40505
TM: Cindy Smith
Ph: 606-293-5656
FAX: 606-299-8604
Tapes: 1", Stereo & Mono

WDRB-TV Ch 41 (F) Louisville, KY

624 W. Muhammad Ali Blvd.
Louisville, KY 40203
TM: Alice Sheffield
Ph: 502-561-7718
FAX: 502-589-5559
Tapes: 1", Stereo & Mono

WDSI-TV Ch 61 (F) Chattanooga, TN

2401 E. Main St.
Chattanooga, TN 37404
TM: Marji Barrows
Ph: 615-697-0661
FAX: 615-697-0650
Tapes: 1", Mono

WDSU-TV Ch 6 (N) New Orleans, LA

520 Royal St.
New Orleans, LA 70130-2114
TM: Patricia Flubacher
Ph: 504-527-0127
FAX: 504-527-0162
Tapes: 1", Stereo

WDTN Ch 2 (A) Dayton, OH

4595 S. Dixie Ave.
Dayton, OH 45439
TM: Janice Barney
Ph: 513-293-2101 ext. 215
FAX: 513-296-7129
Tapes: 1", Mono

WDTV Ch 5 (C) Clarksburg-Weston, WV

5 Television Dr.
Bridgeport, WV 26330
TM: Cheryl Brady
Ph: 304-623-5555
FAX: 304-842-7501
Tapes: 3/4", Mono

WDZL Ch 39 (I) Miami-Ft. Lauderdale, FL

2055 Lee St.
Hollywood, FL 33020
TM: Mary Fuentes
Ph: 305-925-3939 ext. 129
FAX: 305-923-8634
Tapes: 1", Mono

WEAR-TV Ch 3 (A) Mobile-Pensacola, AL-FL

4990 Mobile Hwy.
Pensacola, FL 32506
TM: Polly Weeks
Ph: 904-456-3333 ext. 315
FAX: 904-455-0159
Tapes: 1", Beta, Mono

EXHIBIT 3-11
TV Datatrack: Station Information

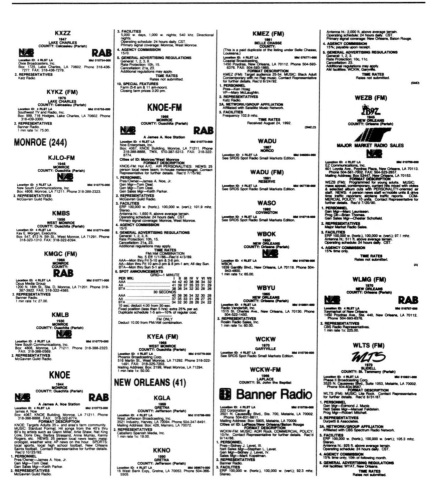

EXHIBIT 3-12
TV & Cable Factbook: Station Listings

Louisiana—Monroe-West Monroe

KNOE-TV
Ch. 8

Network Service: CBS.

Licensee: NOE Enterprises Inc., Box 4067, Monroe, LA 71211.

Studio: 1400 Oliver Rd., Monroe, LA 71201.

Mailing Address: Box 4067, Monroe, LA 71211.

Telephone: 318-388-8888. **TWX:** 510-977-5384. **Fax:** 318-322-8774.

Technical Facilities: Channel No. 8 (180-186 MHz). Authorized power: 316-kw visual, 62.5-kw aural. Antenna: 1890-ft. above av. terrain, 1989-ft. above ground, 2049-ft. above sea level.

| Latitude | 32° | 11' | 45" |
| Longitude | 92° | 04' | 10" |

Transmitter: 2.5-mi. N of Riverton, LA.

Satellite Earth Stations: RCA, 3.7-meter Ku-band; Scientific-Atlanta, 7-meter C-band; Scientific-Atlanta, 4-meter C-band; Simulsat, 7-meter C-band; Comsat, Harris, Pinzone receivers.

AM Affiliate: KNOE, 5-kw, 540 kHz.

FM Affiliate: KNOE-FM, 100-kw, 101.9 MHz (No. 270), 1670-ft.

News Services: AP, CBS, CNN, Headline News, Colorgraphics, National Weather Service, Potomac News Service.

Ownership: Noe Corp.

Began Operation: September 27, 1953.

Represented (sales): Blair Television.

Represented (legal): Cohn & Marks.

Personnel:
James A. Noe Jr., President.
Richard L. French, General Manager.
Kathleen McLain, General Sales Manager.
Ray Frostenson, News Director.
Jack McCall, Program Director.
David Price, Promotion Director.
Denis Baker, Controller.
Gerry Harkins, Chief Engineer.
Ansel Smith, Operations & Production Manager.
Bill Elliott, Chief Photographer.
Laura Z. Roberts, Personnel Director.

Highest 30 Sec. Rate: $1200.

City of License: Monroe. **ADI:** Monroe, LA-El Dorado, AR. **Rank:** 131.

Total Households: ©MSI Consumer Market Data as of 1/1/93. TV Homes, TV% and Circulation ©1993 Arbitron. County coverage based on Arbitron study.

KNOE-TV BPCT-3313 Granted 10/2/64 © American Map Corp., No. 14244

Net Weekly Circulation	State County	Total Households	TV Households	%
50% & Over	Morehouse	11,000	10,800	98
	Ouachita	50,500	50,100	99
	Richland	7,000	6,900	99
	Tensas	2,500	2,400	96
	Union	7,600	7,500	99
	West Carroll	4,400	4,300	98
	Winn	5,800	5,700	98
	MISSISSIPPI			
	Adams	13,100	12,900	98
	LOUISIANA			
Between 25-49%	Bienville	5,900	5,800	98
	Claiborne	6,100	6,000	98
	Natchitoches	12,600	12,300	98
	Rapides	46,000	45,600	99
	MISSISSIPPI			
	Claiborne	3,500	3,400	97
	Issaquena	600	600	100
	Jefferson	2,800	2,700	96
	Warren	17,200	17,000	99
	ARKANSAS			
Between 5-24%	Bradley	4,500	4,400	98
	Calhoun	2,200	2,200	100
	Chicot	5,400	5,300	98
	LOUISIANA			
	Avoyelles	13,400	13,200	99
	Red River	3,300	3,200	97
	Sabine	8,300	8,100	98
	MISSISSIPPI			
	Sharkey	2,100	2,100	100
	Wilkinson	3,300	3,200	97
Station Totals		**326,200**	**321,300**	**98**
Net Weekly Circulation (1993)				**205,500**
Average Daily Circulation (1993)				**128,800**

Net Weekly Circulation	State County	Total Households	TV Households	%
	ARKANSAS			
50% & Over	Ashley	8,800	8,600	98
	Union	17,800	17,600	99
	LOUISIANA			
	Caldwell	3,500	3,400	97
	Catahoula	3,900	3,800	97
	Concordia	7,200	7,000	97
	East Carroll	3,100	3,000	97
	Franklin	7,700	7,600	99
	Grant	6,400	6,300	98
	Jackson	5,700	5,600	98
	La Salle	5,000	4,900	98
	Lincoln	13,800	13,700	99
	Madison	4,200	4,100	98

Other information available in the *Factbooks* includes market rankings; data on Canadian broadcasting stations; the construction permits granted by the FCC; information on subscription TV stations, station boosters, and translators; and low power station applications and grants. (See Exhibit 3–13.) An international directory gives a summary of information on television in other countries of the world. Since many of the facts listed in the *Factbooks* are not in *SRDS,* they fill a data vacuum for the media buyer.

As cable becomes increasingly important to the communications industry, anyone involved in media must know and understand the availabilities, capabilities, and workings of cable systems.

Rating Services

Currently, there are two major rating services accepted by the advertising industry for television and cable, Arbitron and Nielsen, and one rating service for radio, Arbitron.

The rating services publish individual books and summary volumes for each radio and TV market four times annually. The ratings cover a four-week period and are called *rating sweeps.* These sweeps occur in February, March, May, July, and November. In addition, some major markets are rated daily.

Both of the rating services use the same ratio—one rating point equals 1 percent of the total television or radio homes in the surveyed area. In some markets, the station selects counties to be rated. In others, the area of dominant influence of the station that has the most powerful signal in the marketing area is the basis for the rating.

The TV ratings give considerable demographic information about the market, including the audience demographics and programming for every 15-minute segment from 6:00 A.M. to 2:00 A.M. (See Exhibit 3–14.) The service breaks down each rating further into rating shares by percentages and gives the rating trends for the previous four periods. Special prism studies are available that break down numerous other demographics, such as ZIP-coded audiences, affluence, education, living habits, and specific types of product consumption. If one is to become proficient in media, one must become as familiar with these various rating reports as a minister is with the Bible.

It would take a complete course to fully explain how to use the rating services and the associated data and how to figure reach, frequency, and cume for specific schedules. Students can usually obtain rating books from their local broadcasting stations, by writing to the rating services, or, in most metropolitan areas, by inviting someone from one of the rating services or broadcast stations to lecture on the rating system.

EXHIBIT 3-13
TV & Cable Factbook: Cable Systems Listings

Cable Systems—Louisiana

Pay Service 3
Pay Units: 223 (03/01/86).
Programming (via satellite): HBO.
Fee: $35.00 installation; $9.50 monthly.
Pay Service 4
Pay Units: 606 (03/01/86).
Programming (via satellite): The Movie Channel.
Fee: $35.00 installation; $9.50 monthly.
Pay Service 5
Pay Units: 938 (03/01/86).
Programming (via satellite): Showtime.
Fee: $35.00 installation; $8.50 monthly.
Local advertising: Yes. Regional interconnect: Cabletime.
Equipment: Scientific-Atlanta headend; C-COR amplifiers; Amphenol cable; Scientific-Atlanta satellite antenna.
Miles of plant: 86.0 (coaxial).
Manager: Roger St. Dizier. Marketing director: Verna Landry.
City fee: 2% of gross.
Ownership: TCA Cable TV Inc. (MSO).

NEW IBERIA—Star Cable Co., Box 437, 720 W. Dardeau St., Ville Platte, LA 70586. Phone: 318-363-5900. Counties: Iberia & Vermilion. Also serves Erath. Population: 34,225.
TV Market Ranking: Below 100. Original franchise award date: N.A. Franchise expiration date: N.A. Began: N.A.
Channel capacity: 35. Channels available but not in use: 3.
Basic Service
Subscribers: 2,474 (05/01/93).
Programming (received off-air): WVLA (N) Baton Rouge; KADN (F), KATC (A), KLFY-TV (C), KLPB-TV (P) Lafayette. Programming (via satellite): WTBS (I) Atlanta; WGN-TV (I) Chicago; WWOR-TV (I) New York.
Fee: $15.95 monthly.
Expanded Basic Service
Programming (via satellite): Black Entertainment TV; CNN; Country Music TV; Discovery Channel; ESPN; EWTN; Family Channel; Headline News; Lifetime; MTV; Nashville Network; Nickelodeon; QVC Network; Sci-Fi Channel; The Weather Channel; Trinity Bcstg. Network; Turner Network TV; USA Network; Video Hits One.
Fee: $6.50 monthly.
Pay Service 1
Pay Units: N.A.
Programming (via satellite): Cinemax; Disney Channel; HBO; Showtime.
Fee: $7.95 monthly (Cinemax or Disney), $10.50 monthly (HBO or Showtime).
Miles of plant: 126.0 (coaxial). Homes passed: 3,406.
Manager: Erwin Guidry. Chief technician: Johnny Olinde.
Ownership: Star Cable Associates (MSO).

NEW ORLEANS—Cox Cable of New Orleans, 2120 Canal St., New Orleans, LA 70112. Phone: 504-522-3838. Fax: 504-529-2394. County: Orleans. Also serves Orleans Parish. Population: 557,364.
TV Market Ranking: 31. Original franchise award date: May 28, 1981. Franchise expiration date: July 8, 1996. Began: April 21, 1982.
Channel capacity: 54 (2-way capable). Channels available but not in use: None.
Basic Service
Subscribers: 93,130 (01/31/93).
Programming (received off-air): WDSU-TV (N), WGNO (I), WLAE-TV (P), WNOL-TV (F), WVUE (A), WWL-TV (C), WYES-TV (P) New Orleans; allband FM.
Programming (via satellite): WTBS (I) Atlanta; WGN-TV (I) Chicago; American

Movie Classics; Arts & Entertainment; Black Entertainment TV; C-SPAN; C-SPAN II; CNBC; CNN; Comedy Central; Discovery Channel; E! Entertainment TV; ESPN; EWTN; Family Channel; Headline News; Learning Channel; Lifetime; MTV; Mind Extension U; Nashville Network; Nick at Nite; Nickelodeon; Prevue Channel; QVC Network; RAI-USA; The Weather Channel; Travel Channel; Trinity Bcstg. Network; Turner Network TV; USA Network; Univision; Video Hits One.
Current originations: Bulletin board; classified ads; public access; educational access; government access; religious access; leased access; teletext; emergency alert; public service announcements; program guide.
Fee: $30.00 installation (aerial), $50.00 (underground); $19.95 monthly; $15.00 installation, $5.00 monthly (each additional set).
Commercial fee: $18.95 monthly.
Expanded Basic Service
Subscribers: 59,007 (06/24/92).
Programming (via satellite): Bravo; Home Sports Entertainment; Sci-Fi Channel.
Fee: $1.00 monthly.
Pay Service 1
Pay Units: 21,413 (12/01/91).
Programming (via satellite): Cinemax.
Fee: $7.05 monthly.
Pay Service 2
Pay Units: 7,943 (12/01/91).
Programming (via satellite): Disney Channel.
Fee: $8.55 monthly.
Pay Service 3
Pay Units: 44,130 (12/01/91).
Programming (via satellite): HBO.
Fee: $8.55 monthly.
Pay Service 4
Pay Units: 10,472 (12/01/91).
Programming (via satellite): The Movie Channel.
Fee: $8.55 monthly.
Pay Service 5
Pay Units: 18,258 (12/01/91).
Programming (via satellite): Showtime.
Fee: $8.55 monthly.
Pay-Per-View
Addressable homes: 75,108 (01/31/93).
Continuous Hits; Hot Choice; Viewer's Choice.
Fee: $3.95.
Local advertising: Yes (locally produced & insert). Available in satellite distributed, locally originated, character-generated, taped & automated programming. Rates: $100.00/Minute; $50.00/30 Seconds.
Local sales manager: Mike Salgado. Regional interconnect: New Orleans Interconnect.
Program Guide: The Cable Guide.
Equipment: Scientific-Atlanta headend; Texscan amplifiers; Comm/Scope cable; Hitachi cameras; Sony VTRs; MSI & Flexicasting Systems character generator; Scientific-Atlanta set top converters; Scientific-Atlanta addressable set top converters; Scientific-Atlanta satellite antenna; Scientific-Atlanta satellite receivers; ChannelMatic & MSI commercial insert.
Miles of plant: 1286.0 (coaxial). Homes passed: 228,152.
Manager: Ray Nagin. Chief technician: John Babich. Marketing director: John Bowen. Program director: Michele Moore.
City fee: 5% of gross.
Ownership: Cox Cable Communications (MSO).

NEW ROADS—Cablevision of Pointe Coupee Inc., Drawer 410, 3421 Ewing Dr., New Roads, LA 70760. Phone: 504-638-9049. Fax: 504-638-8360. County: Pointe

Coupee. Also serves Morganza, Pointe Coupee Parish. Population: 25,000.
TV Market Ranking: 87 (Morganza, New Roads, portions of Pointe Coupee Parish); Below 100 (portions of Pointe Coupee Parish); Outside TV Markets (portions of Pointe Coupee Parish). Original franchise award date: October 15, 1979. Franchise expiration date: October 29, 1994. Began: February 1, 1981.
Channel capacity: 36. Channels available but not in use: 1.
Limited Basic Service
Subscribers: 12 (11/18/91).
Programming (received off-air): WAFB (C), WBRZ (A), WGMB (F), WLPB-TV (P), WVLA (N) Baton Rouge; KLFY-TV (C) Lafayette.
Programming (via satellite): WTBS (I) Atlanta; WGN-TV (I) Chicago.
Current originations: Time-weather; bulletin board; classified ads; emergency alert; public service announcements.
Fee: $8.95 monthly.
Basic Service
Subscribers: 4,000; Commercial subscribers: 165 (06/01/93).
Programming (via satellite): American Movie Classics; Arts & Entertainment; Black Entertainment TV; C-SPAN; CNN; Discovery Channel; E! Entertainment TV; ESPN; EWTN; Family Channel; Headline News; Home Sports Entertainment; Lifetime; MTV; Nashville Network; Nickelodeon; QVC Network; The Weather Channel; Turner Network TV; USA Network.
Fee: $50.00 installation (aerial), $65.00 (underground); $18.45 monthly; $4.00 converter; $30.00 installation, $3.50 monthly (each additional set).
Commercial fee: $195.00 monthly.
Pay Service 1
Pay Units: 700 (11/18/91).
Programming (via satellite): Cinemax.
Fee: $40.00 installation; $10.95 monthly.
Pay Service 2
Pay Units: 300 (11/18/91).
Programming (via satellite): Disney Channel.
Fee: $40.00 installation; $8.95 monthly.
Pay Service 3
Pay Units: 950 (11/18/91).
Programming (via satellite): HBO.
Fee: $40.00 installation; $11.95 monthly.
Pay Service 4
Pay Units: 250 (11/18/91).
Programming (via satellite): Showtime.
Fee: $40.00 installation; $9.95 monthly.
Local advertising: Yes. Available in character-generated & taped programming.
Program Guide: TV Host.
Equipment: DX Engineering & Jerrold headend; Jerrold amplifiers; Times Fiber cable; Mycro-Vision character generator; Pioneer & Scientific-Atlanta set top converters; Northeast Fiber traps; Scientific-Atlanta satellite antenna; Scientific-Atlanta satellite receivers.
Miles of plant: 140.0 (coaxial). Homes passed: 5,537. Total homes in franchised area: 11,000.
Manager: James Laurent Jr.
City fee: 3% of gross.
Ownership: Cablevision Industries Inc. (MSO).

NEWELLTON—Galaxy Cablevision, Box 526, 204-A N.W. Railroad Ave., Sibley, LA 71073. Phone: 318-371-9400. County: Tensas. Population: 1,726.
TV Market Ranking: Outside TV Markets. Original franchise award date: N.A. Franchise expiration date: N.A. Began: June 1, 1982.
Channel capacity: 52. Channels available but not in use: N.A.

Basic Service
Subscribers: 345 (12/01/90).
Programming (received off-air): WAPT (A), WJTV (C), WLBT-TV (N) Jackson; KLTM-TV (P), KNOE-TV (C) Monroe-El Dorado.
Programming (via satellite): WTBS (I) Atlanta; WGN-TV (I) Chicago; WWOR-TV (I) New York; CNN; ESPN; Family Channel; Nickelodeon; The Weather Channel; USA Network.
Fee: $30.00 installation; $18.00 monthly, $3.00 monthly (each additional set).
Pay Service 1
Pay Units: N.A.
Programming (via satellite): Cinemax; HBO; Showtime.
Fee: $12.00 monthly (each).
Miles of plant: 9.9 (coaxial). Homes passed: 529.
Manager: Billy Eubanks.
Ownership: Galaxy Cablevision (MSO).
Note: Current information not available.

NEWLLANO—See LEESVILLE, LA.

NORCO—See ST. CHARLES PARISH, LA.

NORTH HODGE—See JONESBORO, LA.

NORTH MONROE—Southwest Cablevision, Box 4028, Monroe, LA 71211. Phone: 318-343-5253. County: Ouachita. Population: N.A. (area served).
TV Market Ranking: 99. Original franchise award date: October 3, 1980. Franchise expiration date: October 3, 2005. Began: August 1, 1979.
Channel capacity: 35. Channels available but not in use: N.A.
Basic Service
Subscribers: 986 (04/01/92).
Programming (received off-air): KARD (A), KLTM-TV (P), KNOE-TV (C), KTVE (N) Monroe-El Dorado.
Programming (via satellite): WTBS (I) Atlanta; WGN-TV (I) Chicago.
Fee: $14.95 monthly.
Program Guide: The Cable Guide.
Miles of plant: 38.0 (coaxial). Homes passed: 2,942.
Manager: Jack L. Morgan. Chief technician: Stan Jones. Marketing director: Greg Klugiewicz.
City fee: 3% of gross.
Ownership: Nathan A. Levine (MSO).

NORWOOD—Rural Cablevision, 9111 Interline Rd., Baton Rouge, LA 70809. Phone: 504-928-4137. County: East Feliciana. Population: 421.
TV Market Ranking: 87. Original franchise award date: N.A. Franchise expiration date: N.A. Began: N.A.
Channel capacity: N.A. Channels available but not in use: N.A.
Basic Service
Subscribers: N.A.
Programming (received off-air): WAFB (C), WBRZ (A), WLPB-TV (P), WVLA (N) Baton Rouge.
Programming (via satellite): WTBS (I) Atlanta; WGN-TV (I) Chicago; WWOR-TV (I) New York.
Fee: N.A.
Ownership: Gulf American Cable Group (MSO).
Note: Current information not available.

OAK GROVE—Delta Cablevision, Box 432, Lake Providence, LA 71254. Phone: 318-559-1212. County: West Carroll. Population: 3,500.

EXHIBIT 3-14
Audience Demographics for 15-Minute Segments

NEW ORLEANS, LA   WK1 2/03-2/09 WK2 2/10-2/16 WK3 2/17-2/23 WK4 2/24-3/02

(Full-page ratings data table — TIME PERIOD, SATURDAY 8:00PM - 10:15PM)

This exhibit presents a detailed Nielsen-style audience ratings grid for New Orleans, LA, Saturday 8:00PM–10:15PM, broken into 15-minute segments, with columns for DMA HOUSEHOLD RATINGS (weeks 1–4, multi-week average, share trend), DMA RATINGS for PERSONS, WOMEN, MEN, TNS, and CHILD demographics. Stations/programs listed include WDSU (AVG. ALL WKS, DECISION 94, EMPTY NEST NBC, HOT COUNTRY-SP, NBC MOV-WK-SAT, NURSES-NBC, SISTERS NBC, I WITNESS-SAT, 6 NEWS TONIGHT), WGNO (SAT 8.00 MOVIE, COUNTRY CNNCTN, STAR GEN-AS R, SANFORD&SN SAT), WLAE (AVG. ALL WKS, LONESOME PN SP, A.C.T.VISNS-98, BUSINESS & LAW), WNOL (AMER-WANTD-FOX, NW8 EL COVERAG, ABC SAT-MOV, COMMISH-ABC, TALE-CRYPT1FOX), WVUE (AVG. ALL WKS, NW8 EL COVERAG), WWL (LOCAL EL COVRG, XVII0LM WTR-PR, NEWS 8, EYEWIT NWS-10), WYES (C JAMES-CNTURY, AUSTIN CTY LMT, SNEAK PREVIEW), and HUT/PUT/TOTALS rows for each segment.

SATURDAY
8:00PM - 10:15PM

Rating levels are not the basic criterion for purchasing radio time. Radio programming is much narrower than TV programming in demographic scope, and radio buyers should, therefore, first identify the target audience and then evaluate stations by their share of that specific audience.

You will often hear about the GRPs (gross rating points) of a specific radio or TV schedule. These GRP schedules use a 30-second announcement as their foundation. Although direct marketing commercials are often 120 seconds long, you cannot multiply the GRPs by four. It is not fair to compare a 30-second with a 120-second GRP, but these exposures do *not* reach more audiences. They reach the same audience for a longer period or with more motivating commercials.

NEGOTIATING RATES WITH THE MEDIA

In discussing *SRDS,* we explained that rate cards provided by radio and TV stations are merely guidelines for the media buyer. Even the novice media buyer will seldom pay the printed rates.

The most common way media buyers negotiate rates is to request fixed, nonpreemptible time periods, as set forth in section 1 of a station's rate card, and then negotiate for these fixed periods at the preemptible rates, as set forth in section 2. A more seasoned buyer will negotiate to purchase the fixed time period under the terms of section 1 at an ROS (run-of-station) rate, with the guarantee from the station that the spot will only be preempted under the most unusual conditions, such as the sale of the selected spot to a higher paying customer. Keep in mind that radio and TV stations are in business to make money. Their prime objective is to sell their spots at any price. If there is demand for the time, the spot will go to the highest bidder, but usually under the printed card rate.

Remember, too, that radio or television availability is perishable. Once a time period goes by without a commercial, it never returns. Any income that the station can obtain for that specific time period that would normally go unsold drops to the station's bottom line as net profit. Remember, it costs a station about the same to run a paid commercial as it costs to run a public service or promotional spot. Always think of an open commercial time period as an empty hotel room or a vacant seat on an airplane. Stations need to fill these spots at the last minute, and direct marketers provide the commercials to turn these periods into cash.

To the general advertiser, running an advertising campaign as scheduled is essential. Commitments have been made to the retail outlets, specific merchandise has often been stocked, and all marketing aspects have been coordinated for a predetermined campaign that is expected to move the merchandise to the customer. Any preemptions or variations of the announced schedule affect not only the movement of goods, but also the national advertiser's credibility. General advertisers must also confine their schedules to only those markets in which they have distribution.

Direct marketers, however, are not concerned about when orders come in or where they come from. Their only concern is that the sale is made within the parameters of a profitable advertising allowable. A direct marketer, therefore, can supply stations in any geographical area, at any time of the year, with commercials that the station can schedule in any open time periods.

Thus, to experienced radio and TV stations, the direct marketer is an expedient source for turning unsold time into immediate profit. In the game of profits, the station and the direct marketer become partners. For this reason, the direct marketer—or the direct marketing agency—must "invite" the media to sit on the client's side of the desk and participate in the success of direct marketing ventures. The barrier that normally separates the media buyer from the media seller must be dissolved for their mutual benefit.

Consider that the direct marketer usually has an unlimited budget for any medium that is able to provide sales under the advertising allowable or Magic Number. Consequently, the direct marketer literally has no limit on advertising dollars for a productive station.

Flexibility of Broadcast Decisions

When considering various media for direct marketing, the direct marketer must remember that magazines usually specify a six-to-eight-week deadline for purchasing space. Even direct mail requires several weeks before a follow-up mailing can be based on a previously tested list. Therefore, in the use of most direct marketing media, there is a sizable lapse of time between a successful test schedule and the roll-out of the schedule. In addition, results from direct mail often take 90 to 120 days to evaluate.

Television and radio tests can be evaluated on a day-to-day basis, but, even more important, the media can be turned on and off like a water faucet. When tests are successful, you can add times and stations almost instantly. When an offer stops working, you can cancel or change offers in 48 to 72 hours.

The Per Inquiry Method

One media buying method unique to direct marketers is called PI—"per order" or "per inquiry." Under the terms of the PI contract, the station agrees to run the commercials of the direct marketer in station-discretion time periods and charge the direct marketer an "advertising allowable" only for the orders delivered. That is, if the direct marketer can afford to pay $5.00 for each order and the station delivers 500 orders as a result of the commercial, the direct marketer is billed $2,500. About 40 percent of all broadcast stations in radio and TV and about 85 percent of all cable networks will negotiate a PI contract.

PIs offer the direct marketer guaranteed orders at a profitable level, which relieves the direct marketer of day-to-day monitoring of order costs. More important, it offers direct marketers exposure on media schedules that would sometimes not be within their advertising allowable. On the other hand, a PI arrangement can be a disadvantage for a highly productive offer. Under a PI arrangement, the cost per unit sale is usually at the maximum allowable, and the direct marketer's profits are often less than profits from a straight media buy. That's because the rate set for PIs is usually the maximum the direct marketer can afford. A straight media buy can produce unit sales at a price far less than the advertising allowable.

An even greater disadvantage of the PI arrangement is loss of control over the number of exposures a commercial receives. When you buy certain times, you are assured of receiving the number of exposures purchased. A station taking the offer on a PI basis exposes the offer at the station's convenience. If a station finds it has more lucrative offers, or only a limited amount of time for direct marketing exposures, direct marketers might find that their commercials are not being aired. It is important to remember that on a PI basis a direct marketer's sales volume is at the mercy of the station.

The direct marketer must also understand that a medium does not accept every PI commercial. Top-producing, highly successful PI media are bombarded by hoards of professional and amateur direct marketers who are eager to take advantage of this low-risk, high-return PI plan.

Stations tend to give the lion's share of PIs to established direct marketing offers and agencies. Even the most experienced, successful, and reputable direct marketer, however, will probably have his or her schedule cancelled if the PI offer does not meet the minimum cash return standards set by the media. In peak season periods, the media will not even consider giving a PI offer exposure until the direct marketer can show some positive test results from straight media buys.

Why should the media accept any advertising on a PI basis?

As I explained earlier in this chapter, television and radio time is an extremely perishable commodity. If a station can get even one dollar from a time period that normally would have gone unsold, that dollar drops to the bottom line as net profit. The experienced radio or TV station, therefore, does not try to establish a relationship between its going rates for general advertisers and the income received from direct marketing exposure. The station's primary objective is to limit direct marketing exposures to the offers that give them the highest return.

The philosophy of accepting PIs by any medium follows this logic: If the medium sells its time to direct marketers, direct marketers buy a minimum of one week's schedule to test the medium. In most cases, neither the station nor the direct marketer profits from this one-week test due to the original set-up cost.

Now, let's look at this minimal test schedule from the media point of view: First, it can be highly successful for the direct marketer, delivering orders far under the advertising allowable. The direct marketer, of course, will continue to renew week after week, and the station will be compensated at a far lower rate per exposure than it would receive if it had taken the offer on a PI basis. Second, the offer can be borderline: the income to the medium would then be about equal to what it would have received on a PI basis. Third, the offer can be a disaster: If the medium had taken the offer on a straight cash basis, it still would have received only one test period's worth of income. Fourth, the offer can produce orders slightly over the profitable allowable. When this occurs, the advertiser does not renew the schedule, and the medium receives no additional revenue. But under a PI arrangement, the medium could continue to run this schedule for a long time, receiving continuous income at a rate slightly under its published rate. The medium, of course, has the option of running the offer in an open time, which produces income and profit for the station that it would not normally realize.

Cash Library and Guarantee Purchase Methods

Many stations and networks understand the benefits of taking direct marketing offers on a PI basis. But some radio and TV station managers don't accept PIs. They believe that while a PI method guarantees the direct marketer a profit, the medium loses because it receives a less than normal rate. To respond to this anti-PI argument, the direct marketer can turn the PI concept into a station benefit merely by changing the term "PI" to "cash library."

The cash library is an inventory of commercials that can be scheduled instantly in any unsold periods. These exposures turn these otherwise barren periods into net profit. With the cash library concept, the station rather than the direct marketer, is the beneficiary of the income. Often stations that refuse PIs accept cash libraries even though there are only semantic differences between the two.

Another method of removing the PI stigma is called "guarantee purchase." Using this method, the direct marketer actually purchases a schedule of commercials at *any* rate set by the station (the rate under the guarantee concept makes no difference because the station guarantees a sufficient number of orders against the purchase—and it requires no negotiations). In exchange, the station guarantees to produce the minimum number of order the direct marketer needs to meet the advertising allowable, regardless of how many exposures the station has to run. The guarantee method often causes problems because stations sometimes ask for a purchase contract in excess of what they are able to deliver. Under these conditions, a problem arises in reconciling invoices. If there are several products involved from a single direct marketer or agency, the medium often attempts to juggle the order between the products, giving more exposure to those products that produce the highest income for the medium.

Direct marketers, however, can profitably use the guarantee method to obtain acceptance when the station or network has cash flow problems and needs advance payments to meet financial obligations. This cash-in-advance guarantee often allows a direct marketer to get exposure for a product that would not normally be strong enough for a regular PI and would not pay out on a cash-buy basis.

Guarantees also overcome a problem that stations sometimes have with general advertisers who think they should also be able to schedule advertising on a contingency basis. With guarantees, the station can show the general advertiser a contract for a higher rate than the general advertiser is paying for the same time.

If you analyze all of the various direct marketing options available to the media, you will find that the media have the most to gain by accepting the cash library or PI method.

When a medium is purchased on a PI, cash library, or guarantee basis, there is little skill needed on the part of the media buyer to select where or when the commercials should be exposed. On a cash-buy basis, however, the media buyer must be highly skilled. Because of the direct marketer's demand for an immediate, profitable return, the media buyer must know the maximum rate at which each medium can produce profitable orders and be highly skilled at negotiating rates that will be low enough for the direct marketer to pay them out within a specific advertising allowable. After the rate is negotiated, the commercials must be scheduled in areas that will provide maximum profit.

Seasonality

When the offers fails to pull well enough to meet the advertising allowable, the media buyer must have the ability to renegotiate either the rates or the time periods or number of exposures so that sales reach a profitable level. This renegotiation of rates is extremely important in periods when the media are experiencing seasonal income slumps.

Rates for direct marketers should never be negotiated by rating points, but rather by programming and dayparts that have proven track records for direct response. By constantly evaluating the effectiveness of various exposures, an experienced direct marketing media buyer knows the maximum he or she can pay for an exposure and the area in which these exposures should be concentrated. Consequently, a media buyer must be highly skilled in two basic areas: negotiating rates and selecting commercial placement.

Let's focus on television time-period selection. When selecting periods, buyers must take into account not only the times of the day and the days of the week, but also the seasonal variations of broadcast audience reaction.

As we will see in Exhibit 8–2, years of research and post-analysis of trends and results indicate that January, February, and March are consistently the most productive months for achieving maximum sales results for direct marketers at minimum cost per sale. The period of maximum return is usually between the first and fourth week in January. After that, results usually begin to drop off at a relatively slow rate. The Easter weekend, no matter how early or late it occurs, produces a steep decline in direct marketing sales and a high increase in the cost of achieving sales.

Let's analyze these seasonal highs and lows as they occur in both radio and television. Both media experience the advantages and disadvantages of weather. During cold, damp, inclement weather, people stay at home and watch TV or listen to the radio. Because of the snow and cold of winter, studies indicate that audiences peak during the first quarter of the year. What is even more significant is that the normal demand by general advertisers for TV and radio time declines to its lowest level during this peak viewing and listening season; inclement weather inhibits in-store retail traffic and the need for stores to take inventories and restock merchandise moved during the Christmas rush. As a result, they hold back on advertising schedules during most of January. Cosmetics, giftware, and toy manufacturers have just completed their major advertising efforts for Christmas, and they are in the process of regrouping and rebudgeting. Other major national advertisers are still at work on the year's advertising program. They are also awaiting year-end sales results so they can evaluate their past campaign before embarking on a new one. That's why the direct marketer literally basks in the failure of regular advertisers to take advantage of the peak broadcast audiences in the first quarter.

As for radio, especially the powerful AM stations (5,000 to 50,000 watts), their signal is determined by the setting of the sun. When the sun goes down early, their signal goes out hundreds of miles farther earlier in the day, as compared to the signal strength that occurs at late sunset during the summer. AM radio, therefore, undergoes a tremendous expansion of signal strength and expanded audiences during the hours when people are awake. In addition, wet, slippery roads cause slower traffic, which prolongs the in-transit audiences. Keep in mind, however, that drive-time audiences are relatively unimportant to direct marketers, because it is difficult to get an in-transit listener to write down an address or phone number.

After the Easter direct marketing slump, a slow but steady increase occurs in direct marketing response, coupled with a decrease in cost per order. This pattern carries through most of June. July, the direct marketer's "mystery month," is characterized by variable fluctuations that make it a profitable direct marketing month in some years and a disaster in others. August is normally good, but the August increase quickly turns into a September decline.

In 30 years of tracking results from radio and television direct marketing, there has never been a single year in which September has not won the "worst month" award. Why September is so bad for broadcast and relatively good for direct mail and print is one of the mysteries of broadcast direct marketing. Our rationale is open to argument, but it is worth mentioning. In September, people have just returned from their vacations. They have to buy fall wardrobes for themselves and back-to-school clothing for children. Thus, they have little cash to spend for mail order offers. In addition, the networks present their new programming in September, and most direct marketing commercials are confined to independent stations during this period. The independent viewers very often switch to the networks to see what is new.

Why doesn't this same rationale hold true for direct mail and print? Maybe the direct mail buyer believes that orders on the phone are delivered faster—allowing time to replenish the bank account from the vacation and wardrobe spending spree. On the other hand, print and direct mail can stay in the home and be acted on at a later date.

We find increasingly better results in October, November, and December. This increase would probably be even stronger if there were more time available; it is difficult to buy television time during the fourth quarter because of an increase in demand by general advertisers. This increase in media demand stimulates an increase in the price of media. Of course, supply, demand, and price for the media affect the direct response end results.

THE THEORY OF SALES RESISTANCE

Now, let's get down to the nuts and bolts of purchasing television time. It seems only logical that a correlation should exist between ratings (size of audience) and results (ratio of advertising to sales). If so, it would be logical to assume that the most effective time to buy would be those periods with the highest ratings, particularly if the cost per thousand listeners or viewers remains consistent. If this rationale really held true, it would make the buying of time for direct marketing offers relatively easy. Unfortunately, this is just not the case.

In Chapter 11, we will explain how to keep records to accurately measure the number of orders received from each specific commercial exposure. By obtaining the rating or audience size for each exposure, the direct marketer can compare the size of the audience with the number of orders received. Again, it is logical to assume that if you show the same commercial to twice as many people, you should generate twice as many orders. But again, that is not the case.

Discovery

At first, we assumed that the lack of correlation was due to different audience demographics, so only exposures with nearly identical demographics were compared. Still, no correlation existed between ratings and results. Needing a logical explanation for this paradox, it was easy to come to the conclusion that the ratings were wrong. How can a commercial be exposed to a far greater audience and get a much lower sales response?

This inconsistency was plotted on hundreds of graphs before a pattern began to emerge that indicated a correlation did exist if one compared the same time of the day and the same day of the week. This time and day correlation seemed to exist even when there was a variance of demographics. (Exceptions existed when children's programming was compared with adult programming.)

As the results of hundreds of exposures were analyzed, the graph began to take the shape of a seven-fingered hand with the top of the fingers representing the periods of maximum sales resistance and the lower part representing periods of minimal sales resistance. (See Exhibit 3–15.) In effect, what emerged was the Theory of Sales Resistance. There are times of the day and days of the week on which one could sell almost anything, and, conversely, times when people become highly resistant to any sales message. (See sidebar.)

The periods of least sales resistance occur the first hour after waking, the last hour before going to bed, and all day and night on Saturdays and Sundays.

Sales resistance is relatively low on Monday, builds up until Wednesday (when people start looking forward to the weekend), and then begins to decline until it reaches its lowest resistance level on Sunday.

The point of maximum sales resistance does not occur at any specific time of the day. It comes after the day's "highlight" event—after something that a person has been eagerly anticipating has happened. For example, if that event is a specific TV show, a baseball game, or the weekly poker outing, the curve reaches the highest point of resistance during that expectation and then starts to descend.

In interpreting this theory of sales resistance, it is important to consider the definition of advertising: "An attempt on the part of the seller to plant a buying suggestion in the conscious or subconscious minds of a potential customer that will motivate a buying decision." Given that definition, advertising is an attempt at hypnosis—an attempt to implant a motivating suggestion in the mind of a potential buyer. Because advertising is rather shallow hypnosis, we like to call it *surface hypnosis.*

Given this definition, it is important to analyze the periods when it is easiest to reach the potential customer's subconscious with a buying suggestion. Hypnotists say it is easiest to implant a suggestion when the subject is least alert and most tired and has the least outside distraction. These periods occur during that first hour of the day, before one is fully awake; the last hour, when the thinking system is shutting down; and on the weekends, when one is most relaxed.

EXHIBIT 3-15
The Theory of Sales Resistance

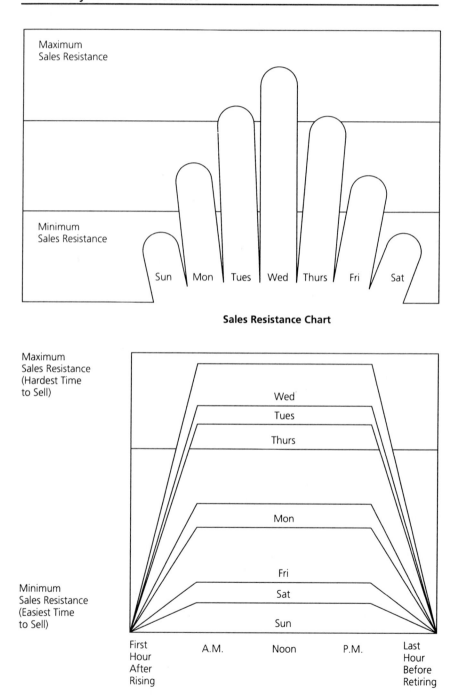

Sales Resistance Chart

I LOVE LUCY, BUT I WOULDN'T LET MY PRODUCTS APPEAR ON HER SHOW

For a long time, the ratings problem had bothered me. Even during my radio years, I had noticed that there was often no correlation between a show's ratings and the results or orders it pulled for a product. Poorly rated shows would pull a larger number of orders, and high-rated shows would pull fewer orders. Yet everyone insisted that ratings were a logical way to buy time.

In the late 1950s, I decided to explore the reality of ratings versus results. I compared shows with similar demographics (situation comedies with situation comedies, cowboy shows with cowboy shows). I compared results from the higher-rated shows against the lower-rated ones. In nearly every case, the studies demonstrated that lower-rated shows actually outpulled higher-rated shows in direct response orders.

Even more surprising was the fact that placing a direct response commercial on a top-rated show—"I Love Lucy" or the "Milton Berle Show"—was like assigning it to a cell in death row. Virtually no one ordered products advertised on those shows, despite the huge audiences. I also graphed the time of the day and days of the week when products sold best, and ultimately a pattern emerged: weekends, late at night, and early in the morning were the most effective hours for direct response.

Our research contradicted everything the advertising community preached and practiced. If the research held up, it would mean that there was a potentially revolutionary alternative to the standard media-buying methods. You could kiss the premium prices for high-rated, prime-time shows goodbye and concentrate your buys in optimum buying periods for a fraction of the usual cost.

To test the validity of my research, I contacted a highly respected professor at Northwestern University's Department of Industrial Psychology. I explained my findings and asked him if they made any sense. After studying the data I had collected and doing some research of his own, he posited a theory that put my findings into a psychological context. He told me that all advertising is an attempt to get a prospective customer to act: to call a number, mail a letter, or go to a store and buy a product. For advertising to be successful, you have to reach subjects when they are most receptive and least likely to resist the message.

To put it in the simplest terms, you are trying to implant a buying suggestion in the conscious or subconscious mind of a prospective buyer. The professor explained that this "surface hypnosis" is easiest to bring about when a person is most relaxed, most tired, and has the fewest outside distractions. This occurs when people first get up, before they go to bed, and on weekends. People build up and let down sales resistance on a daily basis as well as a weekly one.

The professor then added the clincher. He said that if you are trying to reach a potential customer, the worst time to do it is during a popular prime-time show. While watching that type of show, the viewer is fully alert and resents the commercial interruption.

I should note that my theory is less applicable to advertising that tries to gradually improve attitudes and awareness about a product and more applicable to advertising that tries to motivate a decision to buy before the commercial ends. Image or life-style advertising can work during prime time. But it still runs the risk of what I call "negative recall," generating hostility toward the advertising for interrupting an interesting show.

From the moment I confirmed my suspicions about ratings, I eschewed prime time. Immediately thereafter, my agency began to grow by leaps and bounds and my clients' profits soared. What was amazing to me was that others didn't tap this rich vein of viewers. Most advertisers seemed to believe that the poor ratings of non-prime-time shows rendered their commercials useless. To this day, many advertisers still believe that to be the case. ∎

Confirmation

This, of course, is a highly controversial theory, but numerous studies support it. One of Japan's leading universities was able to isolate a community of 100,000 and deliver mail, newspapers, and periodicals at specific times of the day and on specific days of the week. Researchers then measured the motivational reaction to the advertising. Although their methodology was entirely different from that used to measure broadcast (and cultural differences are significant), their curve of sales resistance duplicated the curve in the United States.

An indirect confirmation of the theory manifests itself when you analyze why Sunday newspapers are filled with advertising. Advertisers tend to use the medium that does the best selling job for their specific products. There is no doubt that in most English-speaking countries, the Sunday paper, which carries the heaviest advertising linage, is the most effective vehicle for all types of advertisers. Why? Because on Sunday, people have more leisure time; thus, they read the paper more thoroughly.

A 1982 survey, however, indicated that because of its great size, most Sunday papers are actually the least read of all editions. Often, section after section of the Sunday paper is discarded without being opened. A direct marketer actually has a better chance of having an advertisement seen in the much leaner and much more thoroughly read Tuesday, Wednesday, or Thursday papers. Because people are not as susceptible to a mid-week sales pitch, the Sunday paper receives the bulk of the direct marketer advertising dollars, and in most markets it is the only edition that brings in orders within the advertising allowable.

The demise of newspapers published in the afternoon also adds credibility to the theory of sales resistance. This theory leaves little doubt about why such great papers as the *Philadelphia Bulletin,* the *Chicago Daily News,* and the *Washington Star* failed. The demise of the afternoon newspaper was not due to the quality of news and editorial content, but to the time of its distribution. These newspapers were purchased and read during periods of maximum sales resistance and therefore did not do an effective selling job for the advertisers. Because the advertisers did not get the desired results, they cut back or eliminated their advertising from the paper. With fewer advertisers and fewer readers (many people buy papers as much for the advertising as for the editorial content) the afternoon newspapers' circulation began to decrease. Less advertising and less circulation spelled doom for these papers, and they were ultimately forced to close their doors. According to the theory of sales resistance, any one of these afternoon papers could have been saved by merely changing its time of distribution.

Viewer Engagement

In direct marketing selling, another factor enters into the sales results. First-run, high-interest shows do not usually air in the early morning or late evening, and a customer is more likely to leave the TV to make a phone call while watching a less interesting show. For a more whimsical explanation, imagine a fanatic football fan watching the Super Bowl. The game has reached a critical moment, and suddenly the game is interrupted with a direct marketing commercial. What chance do you think you would have to motivate that potential customer to leave his or her TV set and spend 10 to 20 minutes trying to reach an operator to buy your product?

Another antimotivation factor is worth considering at this point. In Chapter 6, we will explain that commercials with negative recall frequently achieve high recall scores. There is another way to achieve negative recall, even with a well-made commercial: by interrupting someone's favorite show. When viewers are involved in a TV program, they resent any interruption. Thus, when a commercial interrupts a show, the viewer often consciously resolves not to buy the product. This negative motivation factor was explained by a study done by Marschalk Advertising that concluded that 35 percent of viewers with a negative reaction will go out of their way *not* to buy a product, while only 33 percent of those with a positive reaction will go out of their way to buy a product.

The Isolation Factor

In media studies, we've found another significant variable that affects sales: the isolation factor. Remember that a commercial should be as long as it takes to sell a product. But studies also show that if you paid for two minutes and ran only a 30-second commercial—and the other 90 seconds were simply dead air—that isolation would give you a better chance of motivating a sale. Since most television and radio commercial breaks are limited to 120 seconds, the purchase of a commercial of that length almost assures you that your commercial will be isolated, giving you a clean shot at the prospective customer. It gives customers a chance to make a buying decision before several other advertisers try to take their money. See Chapter 4 for further information about this factor.

Radio Buying

Most of this chapter on media has been spent on the purchase of television time, because TV is the more effective of the broadcast media for direct marketing. However, there are certain media buying criteria applicable to radio.

It is important to understand that AM radio stations cover much greater populations and areas than do FM stations, particularly those stations operating on 5,000 watts or more. In AM radio, the lower the frequency, the more powerful the signal and the greater the coverage area. Thus, a station of 5,000 watts at 560 KC can offer as much coverage as a 50,000-watt station on 1530 KC. Furthermore, because AM radio uses skywaves and cloud reflections as well as the ground for coverage, AM stations have a tendency to have great skip signals. For example, WCKY, Cincinnati, Ohio, a 50,000-watt station on 1530 has as good a signal in some parts of Alabama, Georgia, and Florida as it does in Cincinnati. WWL, New

Orleans, sends a strong signal into Chicago after the sun goes down. And WBBM, Chicago, operating on 780 KC, might cover six states in the daytime and as many as 26 states after sundown. Very often, the on-the-road traveler can tune into one of these powerhouse stations and almost ride it across the country.

On the other hand, FM stations transmit on a ground wave, thus limiting their coverage to the tangent line along the earth's surface—about 32 to 50 miles, depending on the height of their tower. Although the signal is clearer and more consistent within their range, FM's greatest asset is its ability to broadcast programming that relies on the fidelity of sound.

Coverage and programming are the most important considerations in buying radio the achieve the best direct marketing returns. Talk stations, which require more attentive listening, usually are far more productive for direct marketers than are music stations, except when the direct marketer is selling CDs or tapes that are compatible with a station's program mode. A rock station would best be able to sell a rock music package, while a station programmed for the music of the 1930s and 1940s would do best selling a big band package. News stations are especially effective for products aimed at a male audience.

Perhaps the best format for effective direct marketing results is the purchase of 10- or 15-minute segments that allow for a 30-second opening commercial, a 120-second middle commercial, and a 60-second closing or 5-, 10-, 15-, or 30-minute commercials that are interesting and informative and use the entire time to sell the product.

Is this type of media purchase currently available on radio? As late as 1980, radio stations held firmly to their formats of limiting the length of commercials to 60 seconds. That philosophy is based on the belief that people will set their dial on the station that is the least commercialized. This commercial limitation was also an attempt to combat television's overcommercialization.

This commercial-limited format drove the direct marketers who found radio so successful in the 1950s and early 1960s into television. During this period, television stations were tailoring their formats in any way that would help bring them more direct marketing revenue. Unfortunately, there was basically no way the direct marketer could make the 60-second commercial work on radio; direct marketers needed far more time just to repeat the phone and mail address when the commercials lacked the benefit of the picture. In addition, a great percentage of the radio audience was in transit. And because this portion of the audience did not have pencil and paper at their disposal as they drove, it was even less likely that direct marketers would use radio.

However, as more and more radio stations went on the air and the advertising dollars per station dwindled, radio began to realize the necessity of getting a piece of the direct marketing pie.

Its first move was to liberalize the 60-second commercial limit, allowing advertisers 120-second commercials in non–drive time periods. When this did not prove effective, many radio networks and stations approached the direct marketer with the proposition, "Tell me what you want, and we'll work it out." This change in radio philosophy opened a new dimension for the direct marketer who can create the commercial for radio; the medium's arms are open wide in a gesture of welcome.

BUYING SALES-PRODUCING TV TIME AT BARGAIN RATES

A common misconception among print advertisers (and some broadcast advertisers as well) is that TV advertising is prohibitively expensive. They see the rates for prime-time shows as high as $850,000 for 30 seconds and shudder. But, would they shudder if they knew they could buy 2 minutes of TV time in a major market for under $400?

The problem, quite simply, is one of perspective. If advertisers view prime time as the only time worth buying, many, of course, will be unable to afford the rates. But that is like looking at a magazine and believing the back cover is the only worthwhile space for an ad. Prime time is not the best slot for benefit-oriented, demonstration commercials. Therefore, this chapter will focus on the bulk of media time that is not prime. For any individual or company with a unique, beneficial product, it is the most valuable TV time that exists.

Capitalizing on Television's Insecurity

The secret of strategic media buying lies in understanding the fundamental insecurity of the TV industry, manifested in its liberal credit policies. Virtually anyone can walk in off the street, and a TV station will extend credit. Stations seldom ask for financial statements or references. Although TV stations continue to suffer tremendous credit losses, few have done anything to alleviate the problem.

In contrast, the print medium is not only quite strict about credit, but also offers cash discounts for prompt payment and exacts penalties if payment is late. Usually magazines and newspapers allow a 2 percent discount for payment by the tenth of each month, and some disallow the

15 percent agency commission if payment is not received by the fifteenth of the month. Because TV stations tolerate 60- to 90-day payment delays, advertisers frequently use television's money to pay other media.

One blatant example of the TV industry's insecurity is its total disregard for rate cards. Virtually every TV station, big or small, network or independent, has a hundred different rates for a hundred different advertisers. Recently a *Fortune* 500 company's invoice for a 30-second spot on a New York TV station was sent to us by mistake. This company paid $9,600 for a 30-second spot on the same night and in the same show we paid $1,200 for a 120-second spot. Another company's invoice sent to us in error shows a prime 30-second spot on a California station listed at $1,400 on its card. This company paid $800 (about 33 percent off). We bought a 120-second spot in the same show on the same night for $175.

Television's insecurity is responsible for this situation. It seems that this insecurity stems from the perishable nature of its product. If a time slot goes by unbought, it is revenue lost. Such impermanence naturally leads to insecurity. Yet this insecurity makes television a potential gold mine for the savvy advertiser. The advertiser's media-buying service or agency, if knowledgeable and skilled, should consistently buy time at "bottom-quarter" rates. If a station offers a hundred different rates to a hundred different advertisers, the effective media buyer should be able to obtain rates that fall in the bottom quadrant of rates offered.

Unfortunately, many agencies are unable to do this. Their media-buying departments are hamstrung by a tradition that locks media buyers into a rigid pattern of buys. For instance, a client will notify the agency that it wants a specific number of rating points in specific markets over a specific period: 200 rating points in 50 top markets over 13 weeks. This method of buying is tantamount to demanding that the agency "cheat" the client. A good media buyer, given room to negotiate, can actually buy 200 rating points in New York or Chicago for less than it takes to buy the same number of points in Houston or Phoenix. A sharp buyer can do this because stations in larger markets are more willing to wheel and deal than are stations in smaller markets. Larger-market stations are more willing to slash rates if they do a lot of business with an agency.

However, the method set forth by the client prevents the media buyer from taking advantage of these low rates. Tell clients they are paying more for TV time in Houston than in New York, and they will explode. They won't understand why they pay more for the smaller market.

The agency, aware of this inequity, not only doesn't negotiate the lowest rates to prevent the problem, but also keeps the rates in line to avoid cutting its commission income. Obviously, the more of the client's money it spends on the media, the more commission it earns. Thus, the standard operating procedure at nearly all agencies is to fight for enough discount to meet the client criteria, and that's it.

The most effective procedure would be for the client to give the agency a budget based on a reasonable cost per thousand, along with a minimum rating-point level for each market. An advertiser could then tell its agency to spend the full budget, while giving it the freedom and incentive to obtain the maximum number of rating points within the budget. Implicit in this arrangement is that the agency will not be penalized for buying the greatest number of points at the lowest possible cost.

The Limitations of Rating Points

Rating points, however, should not be the be-all and end-all of media buying (or even the major criterion). At best, rating points should serve only as a guide for buyers. At worst, they can lead buyers down the path to disaster. Rating points are simply a percentage of the total homes in a given market. If a market has 100,000 homes, one rating point equals 1,000 homes. This 1,000 homes per point holds true if the point occurs at 9 A.M. or 9 P.M., at noon or midnight.

The reason advertisers pay premium prices for prime-time buys is that prime-time shows offer greater reach—that is, the highest number of unduplicated homes. A little arithmetic, however, demonstrates the fallacy in that reasoning. Prime time generally costs anywhere from five to ten times as much per point as fringe time. If you spend the same amount of money in fringe that you would in prime, your cume (the number of people reached multiplied by the number of times they are reached) will be at least four to five times as great. Thus, non–prime time offers advertisers the best value for the money they spend.

Late-night television often gives advertisers the best return for their money. Most agencies refuse to believe that. Perhaps their negative attitude toward late-night advertising is ingrained, a misconception that has been handed down from one generation of advertisers to the next. In the late 1940s, when ratings were determined by random phone calls, there were no ratings after 10 P.M. or before 8 A.M. Thus, the standard belief was that where there are no ratings, there is no audience. Now, of course, the methods allow for 24-hour ratings. In addition, daily ratings in major markets are made available the day following the date of scheduled shows.

The fact is that certain advertisers, particularly car dealers, find that late-night is most productive for them. One reason for late-night advertising's effectiveness is that the advertiser often has a captive audience in that there are few, if any, good shows to tune to. In addition, prime-time shows are often "zapped" with the remote control during commercials to allow the viewer to catch parts of other top shows. In fringe periods, there are fewer good shows to turn to, and thus less zapping.

Improving the Media-Buying Relationship

The traditional method of media buying pits agency buyer against station seller. This buying concept is counterproductive to good media selection. Station representatives and personnel call on an agency for the sole purpose of selling time. Once they have accomplished that—once they walk out with a contract in hand—they feel their job is over. Whether the commercial succeeds or fails to move the merchandise off the shelf at a profitable level is of little concern to the station rep.

This tradition has been maintained by agencies that put a desk between media buyer and seller. They keep the media seller totally ignorant of the marketing strategies and goals of their clients.

To ensure effective media buying, this concept must be scrapped. The buyer and seller must become part of the same team. The agency must convince the station representative that he or she has a greater stake in the success of the campaign than does the agency. If that seems difficult to understand, consider that the station gets 85 percent of an advertiser's expenditures, and the agency gets only 15 percent. As long as the commercial continues to successfully sell the product, the advertiser will renew and renew the schedule. If it isn't successful, the income stops. The agency and the station both lose. Therefore, because of their 85 percent stake, it is incumbent upon station representatives to do whatever they can to ensure that commercial's success, even to the extent of offering better times at lower rates, free spots, or merchandising help.

And make no mistake about it, a station rep can do many things to ensure that success. He or she is the one who determines the specific time, show, and rate for the commercial. The advertising will be infinitely more effective if the rep realizes his or her vested interest in giving the media buyer the best time, show, and rate.

Many agencies will say this arrangement is impossible. They'll explain that they don't expect their advertising to show any immediate measurable results, and, therefore, schedules aren't renewed based on sales.

For agencies that subscribe to investment spending, the team approach is indeed impossible. But for an agency with its sights set on immediate, measurable sales, the team approach is not only possible, it is practical. In the past decade it was impossible for the general advertiser to evaluate the effectiveness of a campaign until long after its conclusion. Pipe Line, Nielsen, and other market research organizations could not report product movement for 8 to 12 weeks after the fact. The installation of code-bar IPC readers now allows advertisers to get shelf movement results within 24 hours, not only for an entire chain, but also broken down store by store and further broken down by ethnic and affluency factors.

Even general advertisers can now evaluate the effects of a campaign within a week of its origin. With the flow of this information, the media buyer must become more than a functionary. Too often, the media buyer is looked on as nothing more than a robot that executes the commands of the computer. The good media buyer, however, is responsible for a great part of the success of any product. He or she has a keen marketing mind as well as a thorough understanding of media and how they work. He or she can deal directly with the client, evaluating results, recommending changes, and fulfilling the function of an account executive. The perspicacious agency will recognize its media buyers' talents and, instead of promoting them out of the job they do best, will keep them there by offering monetary incentives and increased job responsibility so the agency can best utilize their valuable skills.

The Benefits of Flexibility

The key to successful media buying is flexibility. By arbitrarily predetermining media schedules, you are locking a client into a media cell from which there is no escape. The length of a schedule should vary according to product and market. Every market must be viewed as a profit center. Many agencies attempt to secure distribution in virtually every market, no matter what the cost. They refuse to bow to the realities of a bad market, plowing more and more of a client's money into markets where the product isn't selling in an attempt to maintain the product in these markets. A flexible media buyer, however, will recognize that certain markets (for whatever reason) are death for certain products. They will yank the plug from that market's media and let the client's competition get its brains knocked out by the market's natural resistance to that product category.

Finally, there is the hills and valleys' theory of media buying. Every TV station has busy periods (hills) and slow periods (valleys). The unsophisticated media buyer attempts to climb the hills, buying time when time is scarce and rates are high. The sophisticated media buyer looks for the fertile valleys where time is plentiful and most effective in moving merchandise off the shelves. (Seasonal conditions, of course, can affect this buying method and adjustments can be made in such instances.) If the media buyer and station rep are working together to make a product a success, they will have more freedom to plan an effective media strategy in these valleys.

The theory of sales resistance discussed earlier should be the guiding light for all media buys. It provides the parameters (early morning, late evening, and weekends) within which the media buyer will find times when the viewer is least resistant to a motivating commercial. The isolation factor theory previously discussed is also of crucial importance for the media buyer. Keeping this theory in mind, a media buyer will attempt to dominate commercial breaks rather than be caught in a cluster.

This chapter, of course, is more than a series of theories. My agency has put these concepts into practice and found them to be quite workable. In fact, a number of major agencies have begun incorporating facets of this media-buying philosophy to increase the cost-efficiency and effectiveness of their media departments.

Despite this, most media-buying departments and agencies remain hopelessly mired in outdated media-buying techniques. Large agencies often promote their best buyers into oblivion. As soon as a media buyer is recognized as skillful, he or she is immediately promoted to media director or account executive and is relieved of the so-called menial task of media buying.

Agencies and their advertisers must reevaluate both the role of the media buyer and their approach toward media buying to increase the effectiveness of their advertising. If they do not, they will continue to pay increasingly higher rates for decreasingly effective campaigns.

Looking to the Future

During this decade, there will be from 500 to an infinite number of cable accesses to every U.S. home. Even a single fiber optic cable can be programmed to supply an infinite number of infomercials upon the demand and specification of an interactive "x slave x" that will search and deliver the viewer's request. Under these conditions, the media buyer will become the major player in the advertising game. Where the creative department ruled the roost and often determined the media selections, the media universe will become so vast, yet so narrow and targeted, that the selected media will determine the creative patterns. Clients that formerly were aware that only 50 percent of their advertising was effective will suddenly be able to determine which 50 percent isn't!

CHAPTER 4

Creating Direct-Response TV Commercials That Produce Sales

In David Ogilvy's address at the National Direct Marketing Convention in 1982, and in both of his books *(The Confessions of an Advertising Man* and *Ogilvy on Advertising),* he suggested that no one should be in advertising who had not spent at least two years in direct marketing first. That's because direct-response advertising professionals have to be the best in the advertising industry. Direct marketing creatives must produce immediate results. There is NO margin for error for either direct marketing creative or media people. The direct marketer does not have the luxury of continuity of advertising over an extended time. Direct marketing truly disregards past performance, yesterday's success, and fellow direct marketers' opinions. Direct marketing asks, "What did you do for me today?" If that cannot be answered in a positive manner, direct marketers will have few chances to redeem themselves for that specific offer. Continual failure will slam the industry's doors.

Because an immediate, profitable return is the only way direct marketers keep score, that score must be reevaluated daily. The creative objective of all direct marketing exposures must be to motivate an immediate action that results in an immediate or subsequently profitable sale. As is often said in the industry, regular advertisers rely on Nielsen or Arbitron, but direct marketers rely only NCR (National Cash Register).

There is no doubt that the most effective way of selling is on a one-to-one, person-to-person, eye-to-eye basis. If every company could sell its product by having a well-trained salesperson call on the potential customer, there would be no need for any other advertising medium. The next best means of reaching a potential customer on a personal level is through television.

When advertisers use television, they are knocking on the door of potential buyers, who, in effect, invite them into their homes. The visit usually is limited to no more than 120 seconds, which is not much time to motivate a potential customer to take positive action. If you were invited into a customer's home for the purpose of motivating a buying action and given a maximum of 120 seconds, would you take any of this time to tell a joke, mime, sing a song, or entertain the customer with a brass band? Or would you get right down to the business of selling?

Isn't it logical that you would take the allotted time to set forth the problems the customer might have relative to the benefits of the product and then explain how your product solves these problems? In the vernacular of the old, experienced direct marketing creative writer, the secret of direct marketing success is as follows:

Tell potential customers why they should buy your product.
Tell them again.
Tell them what you told them.

Does this mean that direct marketing commercials are dull, drab, unimaginative? No, it means just the opposite. A direct marketing commercial must simply present the benefits of its products or services in the most informative and interesting way. Notice that I use the word "interesting" as opposed to "entertaining." This technique was confirmed at the very dawn of television when 30-minute sales pitches were scheduled over and over. People watched them numerous times, and many were the topic of discussion to an extent rivaling some of the flashiest commercials.

TAKING A LESSON FROM THE PITCHMAN

The boardwalk pitchman and the traveling medicine man always presented their wares in an interesting way in order to attract crowds and hold their attention long enough to make a sale. Whether the pitchman's presentations were 5 minutes or 2 hours, they all used the same format. (See Exhibit 4–1.) The presentation included a **holder,** or the promise of something sensational to come, ranging from free prizes to a never-before-seen miracle. Next came the **problem:** an ailment, a difficult chore, or a substandard product performance. The problem was always followed by a **solution,** with a visual demonstration or verbal description of how the seller's product would solve that problem.

EXHIBIT 4-1
The Anatomy of a Sales Presentation

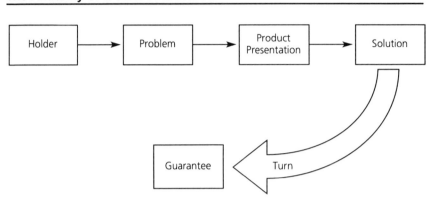

The pitchman used the tell 'em, tell 'em again, and tell 'em what you told them technique. Then came the **turn,** that part of the presentation that asked the potential customer to reach for the money. The turn was always reinforced by a **guarantee** of satisfaction that ended with "or your money will be cheerfully refunded." No other phrase was as powerful in bridging the credibility gap as a money-back guarantee. The pitchman had to make an immediate sale because probably neither the buyer nor the seller would be there the next day.

No creative writer has ever been able to approach the effectiveness of a boardwalk huckster, who often sold 50 percent to 75 percent of his entire audience. His sales presentation was born of evolution. He watched and listened to the responses of his audience and was able to counter their negative reactions. He saw what made them pull out their wallet and what made them walk away. He accentuated the positive, eliminated the negative, and sired the perfect sales presentation.

In the early days of television, we very often used a pitchman as the presenter. We allowed him to work before a live audience on the boardwalk, in a department store, or on a street corner for several weeks before we were satisfied that we had the most effective presentation. (See sidebar.) Although we have not used this technique in many years, there is no reason why it could and should not be used today. One can learn a lot from in-store demonstrations. A direct marketer can often learn more from this person-to-person approach than from all the research money could buy. Let's look at the basic elements of the pitchman's presentation and the television commercial more closely.

The Holder

Many a pitchman held his audience with stinging verbal warnings. He called attention to an imaginary pickpocket in the audience, whom he gave just five minutes to leave. He insulted the audience by shouting, "Anyone who thinks he's so smart that he has nothing more to learn should leave now." With either of these two holders, anyone who starts to leave is suspected of being a pickpocket or a wise guy.

In a TV commercial, the holder is a promise of free gifts, a product's "miraculous" performance, an "amazing offer," "sensational price," or a "revolutionary new concept." The commercials use a series of buzzwords to keep the audience's attention. Some of the great holders of TV history include, "Have you ever seen a bald-headed sheep?" "Give me five minutes and I'll give you a push-button memory!" "How would you like to double your child's grades in school?" "Play the piano in 5 minutes, or your money back!"

The Problem

In the presentation of a problem, the seller of a coleslaw maker demonstrated the old-fashioned "knuckle-busting" utensils Mom used to make coleslaw: clumsy hand graters and dangerous kitchen knives. The problem presented by sellers of health tonics would range from sexual inability, bad eyesight, bad teeth, to the problem of having a husband "who never won a blue ribbon at a fair." The household provided problems such as the "stooping and wringing" that is necessary with an old-fashioned wringer-type mop and the "rubbing and scrubbing" that characterizes cleaning your silver, polishing your car, and removing stains from pots and pans. The more common and catastrophic the malady or problem, the greater chance one has in selling the cure or solution. Ultimately, you create a universal problem by providing a universal cure.

The Product Presentation and Solution

Once you've established the problem or need, you are ready to discuss its solution. You must demonstrate how your product can solve that problem simply and effectively. You mop the floor without stooping, bending, or scrubbing. You touch the silver and it instantly shines. You turn a handle and you have a mountain of coleslaw or a pan full of perfectly textured potato pancake batter. On television, the magic is performed before your very eyes. On radio, the miracle occurs by mental image.

PERFECTING THE PITCH FOR TELEVISION

Lee Ratner and I found our first TV pitchman at a garden show in Chicago. His name was Bobby Green, and he was selling a knife sharpener/glass cutter. He had a good product and what we thought was a good pitch. We approached him and asked if he would like to be on television. He had trouble visualizing what we were talking about. For a pitchman accustomed to working live crowds, a TV commercial seemed like something out of science fiction.

When we started talking about money, we found a language he could understand. We asked him how much he made on an average day. He said $500, which was obviously a lie. Still, we offered him $500 to make a commercial for us and also offered 5 percent of the sales the commercial generated. He agreed to do it.

Ratner and I assumed it would be easy. We rented a film studio, brought Bobby Green and his product in, turned the camera on him, and told him to do exactly what he did at Navy Pier, except that he had to start out the commercial by saying: "My name is Bobby Green. I represent the Grant Company of Chicago." We didn't foresee the effect the camera would have on him. With its beady eye staring Green in the face, he lost his pitchman's characteristic smoothness. In fact, it took him 27 takes to get his first line right.

He'd say, "My name is Bobby Green, and I represent the Chicago Company." Take two: "My name is Bobby Grant, and I represent the Green Company." Take a break. After two days of shooting, he finally got it right. It took so much time because we insisted that the commercial be shot in one single take for the sake of credibility. Rather than using several cameras and cutting to close-ups to cut out mistakes, we decided to start from scratch whenever something went wrong. And, of course, it was extremely frustrating to film 9 minutes of perfect pitch and then have to start from the beginning when a mistake was made.

Still, we thought there was no other way to do it. Our potential customers were naturally wary of the new medium and a pitchman's speed. For them, television was magic, and it was difficult for people to believe what they were seeing. Thus, it was imperative that the camera not waver from the pitchman. It had to look "live." If we allowed any quick cuts or jumpy edits, the viewer would reject the product instantly. It would appear that the pitchman was a magician, not a salesman.

This decision paid off as the knife sharpener/glass cutter racked up incredible sales, moving almost 800,000 units at $2.98 in little more than a year. News of our success spread, and soon we were inundated with pitchmen and their products.

Then came food slicers, magic towels, chemical rug cleaners, one-year car polishes, chrome cleaners, fishing kits, tools, cooking pots, fly killers, gem setters, and the wonderfully named Blitz Hocker, a rotary chopper that revolved to slice food.

These pitchman presentations were the most perfect sales vehicles ever created. They were perfect because the pitchman had chopped, sliced, diced, and thrown away the parts of his presentation that didn't work. He had given the pitch to countless numbers of people all over the country. He would test lines and discard those that didn't make customers reach for their wallets. Bringing the pitchman commercial to television was like bringing a play to Broadway. You play the smaller towns and cities, constantly revising and rethinking the lines until they are just right. By the time the pitchman appeared on television, he knew exactly what to say, how to demonstrate his product, the tone of voice he should use, and even the expressions he should wear on his face. It was a perfect presentation because it had evolved to its highest form.

In the early days of television, the pitchman didn't have to compress his pitch into an arbitrary time limit. If the pitch took 13 minutes, then the commercial was 15 minutes with a 2-minute tag. If it was 25 minutes, then the commercial was 30 minutes with a five-minute tag.

The pitchman commercials were elastic; they could easily be shaped and revised to fit any product. It would be a mistake, however, to think that all pitchman commercials were alike. They were as different from one another as a knife sharpener is from a Mixmaster blender. What they had in common was that they held a viewer's interest.

In these times of 30-second spots, in which information about a product is as hard to come by as water in a desert, it seems incredible that a product's features could be elucidated for up to 30 minutes. But that was precisely the point of the pitchman commercials: the product was allowed to sell itself. Of course, that meant we had to find products that were beneficial enough to justify 10–30 minutes of air time. If a product wasn't unique, if it didn't offer a demonstrable consumer benefit, I crossed it off my list. ■

The Turn and Guarantee

The buyer is now ready for the turn. The seller gives the price and tells how the buyer can obtain the product. The turn will often include extra incentives for an immediate reaction: a free attachment, an added product, or a reduction in price. It is this segment of a commercial that demands an immediate action. As part of the turn, and in order to bridge the credibility gap that may exist between the consumer and an unknown manufacturer, the offer is made with an "unconditional, money-back guarantee." The money-back guarantee is perhaps the strongest single element responsible for closing sales ever developed.

In the construction of a commercial, it is not always necessary to have a problem and a holder. For example, in selling magazine subscriptions or music tapes, no problem exists. Today, few commercials are constructed with a holder, although it is a powerful aspect of selling. Certain elements, however, must be present in an effective direct marketing commercial. They include product benefits, the turn, and the money-back guarantee.

ADVERTISING THE BENEFITS, NOT THE FEATURES

The description or demonstration of benefits is an essential aspect of good commercials. The world *benefit* replaces the word *sizzle* in the old selling adage, "Sell the sizzle, not the steak." It is imperative, therefore, that one knows the difference between a "feature" and a "benefit." This might seem like a simple concept. On numerous tests given to direct marketing professional copywriters, as well as to university advertising students and professors, an amazing number are unable to differentiate between a benefit and a feature. So that you can better understand the difference, Exhibit 4–2 provides examples of features and benefits.

Many creative people find it difficult to make effective, motivating commercials. They can make slice-of-life spots, create aesthetically pleasing animated spots, and dream up comic vignettes that tickle your funnybone. But a realistic, demonstration commercial—one that focuses on the true benefits of a product—is the one that's most difficult to write. The creative departments of many agencies aren't trained to make straightforward, realistic commercials that tell the product story in the simplest way.

We're back to the pitchman technique. The shortest distance between two points is a straight line. Similarly, the shortest distance between seller

EXHIBIT 4-2
Examples of Features and Benefits

Feature	Benefit
Remote control television	Don't have to get up to change channels
Programmable thermostat	Greater comfort and more economical
Rack-and-pinion steering	Easier handling, quicker turns
One calorie per can	Helps you watch your weight
Automatic focusing	Never pay for developing an out-of-focus picture
24-hour automatic teller	Get money when you need it, even in the middle of the night
Golf club with solid metal head	Gives greater distance and accuracy
Ceramic-tile roofing	Lowers heating and cooling costs, saves on roofing expenses
Money-back guarantee	Assurance of satisfaction, purchase without risk
Long-lasting scent	Smell good all day, need to use less product so you save money
Computer fuel injection	Faster starts, smoother ignition, greater mileage so you save money

and buyer is a straightforward presentation. Unfortunately, some copywriters take unnecessary detours on their way to making a sale. They take detours because they want aesthetically pleasing award winners. What often results is an irrational approach to a rational product. Do the ferocious animals in car commercials really motivate anyone to buy cars? Are cute, animated cartoon characters better at selling than are real, live people? Absolutely not!

Too often, the opening shot of a commercial is wasted setting the audience up for a joke or creating atmosphere. These openings, upon repeated viewings, lose their humor or are merely distracting. The first visual and audio elements of a commercial should state the problem clearly and concisely. The potential customer should feel a strong personal identification with the problem presented. The opening audio should reinforce the visual presentation in an attention-getting, authentic, and credible manner.

Take the Roll-O-Matic mop commercial, for example. The opening shot is of a woman laboring to mop a kitchen floor. The audio begins: "One of the most tiring, back-breaking household chores is scrubbing and waxing floors . . . the constant bending, stooping, and straining to wring out your mop." A commercial cannot set up a problem faster, more effectively, than that. The words have an almost visceral kick to them. When the announcer says "bending, stooping, and straining," anyone watching the commercial immediately reacts. Those words are a trigger. Once they're uttered, the viewer immediately thinks, "That's me." Stringing together adjectives with negative connotations builds the intensity of a problem so that the viewer is subconsciously compelled to seek relief, to find an outlet for that intensity. By demonstrating the benefits of the Roll-O-Matic mop, the commercial provides that outlet.

Choosing the manner in which a product is demonstrated is crucial. Because most products can be demonstrated in a variety of ways, the creative team must pinpoint the one demonstration with the most universal appeal. The more problems the demonstration solves, the greater the chances of motivating the viewer to buy the product.

Following this strategy, a Nu Vinyl car polish commercial demonstrates the product in a junkyard and shows how Nu Vinyl puts a lustrous sheen on the oldest, most battered car's surface. (See Exhibit 4–3.) The demonstration had a double-barreled impact. For owners of old cars, Nu Vinyl demonstrates its efficacy beyond the shadow of a doubt. New car owners watching the demonstration are led to believe, "If it works so well on that old piece of junk, just imagine what it can do for my new car." By putting a product in the most difficult situation, giving it a task that seems impossible, you inject drama into the demonstration.

An effective demonstration, however, doesn't have to be confined to one benefit. Because of time limitations, many advertisers are able to concentrate on only one product benefit, believing that trumpeting only the major selling point will have the greatest results. They ignore the many buyers interested in the product's secondary benefits. In the Nu Vinyl spot, the product's multifaceted benefits are demonstrated. The commercial shows how the finish lasts through rains and washes, how it works on the car's interior, and it uses around the house. By spelling out these secondary benefits, a product is automatically made more attractive to a wider range of viewers.

EXHIBIT 4-3
Reed Union Corp.: Nu Vinyl

REED UNION CORP.

NU VINYL

NV-14R-60

Improved formula Nu Vinyl...
The remarkable clear vinyl liquid
that protects and beautifies

almost everything made of vinyl,
leather and rubber...challenged the
competition...and won!

Yes, in tough detergent tests by an
independent laboratory, New Vinyl
lasted more than 3 times longer than
these 2 competing brands.

And Nu Vinyl is easier to apply. Unlike the other brands, there's no waiting...no rubbing...no buffing! Simply
wipe it on. In just minutes your car's
vinyl top can look showroom new.

Nu Vinyl is not a wax. It's a
space-age polymer that actually
penetrates and bonds.

So it always remains flexible...won't
crack or peel.

Nu Vinyl's improved formula also
gives longer lasting beauty and
protection to your car's tires...

upholstery, dashboard...

motorcycle seats...furniture...

shoes, purses, luggage...

almost everything made of vinyl,
leather and rubber.

So get improved Nu Vinyl. There's
no other formula like it. Satisfaction
guaranteed or your money back.

The Parallel Structure Technique

Product solutions can also be demonstrated using the parallel structure technique (PST). This involves placing the viewer in two identical situations: one with the product advertised and one without it. This parallel structure motivates the viewer to objectively analyze his or her need for the product. Consider the commercial for Tarn-X, a product that instantly dissolves tarnish from gold, silver, and copper. (See Exhibit 4–4.) Using PST, the commercial begins by showing a woman confronted with a table overflowing with tarnished plates, utensils, and antiques. The scene cuts to the same setting, but this time the viewer sees the woman dip a tarnished spoon into Tarn-X. When the spoon emerges, it is shining. The before and after (parallel images) are burned into the viewer's mind, and the benefits of Tarn-X are made crystal clear.

The Money-Back Guarantee

There is no more powerful sales tool than a money-back guarantee. How often have you heard people say, "I buy at this particular store because I know if I'm not satisfied, I get my money back." With all the benefits a store can offer the consumer, a money-back guarantee is by far the one most responsible for bringing customers into their store. Thus, it is ironic that so many advertisers take the highly motivational guarantee for granted. Perhaps they don't realize the paramount importance of a money-back guarantee in establishing a product's credibility. The money-back guarantee is especially significant when the customer might be skeptical about the product. For the viewer, treading the fine line between buying and not buying a product, the guarantee is the nudge he or she needs to cross that line and make a positive buying decision. Products such as Miracle White and Lestoil were established on double or triple money-back guarantee⁓.

Exhibits 4–5 to 4–7 provide a sampling of several recent direct response commercials using a combination of the techniques discussed above.

Buzzwords

Many advertisers have also forgotten the importance of certain words: *amazing, revolutionary, new,* and *incredible.* Such words immediately trigger the viewer's interest, because they are the verbal equivalents of exclamation points, adding force to the sales presentation. Of course, these words should be used with discretion. When a product is not "amazing,"

EXHIBIT 4-4
Jelmar: Tarn-X

JELMAR
TARN-X

"Q&A"   :90 Seconds

MALE ANNCR VO: What do you do when you've invited guests for dinner

and forgot your silver serving pieces are black with tarnish?

FEMALE ANNCR VO: Get Tarn-X.

MALE ANNCR VO: Is there an easy way to remove the tarnish from those deep-etched patterns on your serving platter, even after months of neglect?

FEMALE ANNCR VO: Use Tarn-X.

MALE ANNCR VO: Can you keep sterling silver and silver plate pieces looking bright and shiny?

FEMALE ANNCR VO: Yes, with Tarn-X, of course.

MALE ANNCR VO: How do you remove years of tarnish from gold, silver and copper coins?

FEMALE ANNCR VO: Dip them in Tarn-X.

MALE ANNCR VO: How do you keep the family heirloom flatware looking shiny and bright?

FEMALE ANNCR VO: Clean them with Tarn-X.

MALE ANNCR VO: Can anything remove tarnish and discoloration from copper pots and pans?

FEMALE ANNCR VO: Tarn-X does the job.

MALE ANNCR VO: Is there a way to bring back the showroom beauty, sparkle and luster to your favorite gold, silver or platinum jewelry?

FEMALE ANNCR VO: Yes, Tarn-X does it quickly and easily.

MALE ANNCR VO: Yes, Tarn-X does it all quickly and easily.

FEMALE ANNCR VO: Dip them in Tarn-X.

But, unlike silver polishes, Tarn-X removes

only the tarnish, not the precious metal.

Remember the name . . . Tarn-X. It's guaranteed to work for you at home as quickly and easily as it does on TV or return to place of purchase for your money back. Get Tarn-X.

Always available at these leading stores . . .
LIVE ANNCR COPY: Tarn-X is available at:

EXHIBIT 4-5
Schwinn: Bowflex

SCHWINN
BOWFLEX

"Power of the Bow"

:120 Seconds
Page 1 of 2 Pages

(MUSIC: THUNDERING, DRAMATIC, IN & UNDER) ANNCR VO: The power of the bow. In the arms of strong warriors,

it shaped the histories of entire continents.

But not until now has it been harnessed

to help shape the most important body on the face of the earth.

Yours.

Presenting the Schwinn Bowflex.

The idea is revolutionary. The concept is simple.

Bowflex uses a unique series of power rods, or bows,

to give you from 5 to more than 400 pounds of progressive resistance.

The infinitely flexible bows don't limit your body . . .

they set it free. Free from dangerous weights.

Free from motion-restricting weight machines. Free to move in any direction you choose,

at any workout level you desire. In fact, Schwinn Bowflex can help you achieve total fitness . . .

in the comfort of your own home.

Medical research has proven that adding weight training to aerobics is a key contributor to losing fat.

And Bowflex gives you both -- both a complete aerobic workout -- with a unique rowing feature --

and the advanced strength training you need

to keep fit at any age.

Call this toll-free number now for a free brochure . . .

on the only home fitness unit

(CONTINUED)

EXHIBIT 4-5
(Continued)

"Power of the Bow"

that outlines

more than 100 strengthening

and toning . . .

exercises . . .

and can help

improve performance

in almost any sport

or activity.

The Schwinn Bowflex is silent. It's easily stored.

It comes with a 30-day money-back guarantee.

And for the cost of most one-year health club memberships,

Bowflex can help make your whole family fit for a lifetime.

Call now for a free brochure.

The power of the bow.

It's been around for thousands of years.

But in just thirty minutes every other day, you can harness it to help make your body

the best it can be.

And you can do it . . . no matter who you are.

The Schwinn Bowflex. A great body is just around the bend.

PHONE TAG: INFORMATION.

EXHIBIT 4-6
Time-Life's Mysteries of the Unknown

TIME-LIFE BOOKS
MYSTERIES OF THE UNKNOWN

"Skeptic"

:120 Seconds
Page 1 of 2 Pages

(SFX: RESTAURANT SOUNDS & MUSIC UNDER)
BEN: Well, there just might be something to it.

ANNCR VO: Ben Randall commenting on Time-Life's popular series, "Mysteries of the Unknown."

BEN: I've always been a little curious about unexplained phenomena.

PRESENTER: Because of . . . personal experiences?

BEN: Whatya mean?

PRESENTER: Well, like, for example, can you sense when something's about to happen?

BEN: Well, yeah, I mean, everyone's a little psychic but -- ah --

PRESENTER: What about UFO's?

BEN: I don't know . . . lotsa people swear they've seen 'em.

PRESENTER VO: Ever experienced dé jà vu?

BEN: Sort of. Like, I -- uh -- went into this old 19th-century farmhouse and I -- I just knew I'd been there before.

PRESENTER: In . . . another life?

BEN: I'm not ready for that.

PRESENTER: Ready for this?

BEN: "Mystic Places?"

PRESENTER VO: Uh huh, it's from Time-Life and talks about things

like the Nazca lines.

Were they runways for alien spaceships? And . . . did those aliens

interbreed with the ancient Peruvians?

BEN: Did they?

(CONTINUED)

EXHIBIT 4-6
(Continued)

"Skeptic"   Page 2 of 2 Pages

PRESENTER: Read the book. Read about the medieval warriors

PRESENTER VO: who appeared before Stephen Jenkins in 1936. Then . . . he saw 'em again . . . 38 years later.

BEN: That true?

PRESENTER: Read the book. Read about Aleister Crowley

PRESENTER VO: and his bride. They spent a honeymoon night in the king's chamber of the Great Pyramid.

BEN: What happened? PRESENTER VO: Read the book.

Read about Cyrus Teed's belief that people live in the center of the earth.

Admiral Byrd looked into it . . . know what he found?

BEN: I know, read the book.

ANNCR VO: Read "Mystic Places."

It's yours, free, for 10 days. If you keep it, other volumes will follow. One about every other month.

You'll receive "Psychic Powers"

followed by "Psychic Voyages"

and "Phantom Encounters." Every volume written by experts.

They give you all the information. So . . . you can decide for yourself.

BEN: I've decided! I'm ready to order!

PRESENTER: The books?

BEN: The books and . . . the food.

Waiter!

PHONE TAG: INFORMATION.

EXHIBIT 4-7
Guaranteed Trust Life Insurance

GUARANTEE TRUST
STUDENT LIFE INSURANCE

"Trust"

:120 Seconds
Page 1 of 2 Pages

(SFX: CHILDREN'S VOICES, LAUGHTER, BIRDS SINGING, ETC.) FLORENCE VO: Last night, when she was asleep, did you tuck her in?

Kiss him good night, when he didn't know it?

There are so many things parents quietly do . . .

FLORENCE OC: that children aren't aware of. I'm Florence Henderson, and I'm here to talk to you about one of them.

Life insurance for children. An easy way to protect your child, your family and yourself . . . for life.

It starts with one phone call.

Your concern now means your family will be protected if the worst happens. The money will be there.

FLORENCE VO: And most important, it means security for life.

Truly, because this life insurance plan is guaranteed renewable for life.

FLORENCE OC: There aren't many ways to do so much good . . . with so little money.

With one dollar. That's what it costs to try out this policy for 3 months.

And your annual payments are guaranteed to stay low -- just twenty dollars a year.

(CONTINUED)

EXHIBIT 4-7
(Continued)

'Trust

FLORENCE VO: One dollar now, for three months. Then twenty dollars a year.

Easy, affordable, a must. You can depend . . . on Guarantee Trust.

FLORENCE OC: In business since 1936, Guarantee Trust has been quietly providing children's life insurance to caring parents for decades.

Today, over 300,000 policies are in force, and for good reason. Listen --

FLORENCE VO: ". . . never regretted buying the policy for my child."

"Great . . . low cost coverage."

"Made some checks with other companies and yours (Guarantee Trust) is the best."

FLORENCE OC: You'll learn more in this Great Start® Kit, yours free with a toll-free call.

Life insurance for your child. If this is the security you want, call right now.

And this evening, when you kiss your child good night, you can both rest assured

that the good you've done today will last a lifetime. You can trust Guarantee Trust.

PHONE TAG:
INFORMATION.

it would be inappropriate to use the word. But when a product increases your gas mileage substantially or makes mopping the floor an easy job, then "amazing" is accurate.

Perhaps some advertisers refrain from using these buzzwords because they have been overused or they seem like hyperbole. If that is the case, they are making a costly error. If they have a product that is intrinsically exciting, they should convey that excitement to the viewer. Buzzwords are loaded with meaning. They automatically imply that a product is beneficial. Without these words, a commercial for an extraordinary product becomes ordinary.

Providing Information

Another rule for creating motivating commercials is to supply the audience with enough information to make an educated buying decision. It is a rule that is consistently broken. How many times have you seen a commercial that has neglected to give essential information about a product? After viewing such a commercial, the audience is left with many questions and no answers. Without those answers, it is difficult to make a buying decision.

The dearth of information in commercials is based on an outmoded assumption: that store clerks will supply customers with all the information they need. Years ago, this assumption was valid. Before the advent of high-volume discount stores and chains, most consumers shopped at ma-and-pa stores. Those stores had knowledgeable salespeople who provided their customers with accurate, in-depth information about a product. Even larger stores featured demonstrations of new products, and their salespeople had the time and expertise to help customers make educated buying decisions.

In recent years, however, ma-and-pa stores have gone the way of the buffalo. If not quite extinct, they account for only a small percentage of total retail sales. The big discount stores get the biggest slice of the pie, and their clerks are either too busy or lack the ability to give customers accurate, detailed information about a product.

Thus, it is incumbent upon advertisers to inform consumers about their products in commercials. They must assume that there is no one in the store who can provide the essential facts about products. If advertisers have demonstrably beneficial products, why not show those benefits?

The information-filled commercial is a result of a journalistic approach to advertising. These commercials answer the who, what, why, when, and where of a product. Whom is the product for? What does it do? Why is it beneficial? When can it be used? Where can it be bought? If the product is a beneficial one, the more information given about it, the better, both for the consumer and the advertiser.

PRODUCT CATEGORIES THAT WOULD BENEFIT FROM PROBLEM-SOLUTION ADVERTISING

The type of commercial I have described in the preceding pages is one that can work for any product, providing that product has a demonstrable, unique consumer benefit. The products can run from cars to banks to soft drinks to credit cards. Let's examine a few product categories that usually don't use the problem-solution formula outlined in this chapter and explore what would happen if they did.

Food

Food advertising is a haven for animation, jingles, and slice-of-life techniques. For parity products, these techniques probably serve a purpose. But for food that has some demonstrable, unique benefit, information-filled commercials could be extremely beneficial. Food products that fall in this category are high-fiber cereals, unusual spices, salt and sugar substitutes, low-calorie desserts, and many other food or food-related products.

For instance, when an unusual frozen dinner in introduced in a TV commercial, it can be strongly motivational. If it is frozen crepes, it solves the problem of boring, bland, chicken-potpie-type frozen dinners. It offers the solution of interesting, continental dining, and that is a benefit that can be demonstrated in a commercial.

Banks

Financial institutions are bastions of generalization, image-oriented advertising. They infrequently spell out specific services that benefit the consumer. Instead, they rely on a general theme such as "The Bank for Business" or "The Big Bank with the Little Bank Inside." Such themes are fine, but they would be far more motivating if the commercials backed them up with specific, beneficial services.

A commercial for a bank should begin with a common problem: lack of courteous, personalized service. The bank's solution to that problem should then be demonstrated: tellers who greet customers by name, a bank "host" who meets customers when they enter and directs them to the proper area, etc. The benefits of becoming a customer of this bank are spelled out in compelling terms, and viewers are motivated to respond to the commercial.

Cars

Commercials for automobiles fall into what I like to call the "country roads rut." A sizable percentage of automobile advertising consists of long shots of cars traveling scenic country roads or medium shots of cars against breathtaking views. I have no idea what all this fresh air has to do with selling cars, except for the production company that makes the commercial.

Dashboards are an extremely motivating part of auto sales. Yet how often does an advertiser extol the virtues of a car's dash? Commercials convince people to buy cars by offering them a benefit: better gas mileage, lower price, spaciousness, good handling. Some commercials advertising cars do consist of demonstrations ("We drove this car a hundred miles through the toughest terrain imaginable"), but many do not. And often these demonstrations are not conducted so as to motivate the viewer. For instance, a commercial that demonstrates a car's excellent gas mileage cannot merely list that car's miles per gallon and show the car rolling along a stretch of road. It should clearly demonstrate how much money the consumer will save each year in gasoline costs.

Automobile advertisers are also guilty of selling features, not benefits. Too many car commercials emphasize features such as rack-and-pinion steering (benefit: better control and cornering ability), dual carburetion (benefit: more acceleration and power), and independent suspension (benefit: a smoother, more comfortable ride). The growth of commercials of infomercial length should be the absolute solution to automobile advertising. An auto manufacturer should hire the best salesperson for the product in the whole world and let him or her introduce a car or the new line in an infomercial whose length is based solely on the length of the sales presentation. Thirty-second spots can be used as support to direct people where and when to tune in to see the car or new line. In this infomercial, people will find out for the first time what rack-and-pinion steering really is and its benefits over standard or power steering.

DEVELOPING A BELIEVABLE STYLE

Up to this point, we have concentrated on the content of a motivating commercial. But content is only one element in the creation of a commercial that produces sales. The look of the commercial is another element that must be considered. Here is a rule of thumb: The more real the commercial looks, the more believable it will be. In the 1950s, nothing bridged the credibility gap better than the live commercial. Because it was live, the viewer accepted what was shown: a product demonstration could not be tampered with. Thus, what you saw was what you got.

Today, the next best thing to "live" is videotape. Unlike film, videotape has a quality of cinéma vérité. Videotape has a documentary feel to it, whereas film suggests fiction. Over the years, A. Eicoff & Company has resisted the trend toward filmed commercials, relying on videotape because it makes a presentation more believable. An added bonus of videotape, of course, is that it is far less expensive to use, saving clients a great deal of money. However, when selling foods or aesthetic products, film can add to the selling power of a commercial. Be aware that the future of film is in question with the advent of high-definition videotape, which will offer the same quality as film at far lower cost and much lower duplication charges.

Benefit-oriented demonstration commercials should have a "live" feel to them. Television viewers have become increasingly sophisticated, attuned to the medium's ability to tamper with reality. They have built-in cynicism toward products that claim to do amazing things. The only way to break through that cynicism is with a believable commercial.

Most people in the advertising world are aware of this cynicism. Some of them, however, make a crucial error in trying to combat it. For instance, some commercials attempt to simulate ridiculous "real-life" situations. How often do a husband and wife argue about using a deodorant? How common is it for a secretary to tell her boss he has bad breath?

But slice-of-life commercials, even if they are true to life, are still distortions of reality. Viewers are aware that they are watching actors and actresses reciting rehearsed lines, and that awareness prevents the commercial from being as effective as it might be. For these commercials to work, they would have to invoke what Samuel Coleridge referred to as "suspension of disbelief"—the willingness of readers (or viewers) to forget they are reading a book (or watching a movie) and to approach it as if it were reality. While such a suspension of disbelief might work for literature or film, it won't work for a TV commercial.

This is not to say that no slice-of-life spots work. If they appear during a period of low sales resistance when the viewer's alertness level is down, they can make a positive impression. But if the commercial runs during a period of high sales resistance, the alert viewer will instinctively analyze and reject the obviously "staged" slice-of-life situation.

Similarly, animation, fantasy, and humor are advertising techniques that detract from a commercial's credibility. (Animation should be used only when a product demonstration is physically impossible, such as fertilizer's ability to help grass grow.) On the other hand, the demonstration approach can provide the credibility necessary for a viewer to buy a product. A demonstration of a product is exactly what it purports to be. There is no need for suspension of disbelief.

One effective technique for achieving credibility for a direct marketer and attracting the hard-to-sell pseudo mail order buyers is called a wrap-around. This technique calls for a commercial to start with a pleasant, honest-looking order taker who informs the audience that she will be ready to take their orders after they see the commercial. Following this 15- to 20-second introduction, the commercial is aired. The order taker returns at the end to remind people that she is now ready to take their orders. She also provides the phone number and mailing address. This wraparound concept constantly increases the orders and cuts order cost sufficiently to warrant the 15 to 20 seconds taken from the normal commercial time.

WHAT IS THE BEST LENGTH FOR A COMMERCIAL?

The final element necessary to create a motivating commercial is time. There is a general misconception that 30 seconds is a commercial's optimum length. In fact, 30 seconds is an arbitrary number with absolutely no relation to the realities of selling products. It is the standard length of commercials because that's how long it takes a second hand to move halfway around a clock. To designate one specific time as being best for all commercials is like saying all books should be 200 pages, all symphonies should be 45 minutes, and all movies should be 90 minutes. By limiting commercials to 30 seconds, advertisers are also limiting the amount of information they can convey about a product. In many cases, the time limit is unfair to potential customers. They don't have enough information to make a buying decision.

To determine the length of a commercial, an advertiser must determine how long it takes to sell the product. Generally, 1 to 2 minutes is necessary to do an effective selling job. Some products could easily use an hour, and more advertisers are opting for longer commercials, even infomercials, to do an adequate motivating selling job.

THE ISOLATION FACTOR

An even more compelling reason for advertisers to create longer commercials is the isolation factor theory. It is the result of 6 years of research, and it stipulates that if you can obtain sole possession of a commercial break, you can greatly increase the motivational power of your commercial. By "isolating" viewers, you allow them to make a buying decision before they are distracted by other commercials.

Imagine if you were a buyer and you allowed four salespeople into your office at the same time to sell four different products. As soon as one salesperson completed a presentation, the next one would begin the sales spiel. What chance would you have to make a buying decision for one product before you were into the next one?

To dominate a 120-second break, you must create a commercial at least 90 seconds in length. To own that break, your commercial must be the entire 2 minutes. If you don't do either of these two things, you run the risk of irritating viewers by being within a cluster of four 30-second spots. When you gang up on viewers with clusters, they cannot absorb the first pitch before the second salesperson starts talking. The viewers' irritation level becomes so high they often reject all the products being sold. If, however, you isolate your commercial, you become the only salesperson in viewers' homes, greatly increasing the chances that they will make a positive buying decision.

To measure the effect of longer commercials on viewers, we conducted a series of tests in conjunction with TVB. In these tests, we showed panels of women sets of commercials. One set consisted of four 30-second spots, another set included one 60-second commercial and two 30-second ones, another featured one 30-second spot and two 10-second spots, and there were various other combinations. These sets were shown with one 2-minute commercial in order to compare responses toward longer and shorter commercials. We discovered that viewers don't time commercials; they count them. When people are irritated by a commercial, they never say, "Not another 2-minute commercial!" Instead, they say, "Six stupid commercials in a row!"

Of course, I don't propose that all commercials be 2 minutes in length. As I stated earlier, commercials should only be as long as it takes to effectively sell the product. If a product could be sold in 30 seconds, however, an advertiser would get better results by buying an extra 90 seconds of "dead air" to isolate the 30-second commercial. If that sounds like a revolutionary proposal, consider that corporations such as Hallmark, Kraft Foods, and IBM sponsor TV specials precisely because it allows them to isolate longer commercials within these shows. And they have found that these commercials are extraordinarily effective in moving their products.

HOW MUCH SHOULD A COMMERCIAL COST?

Any marketing or advertising executive reading this chapter should now be asking a very logical question: How much should a good commercial cost? The answer is: usually under $30,000. If that seems a ridiculously low figure, remember what inflates the price of commercials: film, jingles, elaborate productions, location shooting, a full cast of actors and actresses. By eliminating the show biz aspect of creating a commercial, you eliminate the major expenditures.

A top-quality videotaped demonstration commercial should cost between $20,000 and $30,000 to produce. If you spend $100,000 more on production, chances are the aesthetics will be nicer, but the results at point of sale will be the same. At the insistence of a client, we have upgraded a $12,000 commercial to $100,000. The client got a very warm feeling on the inside, but the sales remained the same on the outside.

The wise advertiser spends time rather than money to ensure the advertising's success. Admittedly, it takes many hours to create a motivating commercial. But as the sales figures come in, it will prove to be time well spent.

HOW LONG SHOULD A COMMERCIAL RUN?

Finally, I am constantly asked how long a commercial can be aired. I question the judgment of advertisers that spend fortunes on creative and discontinue them after a few exposures. A commercial should continue to air as long as it is capable of motivating sales at or below the advertising allowable. (See sidebar.) Our commercial for Tarn-X ran for 12 years before it was changed. And now Tarn-X commercials have a life expectancy of 3 to 5 years. The Nu Vinyl commercial is actually 20 years old, having been revised twice to upgrade the car models. The longest-running direct marketing commercial was the John Williams version of the Great Moments in Music, which is still airing after 20 years, with only price revisions from $6.98 to $19.95 plus postage and handling.

Commercials should only be viewed if they can be improved, and in direct marketing, the new can always be tested against the old to find out if it lowers the sales cost to advertising ratio. Most often, when we have written new commercials solely because we thought the old was becoming worn, the new seldom achieved the success of the old. I consider this a compliment to our creative department. They do not produce the first commercial until they're sure it's the best possible commercial they can create.

IMMORTAL DIRECT RESPONSE COMMERCIALS

In my keynote address at a recent National Infomercial Marketing Association meeting, I showed portions of a few of the 408 infomercials I produced between 1950 and 1970. Many of these were made by simply taking the pitchman from the midway to the film studio. Few commercials cost more than $2,500 to produce, although many of them were 10, 15, and 30 minutes in length, and about 80 percent of them were highly successful. It was not unusual to start with a total budget of under $5,000, and without investing any additional money in advertising, but merely using the profits from one market to open another, to end up making profits exceeding $200,000 from a single infomercial. Keep in mind that these were run from 1950 through 1970, when such profits were unusual even in medium-sized businesses.

The aspect of my speech that was most incredible to the audience was that nearly every one of the contemporary commercials closely imitated commercials aired 25 years ago. The auto polish infomercial uses a blow torch and acid to show the protective coating of the auto polish, just as was done in commercial for One Year Auto Polish in 1951. The DD9 spot remover used iodine as the stain and hypo solution, as did M-O-Lene in 1950. There were also striking resemblances in the real estate, sunglasses, and bald spot hair spray products, which were all successfully marketed in the early days of television.

As successful as the early infomercials were in producing large returns on small investments, key outlet marketing products (many of which started as mail order items) were even more profitable. A direct marketing offer normally has a life span rarely exceeding one to two years, but a product put into retail distribution can last for decades, although quality, novelty, or knock-offs can limit their lives.

The Roll-O-Matic Mop was a newly designed mop that allowed the user to wring it out without stooping or bending. It originally was a direct marketed infomercial product, demonstrated by showing how it could be wrung out in a Coca-Cola bottle. With an initial budget of $25,000 including the commercial, Roll-O-Matic became the number-one selling home mop in the drug, variety, and hardware stores. Also, for the first time, a key outlet marketed product became the top seller in mass-merchandising outlets such as Kmart and Walmart. In addition to mop sales, the sales of refills became an annuity for the client. Today, after 26 years, the Roll-O-Matic mop is still a leading seller.

Nu Vinyl was the first of the vinyl cleaners and coatings. The initial commercial positioned it as a treatment for vinyl and fabric car tops, with secondary uses for leather and vinyl upholstery and tire treatment. In the first 6 months of exposure, it became the fourth-largest selling item in the automotive departments of drug and variety stores. The quality of the product and name value nurtured the more universal Nu Finish, a once-a-year car polish that gained acceptance by proving it could polish a junk-yard car and could withstand 52 car washes without losing its protective coating. When *Consumer Digest* rated it the number-one car polish for quality, Nu Finish obtained the number-one sales position in the market. It has maintained that position despite strong competition and saturation advertising by its competitors, Turtle Wax and Raindance. After nearly 30 years, Nu Vinyl adheres to the same direct marketing commercials and media concepts, spending about 25 percent of its competitors' budget to maintain its top position.

Tarn-X is an instant tarnish remover that has maintained the number-one selling position in the silver-cleaning market for over 30 years. It still relies on 90-second direct marketing commercials and direct marketing media buying concepts. Tarn-X has become a household word in many countries. From an original investment of only $2,500, Tarn-X products enjoy sales in excess of $15 million, at extremely high profit levels.

CLR is a household cleaner that works particularly well on stains caused by calcium and lime deposits. It instantly removes rust stains from sinks, tubs, and toilet bowls. It cleans coffee makers and decanters and dissolves rust stains from cement and driveways. It was launched in 1969 with a total budget of $45,000, including production and media costs, and is another product that has not needed any injection of money either from the marketers or the banks. CLR continues to run mostly 90-second commercials, all tagged with dealer identification in each market. Using the profits from sales to finance its expansion, it has joined Nu Finish as a prima donna of the key outlet marketing concept, anticipating sales in 1993 of $40 million.

Jovan Musk Oil is a highly successful worldwide perfume, which had trouble breaking into many U.S. markets during its infancy. The mere fact that it used direct marketing tactics and concepts in its commercial production and media planning was enough to get drug outlets, which had turned the product down on several occasions, to put in displays. In all test markets, the products sold out completely before the end of the schedules. Conflict of marketing concepts caused Jovan later to opt for more conventional marketing methods.

Topol Tooth Polish is a smokers' toothpaste. Although it was highly successful using radio, Martin Himmel, the marketer, decided to give the direct marketing concept a try in three test markets. Sales increases of 23–36 percent in those markets triggered immediate expansion into national use. Although Himmel seldom ran the same commercial for more than 4 weeks, the direct marketing version of the Topol commercial ran for over 4 months.

These are only a few of more than 70 successful retail marketing launchings that A. Eicoff has been involved with over the past 40 years. Every one started with minimum capital and attained an extended period of high profitability. ■

PRODUCING THE TV COMMERCIAL

There are two basic ways to create a TV commercial. You can visualize the commercial and write the audio to fit the video, or you can write a radio commercial and then create video to fit the audio. In TV direct marketing, it is more effective to write the audio and simply keep the video concepts in mind as you write.

Effective direct marketing video can range from the simplest table-top close-up demonstration, used for such products as the Knitting Machine and the Salad Maker, to such sophisticated commercials as the picturesque travelogues of Hawaii created for TWA and the animated Disney World spots created for Grolier Books and the American Express Travel Store. (See Exhibit 4–8.)

Between these two extremes is the stand-up pitch—which recreates bygone days of boardwalk pitchmen—and realistic, slice-of-life commercials used for companies such as Avon. Whichever technique is used, it is important to remember that the audio is at least as important as the video in motivating the consumer. Although demonstrating a product is extremely important, a picture is *not* worth a thousand words. Draw me a picture that says, "War declared!"

Although the audio message most often motivates the sale of a product, the visuals help to give that product credibility. Background settings must be simple, believable, and unpretentious. It is more effective to demonstrate a salad maker in an ordinary, middle-class kitchen, than in the dream kitchen of tomorrow.

A commercial's effectiveness and motivational power can be hurt by overproduction. For example, the Avon Company put its desire for an upgraded image ahead of its desire to increase sales. The Eicoff agency was asked to make a recruiting commercial for Avon, which was produced for a cost of about $18,000. Although the commercial produced recruits below the advertising allowable, the president of Avon felt the commercial did not properly represent the Avon image. The commercial was upgraded by revising the settings, talent, and direction, but not the audio. The upgraded video brought the cost of the new commercial to over $40,000. The commercial produced results comparable to the $18,000 commercial, but the executive level of Avon still was concerned that the commercial did not achieve the desired corporate image.

A secondary agency was given the assignment to re-shoot the video using the basic audio track with a few changes. The new commercial was aesthetically beautiful. It was shot in an upper-middle-class neighborhood, in a home with a $50,000 kitchen, as well as in a ballet classroom where the Avon saleswoman was able to send her daughter to school. The commercial—which was produced for $150,000—undoubtedly would have won any direct marketing award contest it entered. Unfortunately, it did not produce Avon recruits at a profitable rate. What would have been a long and effective recruiting campaign was killed by overproduction.

In creating a TV commercial, one of the most important words is *relate*. The viewer must be able to relate to the situation depicted in the commercial. The problem must be a universal one, and viewers must agree with the commercial's contention that they have a problem and it can be solved with the advertised product.

EXHIBIT 4-8
Mattel Group: Knitting Machine

MATTEL GROUP
KNITTING MACHINE

Imagine...being able to make gorgeous knitted items like this beautiful afghan...

or this magnificent pillow -- and WITHOUT knowing how to knit!

Well, if you can turn a crank and sew on a button, you can make any of these items and more -- with this amazing automatic home knitting machine.

Here's how it works. Just thread the machine. This tension bar automatically keeps the stitches perfectly uniform.

Now just turn the handle. That's all there is to it! A few turns and you've made a small tube.

Close the ends of the tube and you have a Granny Circle.

Rows of Granny Circles make this winter scarf...

Continue to turn and make a long tube, to create these adorable stuffed animals.

Yes, there's just no limit to the things you can create -- sweaters, hats, pillows, bedspreads, purses, infant wear...and what a time-saver!

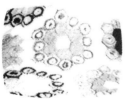

With the Knitting Machine, you can actually make this magnificent afghan in a fraction of the time it would take to knit by hand.

The Knitting Machine comes complete with a skein of yarn, plus step-by-step instructions and patterns to make all the things you see here...

$14.95

and, the price is only $14.95! Best yet, the Knitting Machine carries a full one year warranty. If dissatisfied, return it for replacement or a full refund.

Phoenix Group, a division of Mattel

FORMS USED IN WRITING THE COMMERCIAL

There are two forms you can use when you write a TV commercial. The storyboard is the most widely accepted method. This technique combines an artist's rendering of the video the writer has in mind as the audio is performed. These storyboard renderings seldom look very good when produced. Even when the writer of the commercial does his or her own directing and producing, the video he or she had in mind when originally writing the commercial most often can be improved at the studio. That doesn't mean that one should leave the determination of the video until the commercial is being shot. What it does mean, however, is that the director should be able to vary the camera angles, set placements, etc., to what looks best through the lens and fits the continuity of the commercial.

Another format explains the video on the left side of the page and has the audio on the right. This form is quite acceptable, and the experienced director would rather have this type of video aid than the storyboard. (See Exhibit 4–9.) In selecting the method of presentation to a client, do not risk presenting an inexperienced client the written version, as it is difficult to understand and visualize a commercial in this form without having a great deal of experience and being fully aware of the versatility of production equipment.

EXHIBIT 4-9
Side-by-Side Video Copy Format

Client: Time-Life Books
Product: Home Repair & Improvement
Code: Hom-20-120 (Basic Wiring)
Length: 1:47
Date: As produced 8/80, EUE Video, N.Y.

Video	**Audio**
1. Animated roof blowing off house with Buffalo Bill and Bill Shakespeare rising up. Hands push ceiling down on them and nails shut.	Homeowners are raising the roof over rising repair bills. But there is a way to keep a low ceiling on costs with . . .
2. Beauty shot of series.	Home Repair and Improvements from Time-Life Books. And—
3. Plug goes into socket and shorts out. Black screen clicks on with light bulb.	even if you can't tell a bolt from volt, you can still learn what's watt.
4. Shots of valve handle and tools. Animated plumber's helper.	The series is flush with all the tools and all the rules to plunge into any problem by yourself.
5. Shots of mason's hawk, brick bat, plane, drawer glides . . . awl and level.	You'll find planes and gliders . . . pilots and ripcords. And it's awl on the level.
6. Rapid cuts of brick wall construction and wall papering sequence. Interior/ exterior color photographs of homes.	Simple, step-by-step diagrams give you the know-how in no time . . .
7. Cabinets, woodwork, sinks, showers, wallpaper shots.	and color photographs show you design principles and illustrate the basic concepts. You'll learn to put in cabinets and woodwork without getting chiseled. To install sinks and showers without taking a bath. And to heat your house without getting burned.

(Continued on next page)

EXHIBIT 4-9
(Continued)

Video	Audio
8. Beauty shot. Deck, ducts, bricks, bracket shots.	Home Repair and Improvements covers everything from A-frames to the kitchen sink. Anything to do with decks and ducts . . . bricks and brackets.
9. Painting instructions, track light installation.	You'll brush up on painting and get on track with lighting.
10. Animated scissors cutting off corner of White House.	And you'll learn to cut corners on costs without bringing down the house.
11. Sequential change of entire series of book covers.	Home Repair and Improvements ranges from Basic Wiring to Kitchen and Bathrooms. From paint and wallpaper to plumbing and new living spaces. So whatever your questions, the answers have been nailed down for you right here.
12. Announcer on-camera in workshop.	Start your home improvement library now by examining Basic Wiring for 10 days absolutely free. If you decide to keep it, pay Time-Life Books just $9.95 plus shipping and handling, and we'll throw in this free booklet, "The Home Tool Kit." Future volumes will be sent to you approximately every other month . . . always for a free 10-day examination. You keep only the volumes you want . . . and you can cancel at any time. Order Basic Wiring now and start building your library on a firm foundation.

CHAPTER 5

Creating Dynamic Radio Commercials

A LONG AND PRODUCTIVE HISTORY

Direct marketing in radio began late in the 1920s, when the patent medicine men found a new medium to supplement print. Many patent medicines—such as Garlic Tablets, Lydia Pinkham, and numerous cures for backache, headache, bloody noses, arthritis, rheumatism, impotence, and a vague disease known in the South as "the miseries"—featured highly exaggerated claims promoting absolute cures. Bibles and religion were also highly profitable radio direct marketing subjects.

One great and effective direct marketing campaign was carried on by Dr. Brinkley, an impeached governor of Kansas. He filled the airways with a promise of sexual rejuvenation through a monkey-gland operation that required $700 cash. It was reputed that Brinkley, using his Mexican radio station that also preached anti-Semitism, could perform as many as 150 operations a week and that his calendar was overcrowded.

Following the attack on Pearl Harbor in December 1941, during the short period when all U.S. coastal cities were blacked out, radio direct marketing sold millions of glow-in-the-dark gardenias, allowing people to recognize their escorts, families, or business associates in the dark. It was not unusual to walk into a train depot and see hundreds of passengers with glowing lapels.

Developments during World War II

As consumer merchandise inventories dwindled because of the demands of wartime production, radio's income dwindled. With the exception of nationally advertised products such as Jello, Ipana toothpaste, Fitch shampoos, and Lux soap—all of which used prime time—radio station owners were wide open for any source of new income. It was during the years 1941–1946 that radio openly solicited direct marketing advertisers on a per order (or per inquiry) basis. All types of products that would normally have no consumer acceptance became heavily promoted on the air.

One famous wartime promotion was a weather house. Designed like a cuckoo clock, it predicted the weather by having either a princess come out of the door, indicating good weather, or a witch, indicating rain.

The cuckoo clock promotion occurred after Robert Kahn, who owned a small advertising agency, ran an unsuccessful test on the weather house for a client. The agency never got paid, but it was able to recover 12,000 weather houses in its lawsuit against the client. Having no other way of selling the weather predictor, Kahn gave it one last attempt on December 3, 1941. On Pearl Harbor Day, all weather predictions ceased for national security reasons, and thousands of orders flooded the agency from farmers, carnival workers, airfield employees, and other people whose livelihood depended on the weather.

Another wartime direct marketing offer was aired by Schaeffer, Brennan, Margulies, a St. Louis agency. Chicken was the only unrationed meat during the war period, and a leading producer of chickens was a firm called Blacks. It was Blacks's custom to discard the male baby chicks. Because of the meat shortage, however, the agency convinced Blacks to offer 100 baby chicks for $2.98. The offer became an instant success. Railway Express offices were crammed with boxes of baby chicks piled to the ceiling. It was a boon to Railway Express (which suffered greatly from the scarcity of consumer goods) as well as for radio stations scrounging for income.

Many people who were aware of the progress of radio direct marketing during the war years put many new products on the air when the war ended. Radio—particularly the large, powerful stations—had learned about the profitability of PI advertising, and they accepted new direct marketing products with open arms.

The end of the war brought new horizons to radio. Prior to the 1940s, few of even the very large advertising agencies had radio departments. Rep firms, such as the Petry Company, and advertising agencies brokered time. They actually purchased the time for themselves and then resold it to clients. Dancer Fitzgerald Sample had such a lock on daytime soap operas that, if you had a product targeted to the nonworking housewife, you either used DFS as your agency, or you couldn't get on the air.

The Golden Age of Radio Direct Marketing

Immediately following the war, however, the advent of ABC, a new radio network, and the government's release of new frequencies for radio stations prompted all major agencies to establish broadcast departments.

Because radio media buyers were a rare commodity, most agencies converted print buyers or research people into members of their radio media department. Having such little experience with radio, the new media directors used audience research from four audience-research companies: Nielsen, Hooper, Pulse, and Conlan. These companies measured audience size and demographics using random telephone calls that were made between 8:00 A.M. and 10:30 P.M. They confined their calls to this period so they would not disturb listeners during their sleeping hours. For this reason, there were no ratings before 8:00 A.M. and after 10:30 P.M. and with no ratings, the advertising agency community concluded that there was no audience. Therefore, there was little or no demand for time periods we now call prime.

In addition, although there were 52,000,000 known radios in automobiles, none of the rating services was able to measure the automobile audience. Because it was assumed that this audience was negligible, a great deal of the best time on radio was available to direct marketers at extremely low prices or on a PI basis.

This period, from 1947 to 1955, was the Golden Age of radio direct marketing. Very high audience times were available at very low costs. Saturdays and Sundays, which were particularly lucrative direct marketing days, were wide open for anyone who could provide motivational copy and enough product to meet the demand.

Watches, for example, were unavailable during the war years, so an offer of a Helbros wristwatch for $29.95 on XERF in Del Rio, Texas, produced in excess of 3,000 orders a day and soon exhausted the entire supply.

Many new products were launched via direct marketing, and radio mail order exposure created such high demand in retail stores that the direct marketer found it easy to put products into retail distribution. Such was the case with Kyron, a product that promised the loss of at least a pound a day, with no hunger pangs. The sponsors of the Kyron campaign—which was originally launched through one of America's premier broadcast direct marketing agencies, O'Neil, Larson and McMahon—made $7 million for the entrepreneurs in less than 4 years.

A Chicago partnership launched a direct marketing campaign for a product called Imdrin, which claimed to provide instant relief from the pains and miseries of arthritis. Imdrin became an instant success. Within 2 years, the company moved its product from direct marketing to universal distribution, providing the partnership with profits that exceeded $300,000 a month.

One of the most successful of all direct marketers that converted to retail distribution was Toni home permanent wave. Launched as a mail order offer by a young Minneapolis entrepreneur, Toni soon filled the shelves of all leading drug, grocery, variety, and department stores. From its paltry beginnings, Toni became one of the great products of its era.

Perhaps the longest-lasting product that came up through the radio direct marketing ranks was d-CON, a rat and mouse killer that was launched through a now legendary radio direct marketing campaign. From 1949 through 1955, it was difficult to turn on any major station between 5:45 A.M. and 7:00 A.M. without getting at least one 15-minute d-CON sponsored show. Despite the fact that the total retail universe for rat and mouse killers in 1947 was only $1,800,000, d-CON sold over $3,000,000 worth of product in its first year of mail order exposure and raised this volume to over $5,000,000 a year in the ensuing three years by combining direct marketing and retail marketing. (See sidebar.)

TAKE THAT, YOU DIRTY RAT

I arrived in Chicago in the 1940s with a little advertising experience but uncertain about where that experience would take me. But once I met Lee Ratner, I found myself in the world of direct response advertising.

Ratner had heard that the University of Wisconsin was doing research on an anticoagulant called warfarin. Their research also showed that warfarin was terrific for killing rats. In addition, rats failed to develop an immunity to warfarin as they had to a number of other products. And research showed that humans or other animals wouldn't die from it unless they ingested huge quantities of the stuff.

Ratner obtained rights to the product and told me he wanted to sell it for $2.98. There were many other rat poisons on the market that sold for considerably less. When I pointed this out to him, he responded with Ratner's Rule: Price a product according to what it does, not what it looks like or costs to make. He explained, "If you don't got rats, two dollars ninety-eight cents might seem like a lot. But if you got a bunch of those furry fellows crawling around your home, you'll pay anything to get rid of 'em."

The next step was to give our rat killer a name. Naming a product correctly is crucial to its success. If you want people to have certain expectations about a product, the name should fulfill those expectations. So we racked our brains trying to come up with an appropriate name for the rat killer. At first, we played around the X names: Rat-X, Rid-X, and the like, because to us the X conveyed a sinister, ominous power. Then we got fanciful: Pied Piper, Rodentia, Rat-a-tat-tat. Finally, we sank to the level of the absurd: Ratkill, Rat-Bomb, Rat-Shot. But all the names were inappropriate, or they couldn't be registered as a trademark, or they were in violation of an already existing trademark. So after great thought, and for the sake of expediency, we came up with the name d-Con, short for "decontaminate." It was a terrible name, and we had every intention of changing it as soon as we could think of another one.

But we wanted to get the product out, and we had been wasting time. So d-Con it was. I spent a great deal of time and effort coming up with the copy that would sell the rat killer to the world. We put the spot on the air, but no one bought d-Con. We experimented with different stations and different copy approaches without luck. I told Ratner we should cut our losses and run.

"We can't do that," Ratner said.

"Why not?"

"Because I got a carload of warfarin, $32,000 of the stuff, and I got to get rid of it."

So he didn't let me rest. Instead, we took to the road.

Ratner and I got in his car and drove to downstate Illinois, looking for farmers to talk to. We called on the county agent, who gave us the names of many farmers he knew, who had barns infested with rats. We wanted to talk to the farmers and see why they weren't buying the one product that could eliminate their problem.

But when we asked these farmers about their rodent problem, they looked at us as if we had asked them about the weather on Jupiter. They didn't have rats, they explained. They were afraid we were there to condemn their corn and grain for containing rat droppings.

When we introduced ourselves as representatives of the Wisconsin Alumni Research Foundation and explained that we were collecting data for a study on pest control, their attitude suddenly changed. For days, we heard rat story after rat story. They talked to us like a neurotic to a psychiatrist. They confessed that they were embarrassed about their rats, that rats were a stigma, connoting uncleanliness. Yes, they said, they would do anything to get rid of those rats, as long as no one knew about it. They made it clear they didn't want their neighbors or the postman to know they had a rat problem.

So we returned to Chicago and added one single line to our commercial: "So that no one will know you have a rodent problem, d-Con is always mailed in a plain wrapper." The commercial aired, and farmers across the country mailed in their orders. ∎

The Advent of Narrowcasting

In the late 1950s and early 1960s, as television became a major communication and advertising medium, radio stations began to run scared. Fearing total loss to the new electronic medium that offered everything, radio took steps to give itself a new position.

Block programming made radio a medium of narrowcasting, where each station chose a specific market and went after it with full-time programming. Stations trying to attract young adults programmed rock and roll. Stations that were looking for the 30-plus audience programmed middle-of-the-road music: the big bands and the pop singers, including Eddie Fisher, Frank Sinatra, and Rosemary Clooney. Stations aimed at the businessman found that their audience preferred news. Some stations continued with talk-show formats in an attempt to keep the housewife. The new approach to programming required tight formats with limited commercials, both in number and length. Thus, the radio direct marketers were closed out by format changes. In addition, hundreds of new AM and FM licenses began to segment the audience to such an extent that radio stations could not pull enough mail orders to warrant continuing the commercials, even though the client was willing to allow the stations to run on a PI basis.

Before the new narrowcasting formats, the most successful direct marketing stations had limited regulations relative to commercial length or frequency. For example, WCKY in Cincinnati ran 10-minute segments from 7:00 P.M. to 6:00 A.M., allowing the direct marketer a 30-second opening, a 2- to 3-minute middle commercial, and a 60-second closing.

XERF, XENT, XELO, and XEG, the powerful mail-pulling Mexican stations, played a record and then ran a 2- to 3-minute commercial, repeating the pattern all day long. An hour of time usually allowed for 30 minutes of commercial time. WJJD in Chicago, famous for its mail-pulling Suppertime Frolics, combined 15-minute sponsored shows with 3-minute commercials. On some programs, the station allowed for 5-, 10-, 15-, or 30-minute commercial presentations, such as the "Dean Ross Piano Lesson," which gave the listener step-by-step instructions for 15 minutes, starting with the scale and ending with a near-professional rendition of "The Tennessee Waltz." (See Exhibit 5–1.) When these stations revised their program formats—although they continued to attempt to make direct marketing work—they lost their appeal to direct marketers. The shorter commercials were never effective in motivating an immediate mail order response.

EXHIBIT 5-1
15-Minute Dean Ross Commercial

Friends, I'd like to talk to all of you in radio land who have a problem singing a simple scale like . . . do . . re . . mi. I'd like to speak to those of you who can't carry a tune in a paper bag or who have never been able to read one note of music but envy anyone who can play a musical instrument. Well . . . wonder if I told you that I can teach you to play the piano in less than ten minutes? Wonder if I told you that with my revolutionary new piano teaching method you would be playing tunes such as (Play tune underneath) On Top of Old Smokey . . . (Switch to HOME ON THE RANGE) Home on the Range . . . AND Hymns like (Switch to AMAZING GRACE) Amazing Grace . . . with both hands with just a few hours' practice. Why, before you know it, you'll be playing songs like this (Play TENNESSEE WALTZ) . . . or like this (Play a few bars of GOODNIGHT IRENE). Can you imagine how you'll be the envy of all your friends and neighbors when you sit down at the piano and play?

Hello, I'm Dean Ross, and during my 30 years of teaching, I developed a way to teach you to play the piano, and all you have to be able to do is read numbers. That's right! If you can read numbers, you can play the piano! You see, with my DEAN ROSS method, you just stick special adhesive tabs with numbers on the 88 white and black keys. Now to play the scale, you just hit 31,

(Continued)

32, 33, 34, 35, 36, 37, 38. (Ann follows along and hits keys as he talks.) By merely hitting 31, 33, 34, 35, 35, 36, 38, 37, 36, 35 . . . you're playing a melody like Old Black Joe. As you progress, you'll follow along with 42, 42, 43, 41, 42, 43, 44, 44, 45, 44, 43, 42, 43, 42, 41, 42 . . . and you're playing America. You don't have to be able to read a single note . . . my special method even shows you how long you should hold a note before you play the next one.

So that you become accustomed to reading the numbers and coordinating your hands, the DEAN ROSS method starts you off with a book of 25 songs. Each gets progressively harder . . . you just follow the numbers in the book by hitting the numbers on the piano keyboard. Almost as soon as you sit down at the piano, you'll be playing the melody line of your favorite Country & Western, Patriotic, or Popular song . . . even your favorite hymns like (Play along) Church in the Wildwood . . . or (Play along) Everyday with Jesus . . . As you become more skilled coordinating the numbers on the music and your fingers on your right hand, you do the same with your left hand . . . hitting 22 and 24 like this with two fingers or 22-24-27 like this to give you another chord. When you add the chords of your left hand with your right, you get this (Play Old Black Joe slow and deliberate, then more and more professional). Each time you play it, you'll get better and better, and don't forget, all you have to be able to do is read numbers (finish song). And here's how you do the same thing with America, as the right hand is playing 32, 32, 33, 31, 32, 33, 34, 34, 35, 34, 33, 32, 33, 32, 31, 32, you do the same thing and add the left hand. You see how easy it is to play America. Once you've mastered the easy songs, such popular hits as (Play song) On Top of Old Smokey are as easy as picking out the keys on a typewriter (Finish song). And for those of you who love Tennessee Waltz, you'll find it no harder to play than 31, 32, 33, 35, 31, 32, 33, 35 . . . now add the left hand chords. Each time you play it, it's easier and easier for you and it sounds better and better.

Soon your friends will turn blue with envy when they see you at the piano and hear you playing their favorite song. And if you want to play a love song for someone special, just follow the numbers on the music, 31, 32, 33, 37, 37, 37, 36, 35, 34, 33 . . . and you're playing For Me and My Gal! Now add the left hand. Did you ever think that playing the piano would be this easy? And look how simple it is to play an old wedding favorite like Here Comes the Bride! Play the melody line with your right hand . . . follow the numbers . . . and now add the left (Continue to play).

Remember, the DEAN ROSS method shows you everything you need to know to play the piano. You get 88 numbers for every black and white key, so you merely hit the numbers and play a melody. On each song there's an explanation and drawing showing you what number to hit and how long to hold it. And with our special music converter, you can take any sheet of music and quickly convert the notes to numbers. This special music converter is yours FREE if you order before Friday midnight, so remember, SEND NO MONEY, just your name and address to DEAN ROSS, radio station WJJD, Chicago 1, Illinois, or save COD and postage by sending check or money order for $4.98 to DEAN ROSS, radio station WJJD, Chicago 1, Illinois, that's DEAN ROSS, radio station WJJD, Chicago 1, Illinois. ■

From the very late 1950s through the early 1980s, radio continued its de facto exclusion of direct marketers and longer commercials. However, the loss of cigarette advertising dollars and the loss of a large potential market caused some stations to relax their stringent format concept, opening time periods for direct marketers.

The 1960s and Beyond

Through the 1960s, experienced radio direct marketers, as well as new direct marketing agencies, attempted to make radio work. However, direct marketers who were finding success in nearly all time areas on television (even on the lowest-rated TV stations) were not experienced enough in the new radio to understand the following rules of success:

- It was necessary to have longer commercials on radio than on television.
- The phone number and mailing address must be announced at least four times in the course of the commercial.
- The body commercial should be followed by a reminder commercial reiterating the phone number and mailing address.
- Because radio programming zeroed in on a relatively narrow audience, the advertiser had to confine product exposure to stations with the demographics most nearly resembling the target audience.

The direct marketer also had to learn that stations programming background music, even those with attractive demographics, rarely succeeded in obtaining orders within the advertising allowable. The most productive radio exposure occurred on stations that programmed news, talk shows, or a higher-than-normal amount of disc jockey chatter, such as Wally Phillips offered on Chicago's WGN. As was proven in the Golden Age of direct marketing radio, the most powerful stations—those with the highest wattage and lowest AM frequencies—usually were able to provide far more direct marketing volume than were the small local stations or even the popular FM stations with music programming and coverage limited to about 40 to 50 miles.

Although good radio direct marketers don't have to know much about radio engineering, they must understand that the shorter the wave and the greater the power, the more coverage the station has. For example, WBBM Chicago and WGN Chicago cover 30 to 35 states after sundown with a steady, clearly audible signal. WWL in New Orleans can be heard clearly in Chicago, and WLW in Cincinnati puts a high-grade signal into states from Maine to Minnesota, from Michigan, New York, and New England to Florida. The coverage information that a direct marketer must know is that a 5,000 watt station on 560 KC will send out a signal as strong as a 50,000 watt station on 1300 KC, providing, of course, that the conductivity of the soil, the height of the antenna, and the terrain are relatively consistent. Often, high-powered stations on high frequencies transmit skip, or jump signals. For example, WCKY—50,000 watts on 1560 KC—doesn't cover all of Cincinnati, but it sends a powerful signal into an area from North Carolina to the Florida Keys.

During the late 1970s, direct marketing radio again began to prove itself as an effective direct marketing medium. The *Wall Street Journal* was extremely successful in selling subscriptions using 120-second commercials on news-formatted stations. Saturdays and Sundays were particularly effective, achieving high-quality orders at allowable expenditures. While the *Wall Street Journal* was effective because it could zero in on a business audience, *Playboy* found it difficult to achieve subscriptions because its audience listened to rock stations on which the music was used as background, and the commercials were seldom heard.

Much like the *Wall Street Journal,* the *Kiplinger Report* was able to target a sector of its potential audience using the same news shows. Although it found radio to be an effective medium for short spurts, its campaigns were not effective over the long haul.

Perhaps the most consistently successful users of direct marketing radio are people who sell CDs, tapes, and records. Because it is so easy for music companies to target their exact audience, music stations became very productive for record and tape offers. "The Best of Elvis Presley" was being offered on both radio and television the day Presley died. Both media flooded phone systems with orders. Southern Bell requested the offers be taken off the air because it was impossible to get an emergency call through the system. Seventy thousand phone calls were recorded from 6:00 A.M. to midnight on the day of Elvis's death.

A number of companies have successfully used radio to offer free Christmas catalogs. In the case of catalogs, what's required is a clear definition of the contents of the catalog, a repeat of a free offer, and the address for ordering.

In the 1990s, more direct marketers are learning about radio direct marketing's great potential, and stations are learning more about direct marketing's formatting requirements. Indications are that radio direct marketing has made a complete cycle, and we are returning to the late 1940s, when stations recognized the income potential of radio direct marketing. They now realize that long, interesting commercials do not deplete their audience and are willing to adjust their rates or their selling strategies to make radio profitable for the direct marketer. Unfortunately, there are few people in direct marketing who still remember the Golden Age of radio and who understand the fine points of the medium. Furthermore, most direct marketers avoid radio because it lacks television's glamour.

PRODUCING THE RADIO COMMERCIAL

When you buy direct marketing on radio, keep the following points in mind:

- Make sure that the station will allow you enough commercial time to motivate the audience.
- Make sure that the station audience is demographically right for your product.
- Avoid buying time on stations that provide background music, whenever possible.
- Let the station talent, especially if the talent is a celebrity, do the commercial live in his or her own words from a fact sheet.

- Select stations that offer you a great deal of plus coverage (the extra audience you pick up in the nonurban areas are often real mail order buyers).
- Make a deal for the media cost that will allow you to adjust the rates so that you can continue to have exposure with orders being produced within the advertising allowable.

Selecting a Format

Before you start creating for radio, it is important to select a particular format. Direct marketing radio commercials are usually produced with a live script or a simple recording, so it is both inexpensive and relatively easy to write a 2- to 3-minute body commercial that sets forth the problem, solution, and basic offer; repeats the mailing address at least four times; reiterates the offer; and incorporates a money-back guarantee of satisfaction. This body commercial becomes the middle commercial for a 10- or 15-minute format, which needs only a 30-second opening and a 60- to 90-second closing commercial. The closer should always begin with a summary of the offer, restating the problem and solution, repeating the mailing address at least two more times, and, of course, emphasizing the money-back guarantee.

For radio commercials that offer lessons of some type, a 5-, 10-, 15-, or 30-minute format allows the writer to take the listener through a step-by-step demonstration, promising that anyone can learn to perform a certain function in just a few minutes. In the case of a real-estate investment presentation, the step-by-step procedure takes the listener from poor to rich in 30 days.

It's also effective to run the body or middle commercial, followed by the 60-second summary, three or four times without the interruption of another commercial. Because phone numbers and mailing addresses are so much harder to remember from a radio commercial than from a TV spot, a radio direct marketing commercial must be completely isolated from other commercials. This isolation allows potential customers an opportunity to make a buying decision without being exposed to any commercials that could interrupt their thoughts or confuse them.

Once the format is selected, the commercial should be created so that there is a sense of urgency. To create this urgency, you can make the offer limited; suggest that the offer might never be made again or that it will be withdrawn Friday; or offer a special premium for people who act before a certain date. Of course, the copy must always set forth the promise that the product will fulfill or state the problem that the product will overcome, followed by the logical and motivational reasons why a given product will offer an instant solution. In the vernacular of the old radio direct marketing writer, make the listener sick with a disease and then offer an immediate cure. If there is no real disease for your cure, invent one. The most unsuccessful direct marketed products offer cures for which there are no diseases.

In some cases, the very best direct marketing commercials are not written. Perhaps the most effective radio commercials I've ever produced were those where a fact sheet was supplied to a local or national celebrity and they were told to sell the product in their own way, using any approach or concept they thought would be productive, limited only by the information and restrictions supplied on the fact sheet. If possible, visit in person or by phone with the personality, detailing the advertising allowable and emphasizing the importance of maintaining the profitable aspect to the longevity of the schedule. It is helpful to offer a bonus to the personality in relationship to the success of the advertising.

I remember writing a d-CON commercial that stated: "Enough d-CON was fed a chicken to kill 1,000 rats. Following the ingestion, the chicken was killed and examined by a veterinarian. The autopsy showed no internal damage to the chicken, thus proving that d-CON is safe to use in chicken coops." The announcer on XERF interpreted that statement in his way by saying, "After this here chicken was fed enough d-CON to kill a thousand rats, the veterinarian stated, 'There ain't nothin' wrong with this here dead chicken.'" That interpretation sold thousands of packages of d-CON at $2.98.

What Is the Most Effective Length for a Radio Commercial?

The direct marketing radio commercial has a lot to accomplish in a short time. It must present its audience with a holder, a problem, its solution, a turn, a money-back guarantee, and it must repeat a phone number and mailing address as well. Therefore, the length of the commercial should be determined by how long it takes to sell the product, not by how long it takes for a second hand to pass halfway or all the way or twice around the clock. Until June 1984, government restrictions limited commercials to 120 seconds in length, and radio and television writers were limited to this time frame. Now, however, the FCC has lifted the commercial length restrictions as well as the restrictions on the amount of commercial time allowed in a specific period.

In the 1950s, radio was deluged with a number of 15- and 30-minute commercials that were often formatted as an interview show interspersed with commercials. For example, a diet expert might be questioned about effective methods of weight loss. In between interview segments, the station would insert the sponsor's diet-product commercials.

Fifteen-minute record offers were also quite popular in the 1950s. All or parts of the records in the offer would be played for 15 minutes while the D.J. commented about the music and its era. Of course, the seller would present an offer of the records being played at intervals left open for the commercials.

Another 15-minute show/commercial featured an author or well-known lecturer speaking about his or her field of interest. The lecture would be interspersed with commercials selling the books or magazines covering the subject of the lecture. This is also a common format used in the radio and TV industry to raise funds.

Although it might seem difficult for a copywriter to make such a presentation interesting, it is actually easier to keep the interest of an audience for 15 minutes than for 60 seconds. The writer has time to introduce the elements of interest that are necessary to hold the audience.

When a 5-, 10-, or 15-minute show/commercial is not available or is unnecessary to the selling presentation, the most effective format for direct marketing on radio incorporates a 30-second opening (usually with a holder), followed by about 4 minutes of the station's regular programming. The advertiser then introduces a 120-second commercial, followed by about 3-1/2 minutes of regular station programming. Finally, the 10-minute segment is concluded with a 60-second closing commercial. (See Exhibit 5–2.)

The 30-second opening commercial summarizes the offer that is about to be detailed in the next commercial. The middle commercial sets forth the problem and the solution and gives the phone and mailing instructions for obtaining the offer. It continues repeating a description of the offer. Finally, it repeats the mailing address and phone number. Because radio does not have the advantage of visual presentation, it is essential that the mailing address be repeated at least four times in the middle commercial and at least three times in the closing commercial.

The closing commercial starts off with the mailing address and phone number, restates the problem and solution as set forth in the middle commercial. After offering the money-back guarantee, the closing commercial repeats the mailing address and phone number two more times.

EXHIBIT 5-2
Opening-Body-Closing Radio Commercial Format

Segment	Time	Purpose
Opening	30 seconds	Holder
		Summarize the offer

4 minutes of station programming

Segment	Time	Purpose
Body	120 seconds	State problem
		Announce solution
		Provide phone number/ mailing address at least 4 times

3½ minutes of station programming

Segment	Time	Purpose
Closing	60 seconds	Restate problem and solution
		Announce money-back guarantee
		Provide phone number/ mailing address at least 3 times

This repetition of phone numbers is essential, yet humorous at times. Direct marketing commercials in New York in the 1950s had to use local phone services within the broadcast area before the toll-free 800 number was created. With six separate numbers for people in New Jersey, Long Island, Westchester, Staten Island, Brooklyn, and Manhattan, advertisers often ended up spending more time repeating the phone numbers than selling the products.

Composing and Rewriting

Before you begin writing a radio or TV commercial, think about what claims and benefits it would take to sell you the product. As you write, integrate the benefits with an attention-getting, interest-keeping script that will prevent the potential buyer from changing the radio or TV channel. The first step in creating an effective direct marketing commercial is to write whatever comes into your head, with little regard for continuity or the performance aspects of the product. Your first attempt at any copy should contain the most positive motivational sales message you can think of without any regard for length or substantiation.

Once you have written everything you think it would take to make you buy the product, then begin rewriting your commercial. This first rewrite should focus on a more honest description of the product's performance, while still disregarding continuity or length.

The second rewrite should begin to put the commercial in a logical continuity. As you rewrite for the third, fourth, and fifth times, you should begin to edit for commercial length, logical continuity, credibility, etc. Keep in mind when you begin the creative process that you are not limited to a single voice or an uninterrupted stand-up pitch presentation. Sometimes the method or concept of the commercial is more important.

Remember, great commercials are never written; they are always rewritten!

Other Writing Tips

In creating radio and TV commercials, don't be afraid to use buzzwords like *exiting, new,* and *revolutionary.* Of course, always include in direct marketing copy, "satisfaction guaranteed or your money back!"

To bridge the credibility gap, consider using celebrity and professional endorsements. User testimonials are probably among the strongest selling techniques available to any copywriter: "Let the man who owns one tell how great it is!"

In radio, it is often important to write for the talent. In the heyday of radio, when the airwaves were filled with such well-known personalities as Arthur Godfrey; Gabriel Heater; Grady Cole of WBT, Charlotte, N.C.; Paul Gibson of WBBM, Chicago; and Don Davis of WCKY, Cincinnati, a good radio copywriter wrote a different version of a commercial for each talent. Godfrey did a slow, deliberate delivery, and one created the copy to meet his style. Nightingale delivered 20 percent more copy than Godfrey in the same time frame, while Davis could deliver nearly twice as many words in the same time.

There are few nationally known personalities left on radio, so it is difficult to write for any particular announcer. Often, for this reason, the best results come from giving the talent a fact sheet and allowing him or her to do the commercials in his or her own style.

Finally, when you have completed the most powerful sales presentation possible, you must obtain clearance from the necessary legal and continuity-clearance departments. Still, a copywriter's objective is to write hard-selling copy . . . don't try to be a lawyer!

PRODUCT SELECTION

Many direct marketing commercials can be as motivating on radio as they are on television. For example, if a product is not demonstrable, then a radio commercial can be just as effective as a TV commercial. For example, books, subscriptions, insurance policies, and fertilizers are difficult to demonstrate. Therefore, it is often preferable to use only words to sell these products, rather than pictures.

Though television can be used to demonstrate some books—such as how-to books or home repair—radio often is an equally effective medium. With insurance offers, radio copy can be as effective as television, since most insurance companies find the straight stand-up pitch the most effective presentation.

There are, however, certain types of products for which word pictures can conjure a better image than an actual picture can. This was true in the case of Pinto, the Talking Pony. Pinto was a blow-up, plastic rocking horse with a noisemaker in its neck. When the neck was squeezed, the noisemaker reacted to the amount of air pressure. The copy on radio actually had the horse answering the presenter's questions with grunts and neighs, and the listener could easily visualize the product's appeal.

When you select a direct marketing product for radio, make sure that it has all the elements it would need to succeed in a TV commercial, such as universal appeal, uniqueness, and markup. But radio does not require the product to be demonstrable.

RADIO AS A SUPPORT MEDIUM

Radio alone—or combined with television—can be a highly effective support medium. Since most radio stations have such low ratings, stations should be chosen based on programming that reaches the target audience. Then, saturation campaigns should run over a 3- or 4-day period.

In the case of support for a record club, where the demographics of the target audience are men and women between the ages of 14 and 30, the best rock stations should be selected, and the support should incorporate 40 to 50, 30-second spots on each selected station. When supporting a Sunday newspaper insert, the campaign should run Thursday, Friday, Saturday, and Sunday morning. When a radio commercial supports an insurance mailing, news, talk, and middle-of-the-road music stations with audiences over 35 should set the pattern for the support buy. In the case of an insert, the Thursday, Friday, Saturday, and Sunday pattern should be followed. In the case of a mailing, in which the date of delivery is uncertain, the campaign should begin two days prior to the expected first day of delivery and should continue until the estimated next-to-last day of delivery.

Where the supported product is demographically universal, then the best station in each category should be used: the leading news, talk, hard rock, rock, and middle-of-the-road stations should offer the reach and cume necessary to increase the productivity of the primary insert.

Radio can also be an effective support medium for television when the TV commercial is a show-type presentation, such as a panel discussion or a presentation of how to make money in real estate. The same pattern of reach and cume should be used for television as is used for print inserts.

NETWORK RADIO FOR DIRECT MARKETING

There are literally dozens of radio network combinations, ranging from canned music to news, but the most effective network formats are the news formats of CBS and NBC and the talk format of Mutual. Because of the number of radio network combinations, a direct marketer should stay in constant contact with the various radio networks, particularly for distressed availabilities that either can be purchased at extremely low rates or can be available on a PI basis.

CHAPTER 6

A Look to the Future of Broadcast Direct Marketing

Cable TV and Interactive Technologies

In order to best understand the important role direct marketers played in the birth and growth of cable, it is important to understand that the word *cable* actually has two distinct meanings. Literally translated, cable is merely a piece of wire that attaches to a TV set and delivers something of higher quality or different than you would have seen without that specific cable connection.

THE ORIGINS OF CABLE

There are several stories as to the origination of cable. One attributed it to a retailer in the Portland, Oregon, area, another to a retailer in the Pochono Mountains, but the Cable Advertising Bureau gives Jerry Mangus of Denver the credit for putting up an antenna in 1953 to bring in clearer reception for the purpose of selling TV sets. Mangus at first offered customers a free connection to his tower if they purchased a TV set from him. The customers' cost was limited to the expense of running a wire from the antenna into their homes. Of course, to compete, other retailers had to build towers and offer customers the same opportunity for clear reception. As time went on and subscribers became more distant, many tower builders found a sizeable market for installations and rental fees. These fees soon became more profitable than the TV-set sales.

Superstations

It is important to understand that all the cable company actually provided was a more reliable, stronger signal from local stations. When Ted Turner announced that WTBS, his Atlanta TV station, was to become a superstation whose signal would be available to cable operators via satellite transmission, he was not originating new programming, but merely allowing his normal programming to be picked up and retransmitted by cable operators.

The advent of the superstation provided cable operators with a unique selling benefit that could attract customers who were already getting clear reception from local stations but were unable to receive more distant stations. Other major independent stations saw the superstation concept as a means of becoming a "single source" network, and WTBS Atlanta was soon joined by stations in Chicago, New York, and Los Angeles. Although none of these stations had any intention of producing original shows, they were all sources of local sportscasts unavailable to local broadcasting stations.

Program Origination

Realizing the potential of this new medium, Ted Turner again originated a concept of actually producing shows specifically for the cable operators. His first venture was CNN, a 24-hour news service that he envisioned as a more in-depth presentation of current events that was being offered by the networks. CNN was also designated "cable television." However, it had nothing to do with the logistics of distribution, but rather solely with program origination. Today, with nearly 5 million private satellite receiving dishes, program originators are becoming more and more involved in the logistics of signal distribution. In 1993 there were 5 superstations, 32 national cable program originators, and 24 regional cable program originators. (See Exhibit 6–1.)

EXHIBIT 6-1
Superstations and Cable Networks

Superstations

KTBS   Atlanta, GA
KFBK   Boston, MA (New England coverage only)
WGN   Chicago
KTVT   Dallas (Texas coverage only)
WOR   New York City

National Ad-Supported Cable Networks

American Disability Channel
Arts and Entertainment Network
Black Entertainment Network
CNBC
CNN
Comedy Central
Country Music Television
Court TV
The Discovery Channel
E! Entertainment TV
ESPN Sports Channel
Galavision ECO
Headline News
The Jukebox Network
The Learning Channel
Lifetime
Mind Extension University
The Monitor Channel
MTV Music TV
Nickelodeon/Nick at Night
Nostalgia TV
Prevue Guide Channel
Prime Network College Sports
Sports Channel America
TBS
TNN Nashville Network
TNT
Travel Channel

(Continued)

USA
Video Hits One
The Weather Channel

Regional Ad-Supported Cable Networks

Arizona Sports Network
Empire Sports Network
Group W Sports Marketing
Home Sports Entertainment
Home Team Sports
KBL Sports Network
Madison Square Garden Network
New 12 Long Island
Orange County News Channel
Prime Sports Network
Prime Ticket Network
SportSouth Network
Sunshine Network

Shopping Networks

Home Shopping Network I
Home Shopping Network II
Home Shopping Network Split
Macy/Bloomingdale Shopping Network
Nordstrom Catalogue of the Air
QVC Network I
QVC Network II

Note: A number of movie channels do not currently accept commercials. However, these channels are destined to open to commercial use, if for nothing more than film previews. ■

DIRECT MARKETING'S IMPORTANCE TO CABLE OPERATORS

In the early days of television, there were few sets in use, and rating services measured only private home audiences without regard for the actual size of audience. National advertisers believed the audiences were too limited to warrant even minimal budgets, so TV stations were destined to suffer sizable losses for the first 5 years of their existence. Only local advertisers, who measured advertising success by sales, and direct marketers, who rely totally on responses, found television to be a highly profitable medium. Through most of the 1950s, even the network stations reluctantly accepted infomercials from direct marketers, because they provided a source of income that kept them liquid.

Cable superstations and program originators found direct marketers even more important to their financial stability. When the local superstation went on the air, local advertisers would not pay a premium for national coverage, because their customers were confined to their local area. Both regional and national advertisers refused to recognize the superstation as a viable medium, because the cable operators provided less than 10 percent penetration of any county. Regional media directors had set forth a rule that "if a medium does not have at least 30 percent penetration of a county, it has no penetration." Thus, only direct marketers, who recognized the potential of added coverage and who were concerned only with sales and not with their geographical source, provided major income for the cable originators.

When Ted Turner was struggling to keep his head above water with his superstation and CNN, he gave a speech to the media moguls of Chicago in which he stated, "Those of you who feel that a medium with less than 30 percent penetration is not worthy of a national advertising budget must remember that Jesus started with only 12 converts." As always, Ted was right! It took more than 5 years before the national advertiser recognized the cable networks, and often during this period direct marketers extended a helping hand by paying in advance for future schedules.

ADVANTAGES OF CABLE FOR DIRECT MARKETERS

Cable soon became highly profitable for everyone who had something unique or special to offer to the public. Specific programming allowed an advertiser to zero in on a defined market. Cable's programming flexibility allowed time segments up to 60 minutes for infomercials. Lower commercial standards allowed advertisers to "gaff" their demonstrations and make outlandish product claims without censorship or restrictions.

Cable provided evangelists time for fund raising, sirens an opportunity to lure men into $5-per-minute conversations, and soothsayers a chance to sell "guaranteed" future lottery winners. Cable opened up a panorama of pandering. Today, cable is still enjoying the energy and enthusiasm of teenage immaturity.

One major advantage of cable is its ability to offer advertisers the luxury of narrowcasting, by offering specific programs to small, specific audiences. There are cable originators that confine their production to sports. There are sports cable networks that confine their programming even further to a specific sport. In the future, cable programmers might become as definitive as a specific position on a sporting team. Sound implausible? General Motors will have an interactive channel that can be narrowed to a specific car brand, to a specific model, and even to the variations of the selected model.

With its great flexibility and easy accessibility, cable is destined to drive entrepreneurs of the future, regardless of their business. If they have a product to sell to the consumer, cable will stand ready, willing, and able to zero in on the prospect. If you sell business to business, cable will knock on the door of the prospective customer and allow a seller to make a full presentation without the expense of time and travel.

For teachers, the students will be waiting at the other end of the line. Even those that have only a philosophy to sell might find themselves talking to a single, intense listener. But the binding element to all of these invited and uninvited entrees is the direct marketing technique of selling. The infomercial, whether it be one minute or several hours in length, will be the principle tool in gaining maximum results for every field of sales endeavor. (See sidebar.)

THE APPEAL OF THE INFOMERCIAL

Imagine yourself sitting in front of a TV set, your attitude toward commercials much different than it is in the 1990s. You don't view them with disdain, automatically tuning them out when they interrupt your favorite program. Instead, you view them as a valuable source of information, as something with the potential to both sell and educate.

As you're sitting there, you see a man standing beside a desk, and he says, "Don't touch that dial! Because the next few minutes could be the most important minutes of your life. What you're about to see and hear could very well start you on the road to a newfound happiness . . . greater success than you ever dreamed possible . . . income beyond your wildest imagination. Ladies and gentlemen, how would you like to have a push-button memory?"

Now let me interrupt this commercial for a question: Who among you is not intrigued by what is taking place on the TV set? Unlike any commercial you might see today, it makes you want to continue watching, because you're curious about the product. What is a "push-button memory"?

How would you like to be able to remember first and last names of everyone you meet? I mean, every time you're introduced to a new person, you'll remember that person's name automatically, so if you meet again in a year—or five years—that person's name would pop into your memory automatically. Well, tonight you're going to get some memory tricks and formulas from Mr. Harry Lorayne . . . Mr. Lorayne's fantastic memory is not due to a photographic mind, but rather to a series of memory tricks, or formulas, which he has been able to teach to anyone in a few short hours."

The commercial then showed Harry Lorayne at work, demonstrating his amazing memory. The demonstrations were fascinating and convincing, and the viewer—like anyone witnessing what seems to be magic—wanted to know how the tricks were done. At that point, Lorayne introduced the product: a book called *How to Develop a Super-Power Memory.*

He ended the commercial with the offer, explaining how to order the book. In any direct response commercial, this is the crucial point, where you make the sale. The key to making the sale is to make it as easy as possible for the viewer to order. The announcer must make ordering the product a logical, natural process. Everything in the commercial has been leading up to the close. If exactly the right words aren't used, you've blown it. Here is how Harry Lorayne ended his pitch:

"If *How to Develop a Super-Power Memory* doesn't teach you how to remember names, faces, numbers, events, facts, and ideas, if you don't startle your friends and employees with fantastic new super memory, if all facts, names, and figures aren't embedded in your mind so you'll never forget, then this book costs you absolutely nothing. Remember, you don't have to study this book. You don't have to give me months, weeks, even days. Give me one night! Now here's how to get your copy of *How to Develop a Super-Power Memory* on a no-risk, free-trial offer."

One successful and outrageous commercial of the pitchman era was the one for Vita Mix. The commercial ran for 30 minutes and virtually deified the Vita Mix machine. It was pure pitchman all the way, pulling out all the stops to convince people that Vita Mix was the greatest kitchen aid since the stove. On paper it seems a little ridiculous, perhaps, but when it aired, it was an irresistible presentation that appealed to anyone with a hungry family to feed. I have used the basic elements of the commercial (if not the style) throughout my advertising career. Those elements can be roughly defined this way: tease 'em, please 'em, seize 'em (TPS). You tease viewers by raising their expectations. You promise viewers a product that is better and more useful than anything they have ever seen. You please them with the demonstration of the product. And finally, you seize them with the offer, an offer so attractive that ordering the product seems like a perfectly logical thing to do.

In major interactive tests being carried on throughout the world, reliable projections indicate that one in three U.S. cable homes will be served by some interactive TV system either through cable or telephone lines. Canada and the United Kingdom, which have included interactive TV as part of their pay channels, have found that the interactive aspect is used about 8 hours per week per home. Eighty percent of the time is used for interactive games and contests. Time-Warner Quantum has offered multiplex programs, shown at different times on multiple channels, and have recorded 900 percent increases in movie revenue.

TCl/AT&T and U.S. West are using 150 test homes where they offer 2,000 movies on demand. These tests indicate a 38 percent increase in movie revenue. In Spain, about 10,000 interactive units have been sold at about $125, and Canal Plus ended its first year with 87,000 homes. Dispensing incentive coupons and direct marketing products have exceeded the highest client expectations. ISI interactive system in the Netherlands ran a two-for-one McDonald's promotion on hamburgers resulting in 69 percent of the total interactive subscribers printing coupons to take advantage of the offer.

Interactive TV advertising produces astonishing figures that indicate 60–89 percent participation, with a 21 percent increase in sales and 38 percent in-store coupon redemption.

Some interesting data about American infomercials is that 90 percent of all TV stations and 100 percent of commercial cable channels accept infomercials. In 1988, direct marketing sales, including infomercials, reached $350 million. By 1992, sales had reached $750 million. By 1995, sales are expected to exceed $1 billion, with projections for the year 2000 at $10 billion. Considering that the direct marketer spends about 33 percent for advertising costs, broadcast stations can expect $333 million in advertising revenue by the end of 1994. ■

There is no doubt that the advent of cable is destined to change the way the world lives, and especially the way the world shops. According to *Newsweek* magazine (October 11, 1993), "Today's wars are fought over tiny strands of high strength glass, called fiber-optic cable, and the pulses of light they transport. Whoever controls these information pipelines and whoever figures out how to use them to deliver something valuable to a society that consumes information voraciously will get very, very rich."

SHAKEUPS IN THE CABLE INDUSTRY

There are many major players in the interactive hardware and software game, including the Japanese video-game giant Sega, the computer-chip leader Intel, MCI, Time Warner, Inc., U.S. West, one of the Baby Bell companies, and RCA. All plan to expedite an expanded interactive cable venture and high-definition TV transmissions via cable. They see the great potential in subscriptions and sales in the 92 million TV households in the United States, and the great expanding European and South American markets. (As of December 1994, the hardware necessary to access the super fiber-optic highways is not economically plausible. Such hardware would cost about $14,000 per year, per connection.)

Impact on Marketing

What does all this really mean to the U.S. marketing community? First of all, the advent of high-definition TV (HDTV) will make it possible to present products with motion-picture quality. The difference between high-definition and standard TV is the quality difference between a 33-1/3 RPM record and a CD. People who watch HDTV will wonder how they were ever able to watch programs on the present-day standard channels.

Government plans for switching from standard TV to HDTV involve issuing a new UHF channel to all TV stations. HDTV takes a double channel width, so each of the new channels issued will be wider than anything available on VHF. In the beginning, TV stations will be required to simulcast both HDTV and regular signals for 5–10 years, at which time the regular channels will be phased out and all stations will be UHF.

This transition will be very costly for TV broadcasters, particularly those in small ADI areas. The new hardware will cost $2 million or more, and the cost of simulcasting, without added homes or advertising revenue, will cause many stations to operate at a loss. Many stations under this program will probably opt to close. When you examine this method of conversion, it is difficult to understand how the FCC could come up with such a program. HDTV can easily be transmitted through fiber-optic cables or from a satellite, bypassing off-the-air transmissions. In addition, fiber-optic lines will assure high quality transmissions without the high cost of the simulcast conversion. Digital transmissions of high-definition signals would also facilitate conversion, eliminating many costs.

With the various cable and telephone companies accessing nearly all homes with fiber-optic cable, and with the advent of small, easily pro-grammed dishes for homes outside of the fiber-optic cable area, there seems to be little need for off-the-air broadcasting. TV broadcasting as we now know it will ultimately be changed to cable and satellite signal delivery. This change, which will ultimately be worldwide, will actually open an infinite number of access channels to every home and business. Not only will videophones be commonplace, but also anyone will be able to buy or rent channels into both computers and TV sets. These accesses will completely change world marketing methods. Our world, in effect, will become a direct marketing universe.

The Benefits of Unlimited Length

With direct-to-home unlimited access, manufacturers and service organizations will be able to give their best salespeople as long as they need to sell their product or service. Commercials that are 10, 20, or 30 minutes long, and even 1- and 2-hour presentations will be commonplace. These infomercials will be used to introduce new product lines such as automobiles, computers, and home appliances. Entirely new and unique products will be demonstrated and fully explained. For the first time, the consumer will actually learn the benefits of "rack-and-pinion steering," "turbo," "fuel injector," "V-6," and "V-8." The consumer will be able to dial in and learn the benefits of each washer, dryer, refrigerator, and oven. Channels will be narrow enough to explain specific medical procedures and the value and dangers of various types of drugs. Business-to-business access will allow purchasing agents to completely evaluate various products or methods before making a buying decision. Every vendor will have an opportunity to have a clean shot at its potential consumer.

Entertainment TV or cable, which presently carry 30- and 60-second commercials, will be used to support the company access cable. These commercials will suggest that to get full information, one should tune to channel 1245. Interactive cable will allow the viewer to zero in on specific products or even to specific features and benefits, ask questions, and order the product.

CABLE AND THE CONSUMER

Why will the public be so eager to participate in this new marketing revolution? First, traffic conditions make it more difficult to reach shopping facilities, and parking space is becoming scarcer and more expensive. The constant increase in the price of gas also inhibits shopping trips. In addition, with over 70 percent of all homes with both spouses in the work force, families will have fewer hours to devote to the shopping chore. Thus, the use of cable shopping will give families more time to enjoy leisure activities.

Will people buy cars, appliances, clothes, etc., via cable? Not necessarily. A consumer would probably still want to drive a car before purchasing or try on clothing and shoes before making a buying decision. But cable infomercials will have helped them make a decision before they leave their homes.

There is one market that seems tailored for interactive cable shopping. In the next ten years, the average age of the U.S. citizen will rise dramatically, according to U.S. Census forecasts. The senior citizen market will be highly lucrative. Because senior citizens tend not to go out as much, and because many of them watch television more than younger people, the "golden years" will be golden to the company that learns how to use interactive cable. With the widespread use of interactive systems, the elderly will be able to buy products without leaving their homes. In cold climates, especially, cable will be the ideal advertising vehicle to reach this burgeoning market.

THE MEDIA DEPARTMENT IN THE AGE OF CABLE

Advertising agencies will find their media departments increasingly important in the success or failure of every campaign. When cable channels begin multiplying the way radio stations did after World War II, media buyers will be forced to have an almost encyclopedic grasp of the most cost-effective cable media.

It will be virtually impossible to run fixed schedules on hundreds of cable stations. To do so will mean risking millions of dollars. Instead, media buyers must arrange flexible schedules, which will be renewed only if they pay out. The media supervisor will assign media buyers specialties the way a general assigns officers to regiments. One media buyer will be responsible for cable/direct response, another will be responsible for cable ethnic stations, and so on. If this is not done, chaotic buying patterns will result.

Agency executives will require media buyers and media representatives to work as a team. The buying specialist will be familiar with the territory and have a close working relationship with all the media in the territory. Agencies must utilize this system to receive preferred rates and quality availabilities.

CABLE AND NEW MERCHANDISERS

Cable will open the airwaves to a new generation of entrepreneurs. Interactive TV holds virtually limitless possibilities for those willing to experiment. In the not-so-distant future, I foresee stations that will develop merchandising techniques copied after Marshall Field's, Bloomingdale's, and Walgreens. Each station will offer a certain type of merchandising to certain types of subscribers. Some will feature bargains, and others will sell only the highest-quality merchandise. The discount cable outlets will be able to offer merchandise at lower prices than any store by eliminating the intermediary and such price-inflating costs as clerks, rent, pilferage, supervisors, and credit losses. The flip side of the coin will be the "Bloomingdale's of the Air," and it will be able to bring a daily fashion show into the subscriber's living room before the clothing is even in the stores!

For these cable "stores," subscriber lists will be as valuable as mailing lists are to direct marketers. Rating points will mean nothing in this environment. Profits will not be determined by how many people they reach, but who they reach and what they buy.

Perhaps the best advice I can give to those who will be involved in cable direct marketing is this: Don't base your actions on what has happened in the past. Trying to use standard advertising practices with cable will be like trying to force a round peg into a square hole. Remember that minds are like parachutes. They only function when they are open. If you don't go into cable with preconceived notions about how it should work—if you are able to synchronize your approach with the ultimate reality of cable— then you will land on your feet on fertile ground.

THE IMPACT OF NEW TECHNOLOGIES

The world is standing on the threshold that marks the end of the Industrial Revolution and the beginning of the Communication Revolution. The Industrial Revolution was responsible for centralizing populations into giant urban complexes, but the Communication Revolution is destined to reverse this trend. Inner-city populations will drift to more distant suburbs, small towns, and rural areas. This movement will accelerate because of intolerable traffic conditions; ever-increasing costs of public transportation, gasoline, parking, and urban taxes; the mounting fear of crime; and the rapid rise of multiple household wage-earners leaving less quality time for togetherness.

How soon will all this occur? Television, VCR, and color TV took 10–18 years to reach 50 percent penetration and, in the case of TV, another 15 years to peak out. (See Exhibit 6–2.) Many experts believe that the penetration of both interactive and high-definition TV (HDTV) will closely follow the pace of the conversion to color. However, there are many reasons why such changes will take place at a pace somewhere between the pace set by the acceptance of TV and VCRs.

The momentum of the Communication Revolution will be fueled by the capabilities of fiber optics, satellite communication, and new concepts in interactive TV, cable, and phones. Furthermore, HDTV will give viewers both the illusion of being present at a live event and the ability to participate interactively in the event. Hand-out literature, financial statements, and graphs will be printed out in the viewer's home as they are transmitted.

Twenty-first century hardware will produce dramas that have the sets in one location, the actors and actresses scattered (even on different continents), and the director pushing buttons at the communications center,

EXHIBIT 6-2
U.S. Household Penetration: The First 30 Years

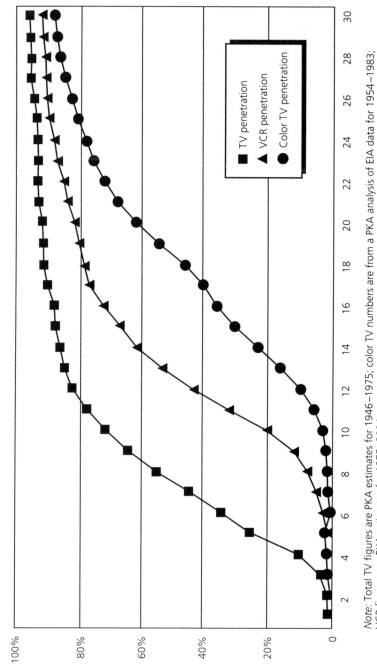

Note: Total TV figures are PKA estimates for 1946–1975; color TV numbers are from a PKA analysis of EIA data for 1954–1983; VCR figures are PKA estimates for 1975–2004.

Source: ©1993 Paul Kagan Assoc., Inc., Carmel, CA estimates.

yet the audience will see the production as if they were sitting in the theater. Meetings will be carried on with various participants enjoying the comforts of their own homes, yet they will perceive and interact with every attendant as if they were all present in a conference room. Convention exhibits will be brought to your very door, not from a convention hall but from the showroom of the manufacturer, who will present the product using the best and most knowledgeable presenter available. This salesperson will not only detail the benefits of the products, but also will reply to questions from viewers.

By far the greatest change will come in the marketing field. Not only will the consumer be able to buy all the necessities of life with a push of the button, but also the entire world will open up for the marketer. Americans will be able to shop at Harrod's in London, LaLeque in Paris, or the Bazaar in Istanbul as easily as they shop at their local department store. Art aficionados will buy African, South American, or European art directly from the artists and galleries of each country. Interactive potential will allow auctions to be carried on with participants from every part of the world.

There will also be vast changes in all levels of the education system. As of 1994, 11 universities have formed an interactive network that will allow professors from any faculty to lecture and allow the professor to see the students in the same way that the students view the instructor. Questions and answers will be handled as if the professor were present in the classroom. All this can be accomplished with the interactive hardware now available, without high-definition or three-dimensional pictures. When those two aspects are introduced, the only difference between the projection and an actual classroom will be that the students can't shake hands with the professors. Of course, as this entire concept is a function of interactive video and audio, students at home or for some other reason not present in the classroom will still be able to attend the lecture.

High-definition pictures will make it possible to present products with motion-picture quality. It will be the ultimate method of producing and distributing motion pictures, saving millions of dollars in production and film distribution costs. Because of the speed and ease of producing computer-generated special effects and in the distribution of the finished product, a central distribution source can supply central projection to vast numbers of theaters that today need $5,000–7,000 prints that are often damaged in projection.

What role will pay channels have in this changing world? People will decide what they want to watch, but the masses will stay with free channels.

Historically, only a small percentage of people will tune into the premium channels, and then only if there is a blockbuster offering. Games will be popular, particularly if the advertiser pays, rather than the viewer.

In addition to shopping and games, the new interactive media will allow viewers to order specific movies, replays of old shows, sporting events, and current programs on demand at specified times. Printers in viewers' homes will produce coupons for participating sponsors. The sports viewer will be able to select camera angles are replays at will. Drama aficionados can become directors by changing the plot or the ending. Of course, there will be numerous TV games that will allow viewers to participate, comparing skills with the contestants.

All this technology will allow mass retail merchandisers to present their wares in optimum settings; emphasize the many consumer benefits, the style, construction, and function; and offer the consumer a variety of models, sizes, colors, and materials. On top of all this, the media will build an intricate database, poll viewers, and get thousands of opinions on local, regional, and international subjects. You can understand the vast changes that will occur in consumer buying. There is no doubt that the marketer will be the source of substantial income to both the hardware and software providers in the interactive industry.

Interactive TV translates into some form of direct marketing. Access availability will be relatively easy and inexpensive to obtain. The real competition in the next decade will be for the sponsors that can create the concepts and unique presentations that will attract the largest audiences. (See Exhibit 6–3 for the major interactive players in the next decade.) Interactive, high-definition, 3-D broadcasting will open world markets to a new generation of entrepreneurs with virtually limitless possibilities.

EXHIBIT 6-3
New TV: Competition for the TV, 1993–2004

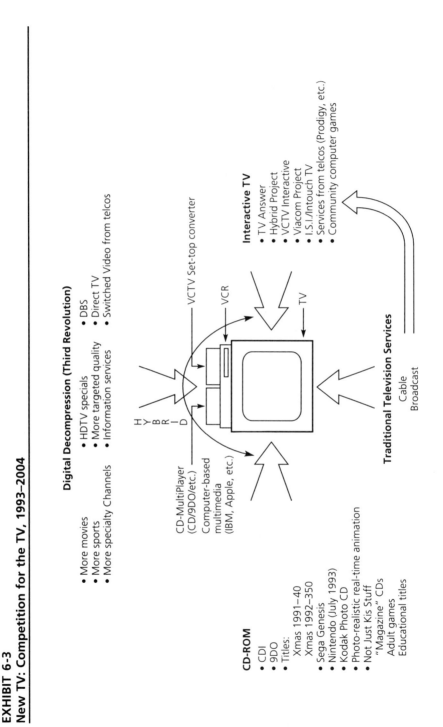

Digital Decompression (Third Revolution)

- More movies
- More sports
- More specialty Channels

- HDTV specials
- More targeted quality
- Information services

- DBS
- Direct TV
- Switched Video from telcos

VCTV Set-top converter

VCR

CD-MultiPlayer
(CD/9DO/etc.)
Computer-based
multimedia
(IBM, Apple, etc.)

H Y B R I D

TV

Interactive TV
- TV Answer
- Hybrid Project
- VCTV Interactive
- Viacom Project
- I.S.I./Intouch TV
- Services from telcos (Prodigy, etc.)
- Community computer games

Traditional Television Services
Cable
Broadcast

CD-ROM
- CDI
- 9DO
- Titles:
  Xmas 1991–40
  Xmas 1992–350
- Sega Genesis
- Nintendo (July 1993)
- Kodak Photo CD
- Photo-realistic real-time animation
- Not Just Kis Stuff
  "Magazine" CDs
  Adult games
  Educational titles

CHAPTER 7

Support Advertising and Trade Support Marketing

Perhaps the most significant and newest of the advertising concepts to be implemented in the past 50 years is support advertising. Before we discuss the various aspects of this relatively new marketing approach, let's examine why and how support advertising was conceived and its relationship to broadcast direct marketing.

THE EVOLUTION OF SUPPORT ADVERTISING

Broadcast direct marketers must use a two-step process whenever a direct marketing offer provides the consumer with a myriad of choices or options, such as titles, style, color, and size, or whenever it is imperative to the offer that the buyer sign a commitment or provide a signature (e.g., for insurance or a conditional sale). The customer orders by phone or letter and the seller follows up the inquiry with the necessary materials for the final closing.

The time lapse of this two-step direct marketing process often delays the potential buyer's receipt of the second part of the offer, which in turn results in the purchaser forgetting about the initial inquiry or reevaluating the offer and ultimately losing interest. Because of this delay, too often the conversion of the inquiry to a sale falls below a profitable level.

An example of a multiple-choice case is a CD club offer in which the prospective member is allowed to select any 12 CDs or tapes from among hundreds. The cost for the 12 is $1 if the buyer agrees to purchase 12 CDs at the regular club price within 12 months. If the initial club offer is made on TV, the direct marketer must use a second-step mailing showing the potential member the selection from which to choose. It would be virtually impossible to expose such a large selection of options on TV or radio, and the viewer wouldn't have enough time to choose.

In offers in which it is necessary to obtain a buyer's signature to verify a commitment, a two-step is also necessary. In the case of an insurance offer, most states require the signature of not only the insured, but also the beneficiary. Again, a follow-up mailing piece is imperative, and the time delay greatly decreases the final conversion rate.

In an effort to increase the closures on a two-step process, the marketing team at Columbia Record Club and A. Eicoff & Company agreed to use a concept that Eicoff had implemented successfully for Liberty Mutual Insurance to sell hospitalization insurance. Columbia ran its regular print ad—complete with the record selection and commitment coupon—in the Sunday newspaper. A TV campaign reinforced the print ad by calling viewers' attention to the ad, the offer, and the newspaper and section in which the ad could be seen. The 30-second commercial used 15 seconds to summarize the offer and 15 seconds to specifically present time, place, and date of the primary insertion.

One major problem was determining how to arrive at the budget for the support media. How much money should we appropriate to call attention to a newspaper ad? Should a relationship exist between the cost of the primary medium (the newspaper ad, in this case) and the supporting media (TV station)? If the newspaper ad appears on Sunday, when should the support program begin? Should the schedule start the week prior to the newspaper exposure? Should it run on Tuesday, Wednesday, Thursday, Friday, and/or Saturday? Should any of the schedule run on Sunday (the day of the exposure) or on the following Monday, since the Sunday paper often stays in the home for several days?

Using seat-of-the-pants logic, we decided to begin the secondary media campaign on Thursday and run it through Sunday morning. Support expenditures were based on a percentage of the cost of the primary medium. But what percentage would be most efficient? Would 50 percent of the cost of the primary medium be too much? How about 75 percent, 100 percent, 200 percent, or even 1,000 percent? Although the basic concept proved to be highly effective, and every test delivered above the most optimistic expectations, it was soon learned that there was a fallacy in the idea of basing the media cost on any percentage of the primary media cost.

Reevaluation of the support concept clearly showed no relationship between the two budgets. For example, if a direct marketer scheduled a four-page, full-color insert instead of a single-page, black-and-white ad, any relationship between the cost of the two media would suggest that the budget should allow six to eight times more money to call attention to the larger, more attention-getting ad than to the less obvious one. Further analysis indicated that the size and color of the primary exposure should neither increase nor decrease the size of the secondary budget. Instead, the same amount of support should be used to call attention to any size and type of primary exposure. Years of controlled testing and post-analysis proved this concept to be the proper formula to achieve the greatest sales at the lowest cost per sale. See Exhibit 7–1 for an example of support advertising.

THE EFFECTIVENESS OF SUPPORT ADVERTISING

Support advertising is so effective that it works for virtually every direct marketer. In 15 years of constant evaluation of support programs carried on at A. Eicoff & Company, the post-analysis never found a single support program that did not produce sales at a lower cost than when the primary medium was run without the benefit of support. This does not mean that support is capable of changing an unprofitable offer into a profitable one. But when support is used in an attempt to turn around a direct marketing offer, the resulting ratio of advertising cost to total sales is always lower, despite the added cost of the secondary support media. And now support advertising is being used more extensively because of the constant sales increase factors that normally range from 50 percent to 800 percent.

It is rare that the primary media results do not improve the total results enough to warrant the increased cost of the support media and the premiums that support might use for measurement. More important, support has often pushed marginal offers into the "win" column. For example, many ads were made profitable when they were exposed on a weekday, although prior tests indicated that the offers were effective only when they were scheduled in the Sunday paper. Other support programs proved that borderline tests could be turned into highly profitable campaigns when properly supported.

In one case history, a direct marketer found the Sunday edition of the *Boston Globe* an unprofitable medium even for offers that were highly profitable in nearly every other Sunday metropolitan paper. However, when TV was used to support the *Globe* ad, direct marketing offers went from losers to winners. In Boston, run-of-paper insertions on Wednesday or Thursdays often were made profitable with support.

EXHIBIT 7-1
Hellmann's Real Mayonnaise Commercial

VIDEO

AUDIO

1. Open on MS of 8- or 9-year-old boy in front of picnic buffet. There are several summer salads and he can't decide which one to take. We hear his thoughts. He sighs and looks indecisive.

1. *CHILD'S THOUGHTS V/O:* Oh, there's potato salad . . . Great! Gee, the coleslaw looks good, too . . . Well, maybe some of Mom's macaroni salad . . . *ANNCR. V/O:* (MUSIC UNDER) Simple decisions aren't so simple . . .

2. Diss. to ECU of woman's hand folding mayonnaise into macaroni salad.

2. When your family's favorite summer salads are made with Hellmann's Real Mayonnaise . . . because nothing brings out the best in a salad like Hellmann's.

3. Diss. to tabletop view of the fresh ingredients necessary to make the summer salads. We track through them until in a CU position of jar.

3. The finest mayonnaise ever to make a good salad . . . great! And now is an especially good time to enjoy Hellmann's because you can get a 32-ounce jar free!

4. Hold above scene. Hand rests recipe card against jar. SUPER: FREE WITH PROOF OF PURCHASE FROM FOUR 32-OUNCE JARS. SEE LOCAL NEWSPAPER FOR DETAILS

4. That's right, a jar of Hellmann's Real Mayonnaise—plus this recipe for our classic macaroni salad— absolutely *free.*

5. Diss. to FSI ad on tabletop next to bowl of macaroni salad. SUPER: Newspaper Names

5. Look for this ad in the coupon section of Sunday's newspaper to take advantage of the free Hellmann's offer.

6. Diss. to plate of picnic food, hot dogs and summer salads, on tabletop with jar in background.

6. Hellmann's Real Mayonnaise . . . it makes a summertime salad . . . great!

7. Diss. back to child. As he sits down against a tree, we see he has taken a big spoonful of every summer salad. He looks perplexed.

7. *CHILD ON-CAMERA: which one* do I eat *first?!*

8. Diss. to beauty shot of jar. SUPER: Store Names

8. *ANNCR. V/O:* Look for the Hellmann's display—and the free offer—at these fine stores.

Grolier's "Dr. Seuss Book Club," for example, worked in very few publications. Where the advertising allowable was X, the best inserts were producing members at X plus 50¢. When support was added to the overall formula, the most effective markets still did not produce at profitable levels, but the X plus 50¢ was reduced to between X plus 10¢ and X plus 25¢. A reevaluation of the best primary medium combined with the support schedules was ultimately able to lower the cost for Grolier to a profitable level. Unfortunately, so few markets maintained their profitability that it was not worth pursuing the program.

Long before direct marketers used television and radio, many media used support to promote themselves. For example, it was not unusual for a billboard to state, "Watch this space for a surprising announcement." During the introduction of Folger's coffee, an effective billboard campaign announced, "We're bringing a mountain to (name of market). Watch this billboard." These are sometimes known as "teaser" ads, but they are variations on the support method. Radio and television often use their own medium to support and promote future programming.

One highly visible use of support advertising is the support of direct mailings by broadcast. *Reader's Digest* and *Publishers Clearing House* annually spend millions to inform the public of the huge prizes they can win by merely opening the mailing piece and returning it. In 1984, the first prize of one of the subscription sales companies reached $10 million. In the highly competitive market of subscription sales, it is likely that the prizes offered by merchandising companies reach sums beyond those awarded in the largest state lottery. These mailings are sent third class, and the post office is under no obligation to deliver at any specific time. Therefore, the support program for these mailings must extend over a longer-than-normal period. Such support should start about 1 week prior to the first delivery and extend for about 10 days to 2 weeks.

It is possible to support print media by running commercials on television or radio a mere 3 or 4 days in advance of the publication in which the ad will appear, since the day of publication is always exact. Too often, the support media for large-prize contests mistakenly focus on the joys of winning the contest, rather than on promoting the tremendous savings available on magazine subscriptions.

TESTING YOUR SUPPORT ADVERTISING

One important question asked by direct marketers who are starting to use the support concept is, How can we get a true measurement of the results?

If our results are improved, how do we know that they would not normally have been better? How is it possible for us to compare a supported market with a nonsupported market?

The most accurate way to measure the effectiveness of support is to select eight or ten markets that are similar in nature. If possible, use past performance as a guide. After you have selected the test markets, randomly choose one-half that will be supported—then run the other half without support.

After the test is completed, an accurate post-analysis can be obtained in the supported markets by combining the costs of the primary and support media and dividing it by the number of orders. Unsupported markets can be evaluated in the same way, using only the cost of the primary media. Next, you evaluate the results of the unsupported markets against the results you achieved in the past. If the nonsupported markets averaged a 10 percent increase, you can assume that the supported markets will also have increased by 10 percent. Using these comparisons, you can get an accurate evaluation of the effectiveness of the support program.

If your cost per unit sale with support is equal to or lower than the unit cost in the nonsupported markets, and the total cost falls within the parameters of the advertising allowable, then the support schedule has been profitable. The support program can be considered successful—even if the unit sales cost is the same—only if it has produced greater sales at a profitable level.

Another way to measure the effectiveness of a support program is called the Little Gold Box method. This concept calls for the support media to offer an extra premium for the customer who marks a box with an X or who writes the number of an additional choice in a specific box within the ad. This method, of course, provides a fast and easy way to find out how many people actually saw the support commercial.

Keep in mind, however, that the use of this method does not allow you to ascertain how many people would have responded to the primary ad had they not been exposed to the support commercial. The additional premium also adds to the cost of the support program. There is evidence, however, that the support premium can actually increase the number of returns beyond the quantity one would normally get from a support program not offering a premium. This premium concept is still being evaluated for its effectiveness.

Before we get into the nuts and bolts of actually initiating a support program, we should cite some other examples of the effectiveness of this concept in areas other than direct marketing. For example, support is an extremely effective device for increasing coupon redemption. In numerous case histories in which successful coupon redemption programs were projected to produce redemptions at 2–3 percent of the total circulation of the primary medium, the support program increased redemptions 6–10 percent.

In a case history for Job Squad, a Scott Paper Company product, the support program for an ad in the Peoria, Illinois, *Journal-Star* increased redemption from the projected 3 percent to 11 percent. In Waterloo, Iowa, where the primary ad erroneously carried the line "Available only to residents of Illinois," the coupon redemption expected was 3 percent but exceeded 12 percent. Although the results of coupon support are not always that spectacular, it generally increases redemption rates by over 200 percent. The only problem, of course, is that this high level of coupon returns can throw the advertising budget out of kilter, since coupon redemptions are usually considered part of the overall advertising budget.

What Elements Are Necessary for Effective Support?

A series of carefully controlled tests revealed that support is most consistently successful when the primary medium has at least a 35 percent penetration of the ADI (area of dominant influence) of the support media. If the primary medium does not penetrate the ADI of the secondary media to that extent, it is imperative that the direct marketer supplement the primary medium with additional primary media. Those primary media might include suburban papers, national publications, or direct mail. It should run within the same period, and the total circulation of all primary media should be a minimum of 35 percent.

For example, the *Des Moines Register* can be used as the primary medium without any supplements, since the *Register* covers approximately 63 percent of the Des Moines TV stations' ADI. The *Atlanta Constitution,* the *Denver Post,* and a number of other dominant newspapers also enjoy a high enough market penetration to meet the 35 percent ADI coverage requirements. The *New York Times, Chicago Tribune,* and *Dallas News,* however, do not have sufficient penetration to warrant a support program without supplementing their circulation with other newspapers or publications. *TV Guide,* for example, adds about 15 percent penetration in New York City. The *Chicago Sun Times* adds about 23 percent to the *Chicago Tribune's* penetration. The *Fort Worth Star* adds 19 percent to the circulation of the *Dallas News.*

The Formula for Buying the Secondary Supporting Media

Heavy mailers with high market penetration, such as Publishers Clearing House, have often scheduled as many as 1,100 gross rating points per market to support their 30–40 million piece mail drops. Experience, however, indicates that 1,100 GRPs is overkill. Although these support programs have often proved effective, such intensive support often does not provide maximum efficiency. Intense research in this area indicates that 300–450 GRPs are sufficient to achieve the maximum profit balance between sales volume and cost efficiency. The 150 GRP variation occurs because of the different variables in markets, such as the number of TV stations, the penetration of cable, the media cost of the market, and the offer potential in the specific market.

When testing support advertising, you start with parameters, and maximum efficiency is obtained through a continuing program of careful post-analysis, which should constantly review the margin of error. Every market reacts differently to each campaign. After readjusting to post-analysis demands, it is not unusual for the most sophisticated direct marketer to support with 280 GRPs in one market and as many as 600 GRPs in another. The maximum efficiency levels are volatile, and they can be kept within the maximum profit boundaries only by constant trial and error and continuous post-analysis.

The most important requirements of an effective support program are (1) the minimum 35 percent penetration of the primary medium, (2) the basic 300–450 GRP support media parameters, and (3) the understanding that market demographics are not as important to the support media as ADI reach.

TRADE SUPPORT MARKETING

No textbook on direct marketing could be complete without a chapter on trade support marketing (also known as key outlet marketing), a direct outgrowth of broadcast direct marketing. An old platitude states, "Necessity is the mother of invention." So it was with trade support marketing, or TSM.

In the early days of television, direct marketing commercials provided stations with enough income to help keep them on the air. Station management during this era looked on direct marketing as a necessary evil.

Although stations found it much more prestigious to run 30- and 60-second spots for Procter & Gamble or General Motors, when it came time to meet the payroll, it was the record offers, salad makers, slicers, dicers, knives, and vitamins that paid the bills.

When Newton Minow took over as chairman of the Federal Communications Commission in 1960, he announced to the broadcast industry that radio and TV stations were overcommercialized. He let it be known that those stations that carried commercials over 120 seconds in length would find it difficult to obtain a license renewal. In addition, Minow pointed out that because of the high percentage of fly-by-night entrepreneurs using television for direct marketing, the FCC would frown upon broadcasters that allowed direct marketers to use their facilities.

When these FCC directives were released, it behooved direct marketers to find another way to sell their products. From 1961 to 1963, many stations changed their policies to conform with FCC guidelines. Yet, still in need of direct marketing income, they closely monitored the reliability of direct marketer sponsors and the lengths of direct marketing commercials.

At this point, I am forced to switch to a first-person narrative, because I played a significant role in creating a solution to the direct marketers' dilemma. I believed that if successful direct marketing offers could be transformed into retail products, a direct marketing approach could still be used to move products. (See sidebar.)

THANK YOU, NEWTON MINOW

It could have been a disaster.

In Newton Minow's famous "vast wasteland" speech, which probably did more to hurt good TV programming than any single event in TV's history, he promised to clean up the airwaves. With that speech, he pounded the nails in the pitchman's coffin. He railed against the glut of ten-minute-and-longer commercials that "polluted" the medium. For Minow, direct marketing was a sleazy, disreputable business that had no place in the idealistic Kennedy era. Remember, this was the time of the "New Frontier," when money-making entrepreneurs were frowned upon. (Ironically, that included Joseph P. Kennedy, who epitomized that type of entrepreneur.)

Minow's vision of television was one of cultural enrichment, free of the crass commercialization of the 1950s. Of course, this was upper-class snobbery and nothing else. From his lofty perch, Minow was deciding what people should watch without considering what people wanted to watch. In effect, he was telling the pitchmen, who survived by direct marketing, that they couldn't belong to the club, that the club was for big businessmen who could afford to play the TV game by the rules.

My agency heard the FCC's thunder and was rocked to its very foundation. Virtually overnight, my billings plummeted from $4.5 million to $400,000. Stations that had accepted our commercials for years suddenly treated us like lepers. Many refused any direct marketing spots under any conditions, fearful that the FCC would revoke their licenses. Others accepted direct response spots only if they were no longer than 2 minutes. To tell a pitchman he had only 120 seconds to sell a product was like telling a conductor he had 2 minutes to conduct a symphony.

For us, it was the bottom of the ninth, two outs, and nobody on base. If we didn't find somebody or something to come through in the clutch, the ball game was over. But all entrepreneurs function best when their backs are against the wall. We put all our chips on one idea—a long shot, to be sure, but one that would pay off if it worked.

The idea had been simmering in the back of my mind for a long time, and now was the time to try it. Basically, it involved finding a chain of stores that would agree to exclusive distribution for direct response items. At the end of the commercial, we would merely substitute the names of the stores for the phone number and address found in direct response spots. I dubbed this new concept key outlet marketing (KOM). Today, the name has been upgraded to trade support marketing, but it's the same old concept.

At the time, many people thought KOM was a harebrained scheme, born out of desperation and doomed to failure. How, they asked, could anyone convince a chain to take a lower profit margin and give mass display to a direct response product? They looked at the entire program with a skeptical eye and wondered how one could make a financially effective, 120-second commercial when the cost of TV time was soaring and major advertisers were cutting their 30-second commercials to 15 seconds to accumulate more GRPs for their sales presentations.

Major buyers for mass-market outlets had been GRP conditioned, and there was no way to differentiate a rating point for a 15-, 30-, or 120-second commercial. The cynics sneered, "Can a

120-second commercial motivate enough sales to warrant its extra cost?"

KOM was such a perfect concept, it was hard to believe it was legal. But of course it was. It circumvented the Robinson-Patman Act in that it did not discriminate against any one store. Rather, it worked in the same manner as a franchise operation.

No matter how perfect KOM seemed in theory, it had to be implemented. And so I began my search for an intermediary, someone with the "in" to deal effectively with the chains. What I was looking for was a first-class close-out man. A close-out man was a guy who bought up products for next to nothing and resold them to the chains. This type of salesman and chain stores were blood brothers, and I needed the best close-out man to get my products into distribution. After much searching, I found Manny Gutterman, "King of the Close-out Men." The chains treated him like royalty. When he gave the chains a product, he gave them something they could sell at a big profit.

As soon as I met Manny, I knew we could do business. He was a tough, hard-nosed salesman who "called 'em like he saw 'em" and had contacts on top of contacts. Manny was a legend in the business, and like all legends, it was tough to know which stories about him were true. What was true, however, was his clout.

Manny could get away with murder and often did. For instance, he once called Morrie Axelrod, the vice president for merchandising at Thrifty Drugs in Los Angeles, and told him, "Send me an order for 36,000 Handi-Screens at $2.10 each."

Axelrod responded, "What are Handi-Screens?"

Manny screamed back, "What the hell do you care what they are—we're gonna spend $20,000 a week to sell them! Just send me the order!" And Axelrod did just that, although he had no idea what he was buying. Manny enjoyed such shows of strength. And when he agreed to help me with my key outlet products, I was sure that I had found a general who would keep the troops in line. ■

My trade support marketing (TSM) concept called for using the names of the retail outlets that carried the product instead of the phone number and mailing address of the direct marketer.

Common sense dictated that this method should sell even more products at higher profit levels than the usual direct marketing method. First, only about 50 percent of Americans would buy anything by mail; putting the product into retail distribution would increase the sales potential by 50 percent. Second, given the hard-sell commercial used by direct marketers, a credibility gap existed. The addition of the name of an established, reputable retail chain would help to establish product credibility. And, third, the fact that the merchandise was highly visible in stores encouraged impulse sales by customers not exposed to the commercial.

The TSM concept, however, needed a number of concessions by the retail chains. For TSM to be profitable, the chain stores had to inventory large quantities of the TSM-advertised product because the concept limits the number of retail outlets that offer the product. Often individual stores within the chain were required to inventory as many as 288 units of a TSM product, whereas in-store displays for even a fast-selling, nationally advertised products were given shelf space for only 12 units. In addition, we asked each retail outlet to give the TSM products prime, end-counter display space. We also asked stores to use large window and in-store banners to give even more visibility to the promotion. Merchandise was often shipped in display cartons with headers that highlighted the TV advertising. Finally, because of the high intensity of the advertising campaign and because the cooperating chains were given an exclusive franchise (they were often sold with the understanding that they were the only game in town), they were offered only a 30 percent discount on merchandise, whereas the normal discounts were 50–55 percent. In order to make TSM work, the marketer also required a biweekly count detailing the sale of the product from the shelf.

When you consider that chain buyers were notorious for demanding extra discounts, charging for in-store display space, and demanding free goods and prepaid freight, TSM's demands seemed impossible. Couple this with the policy of most chains to deny the right of the marketer's own staff to adjust or count inventories, and TSM seemed like a long shot.

However, certain unusual marketing conditions occurred that allowed TSM to obtain all the concessions needed from the chains for the successful launching of TSM. At the time I introduced this concept, the completion of superhighways and freeways altered the geographic size of cities. With these highways came the neighborhood shopping centers that attracted prime supermarket, drug, and discount tenants—retailers that attracted traffic for the smaller stores. As cities grew, major chains opted to have a store within easy driving distance of all major residential communities.

Most important to the success of TSM, however, was the growth of discount operations. Discounters forced chain stores to drop their prices to competitive levels, and the 50 percent discounts on nationally advertised products suddenly dropped to a realistic 15 percent or 20 percent when applied to the actual selling price. For example, the $1 suggested retail product had to be marked down to 79¢ to compete with the discounter. The appliances that carried a factory suggested list price of $24.95 suddenly had to be marked down to $18.88 to meet competition. The large "false" discounts on nationally advertised brands vanished into discount prices that made the chain stores take note of a highly promoted product that offered them a full 30 percent markup. These conditions made TSM flourish. Keep in mind, also, that under the TSM plan, retail chains were often given an exclusive franchise in exchange for the lower markup and their cooperation.

Four Case Histories

In 1961, when the FCC anti-direct marketer dictum first hit, Winston Sales Company of Chicago was having phenomenal results with a 296-piece fishing kit that sold for $8.95. The 5- and 10-minute direct marketing commercials starred Bill Stern, a popular sports announcer, and Frank Gifford, a national football hero. When the fishing kit was forced out of direct marketing, the Sommers Drug chain in San Antonio, Texas, agreed to be the guinea pig for the first TSM test.

Within a short time, Sommers sold 56,000 fishing kits, and news of this half-million dollars in sales brought demands for the kit from chain stores coast-to-coast. Within 90 days, a total of 800,000 units were sold in 18 markets, and TSM was on its way.

The Grant Company of Chicago was offering a hair-cutting comb called Hair Wiz. The commercial claimed that anyone who would read numbers could cut hair without making a mistake. Because haircuts then cost $4–6, it was impossible to keep the $3 Hair Wiz in stock. Over five million Hair Wizes were sold in two years, and as late as 1985 (23 years after it was introduced), the Hair Wiz was still selling about 200,000 units a year. The Hair Wiz replacement blade remains an annuity for the Grant Company.

The Donnatelli Honey's Cream Facial was first introduced through direct marketing ads in magazines. The direct marketing program was so successful that Rhodes Pharmacal, the distributor, opted to test TSM. The Gray Drug chain in Cleveland, Ohio, was selected for one of the early tests. After the campaign had run 2 weeks, the initial sales reports indicated that the product had already sold 40,000 units at $3.98. What made this movement so spectacular was that the $160,000 in sales constituted 50 percent of the entire cosmetic sales in the chain's Cleveland stores for that 2-week period.

Eight weeks after the introduction of the small, portable Dexter hand-sewing machine in the Chicago Walgreen's stores, Charles Walgreen, the president, invited the manufacturer of the Dexter, the sales representative, and the advertising agency supervisor to a special meeting. He wanted to reward them for the sale of 100,000 units ($500,000 in sales) during the first 7 weeks of the campaign's exposure. Walgreen presented a gold-plated Dexter sewing machine for sales achievement.

Later Developments

These case histories represent a small part of an endless parade of winners, which included kitchen gadgets such as handy screens (a screen cover for frying pans that kept the grease from flying), self-sharpening knives, and numerous other products, such as cosmetics, magic cards, lawn and garden tools and chemicals, carpentry tools, books, and records, which had the characteristics necessary for successful direct marketing offers.

As news of TSM marketing continued to spread, many companies hopped on the bandwagon. Popiel Brothers introduced the Vegamatic, a kitchen device that chopped, minced, shredded, sliced, and would make potatoes perfect for french fries, all in one operation. Vegamatic was a sales phenomenon, but Sam Popiel, wanting to milk his success to the fullest, offered the product to anyone who would agree to promote it. There were no protected territories. The success of TSM had been so overwhelming that even when several distributors offered the Vegamatic to a variety of retailers in a single market, the chains couldn't say no. Popiel followed Vegamatic with several other successes, including Dial-A-Matic Food Slicer and Popiel's biggest winner, the Pocket Fisherman, of which Popiel reportedly sold 35,000,000 units worldwide.

Soon after the entry of Popiel Brothers into TSM, Ron Popiel, Sam Popiel's son, founded Ronco, an independent company that not only rode the success of the Vegamatic and Dial-A-Matic, but also introduced many new products, including a wireless radio microphone, in-home and automobile smokeless ashtrays, and almost 40 other products that had varying degrees of success.

Two successful followers of the TSM concept were the Keves Brothers, who started an operation called K-Tel. Their first TSM product, called Wonder Brush, used a commercial that demonstrated the removal of hair and lint from fabric. Unfortunately, the product was easy to copy, and in less than 3 months, K-Tel had dozens of competitors offering the same type of product for less money. K-Tel then turned its TSM efforts to repackaging records and tapes and was able to establish TSM as a worldwide marketing concept for previously released, but uniquely packaged record albums. K-Tel's success lasted about two decades until the company exhausted the record inventories of the major recording companies.

Keep in mind that when a chain has an exclusive on a fast-selling item, the volume makes the product important, and although the discount is only 30 percent, the high volume of a successful TSM promotion delivers excellent profits. When the distribution is expanded, however, it might mean added volume for the marketer, yet the increase occurs at the expense of the sales and profits of the original outlets. As soon as this profit drop occurs, the chains discontinue the product. Any loyalty the chain had for a fast-moving, low markup product quickly disappears, and sales wane. Even when a TSM product is producing at a high sales level, it is not unusual for the chain to buy and offer copies of the successful TSM product at a lower price with a sign that says, "As seen on TV."

As in all marketing, the greatest potential for profit in TSM lies in products that are consumable or that necessitate refills or repeat purchases. An important lesson to learn is that it is as easy to sell a consumable product as it is to sell a product that is purchased only once. However, if you stick to the TSM concept of testing the product—just as you would in direct marketing—and if you control the advertising and limit the number of retail outlets to assure profits at a level that will maintain the franchisers' interest, it is possible to produce high profits with a nonconsumable product.

Other effective uses of TSM are (1) stimulating the sales of products that would normally sell slowly when conventional marketing techniques are used and (2) putting new life in products that have had a past history of profitability, but which have slid into obscurity.

The reason TSM is so effective for these two categories is that sales can be quickly stimulated with a detailed, straightforward presentation of product benefits. In addition, TSM advertising budgets are determined by the ratio of anticipated sales to the advertising allowable, rather than by the traditional method of budgeting advertising campaigns based on pre-determined campaign lengths and gross rating point levels.

A specific example of putting new life in a stagnant product occurred in a controlled test for a garden product that was teetering at the edge of disaster. For this test, four comparable markets were chosen. A national advertising program that was already scheduled was allowed to continue without interruption. But additional budgets were appropriated to supple-ment the national campaign with spot TV in the four selected test markets. In two markets, 400 gross rating points were used, along with 30-second commercials. In the other two markets, much smaller budgets were appro-priated to set up normal TSM schedules with 90-second commercials. In markets that used the traditional GRP method, sales for the product increased approximately 2,800 percent. In the two selected markets where the TSM creative and buying techniques were used, the sales were up 9,800 percent and 11,232 percent, respectively. In effect, the TSM buying and infomercial technique proved 19 times more effective than the conventional method. In this case, as in numerous others, the TSM technique saved a viable product from failure.

Limiting distribution to specific outlets and then supporting the retail outlets by adding their names to the TV commercials is not a new technique. The unique factor in the TSM concept lies in actually using direct marketing creative concepts coupled with direct marketing media buying techniques and controls. Unlike 120-second direct marketing commercials, TSM commercials are cut to 90 seconds because it takes less time to show a tag line listing stores than to repeat a phone number and a mailing address. Another difference between direct marketing and TSM is that the media schedule is purchased for 3 or 4 weeks instead of 1 week. The rationale for the longer schedule is that motivated buyers do not act as quickly in buying from a retail outlet as they do when required to make a phone call. In the case of TSM, the consumer views the commercial, makes a positive buying decision, and then might wait to purchase the product for several days. If the outlet named is where the consumer normally shops, he or she will often wait until the next shopping trip.

Testing TSM

Because the TSM concept so closely parallels that of direct marketing, each campaign must deliver an immediate profit by motivating sales within the parameters of the Magic Number, or the schedule is not renewed.

Under the TSM concept, test markets are selected in the same way they are tested in direct marketing. You do not seek the average market—or the markets that the industry has designated as test markets. Instead, you select markets with the following characteristics:

- You can make the most advantageous media buys.

- The selected retail chain(s) offers the best cooperation in allowing you to inventory the proper amount of merchandise.

- The outlets give the merchandise the best displays.

- Experience has indicated that the chain headquarters provides prompt reports of product movement.

Most often, the best test markets are those in which a single chain dominates the market, such as in the Tampa-Orlando, Florida, area, where Eckerd Drugs has over 230 outlets, or in Portland, Oregon, where the Fred Meyers chain is dominant in drug and variety sales. One can, however, conduct successful tests in New Orleans, where it is essential to have distribution with Walgreen's and Katz and Bestoff because no one chain has enough outlets to properly cover the ADIs of the TV stations.

As one becomes more experienced in the TSM method, markets can be indexed to sales expectations. Such markets, for example, as Sacramento and San Diego, California; Portland, Oregon; New Orleans, Louisiana; and Louisville, Kentucky, index in the 90–101 class. These indexes are determined by a program of continuous post-analysis of market reactions, and markets are continually being reindexed.

If markets in the 90–101 range are used as the projection criterion, Chicago indexes at 109; Detroit, at 106; Los Angeles, at 111, etc. The index number indicates that the same dollar expenditure that will move 100 units of a product in Portland, Oregon (100 index), will move 109 in Chicago and 111 in Los Angeles. These index numbers are usually consistent within ±5 percent, providing the product being marketed is not subject to unusual ethnic, geological, climatic, or demographic conditions. For example, the index would not work for snow shovels, mosquito killers, suntan lotions, rat killers, etc.

An evaluation of the market index numbers shows that New York, Chicago, and Los Angeles are better markets. Why not, therefore, use them as test markets? Although the larger markets are consistently more productive, the media cost of a 3-week TSM test in Chicago or Los Angeles ranges from $36,000 to $60,000 per market, while a 3-week TSM test in Portland, Orlando-Tampa, etc., would cost only $6,000 to $7,200 per market (1985 estimates). Once a product proves successful in a small market, it should be tested in larger markets.

As in most new concepts, initial tests are based on a combination of experience and educated trial and error. There are, however, certain criteria that must always be present:

- The amount of merchandise sold into the selected market must be sufficient to produce profits that satisfy retail outlets.
- The profits produced by a successful market must be sufficient to warrant further expansion into new markets.
- The TV or radio budget must be large enough for the stations to accept the schedule at maximum discount rates.

In effect, the budget must sufficiently meet at least the minimal demands of the marketer, retail outlets, and media, and yet must also be able to keep the capital risk at a minimum.

To meet these requirements, the trade support marketing budget in 1961 for a 100-indexed market was about $800 per week, or a total of $2,400. Despite the fact that these budgets had to meet the demands of all parties, schedules of this size were sufficient to do the desired job. As broadcast rates continued to rise, TSM markets that required $800 per week in 1961 require at least $3,000 per week in 1994. Thus, the cost of a 3-week TSM program in a 100 indexed market rose from $2,400 to $12,000 in 33 years. During this period many factors influenced the size of budgets and the selection of markets, yet testing procedures remained relatively consistent.

A Test Program

To clarify test procedures, let's set up a TSM test program. Based upon the mathematics of TSM set forth in Chapter 10, let's say we have established a Magic Number of $3 per unit. Next we have selected New Orleans with a required budget of $2,100 per week, or a total of $6,300; and we also selected the Tampa-Orlando area (dual markets) which requires $3,000 per week for Orlando TV, for a total of $6,000 and $3,500 per week for Tampa, for a grand total of $10,500.

Based on the $3 advertising allowable, we must sell a minimum of 2,100 units of product in New Orleans and 6,500 units in the Tampa–Orlando markets. Keep in mind, we have determined all of our costs and added in a minimal acceptable profit. The only unknown in the formula is the cost of advertising necessary to move a unit to the consumer; that is what we are trying to determine by our tests. This cost could ultimately turn out to be over or under the $3 allowable.

To give ourselves the best chance to evaluate the test, the units of product distributed into each market should be 25 to 30 percent over the number of units necessary to achieve the minimum acceptable profit. According to this formula it is necessary to have about 2,750 units in distribution in New Orleans, and about 9,000 units in Tampa-Orlando.

The next step requires the presentation of the product, the commercial, and the projected advertising program to the selected chains in each market. The fact that TSM has had such a successful track record, coupled with the fact that the chain does not pay for the merchandise until it is sold (guaranteed sale), helps overcome any objections the selected chains might have to participating in the test.

Once the merchandise is on display in the stores and the advertising schedules begin, one of three results can occur. First, during the initial 3 weeks, the chains may request the schedules be taken off the air because the product has been sold out prior to the completion of the schedule. When this occurs, it indicates that the predetermined advertising allowable is too high. The advertising schedules should be cancelled immediately until the market can be reinventoried with more merchandise. When this is accomplished, a new advertising schedule should be purchased for an additional 3 weeks.

Second, at the end of the 3 weeks, about 80 percent of the required product sales might have been achieved. In this case, it is almost certain that the product will still be successful, because sales usually lag at least 1 week behind the advertising. As soon as the required number of units have been sold to achieve the advertising allowable, restock the market and reschedule the advertising. Once you have two or more successful test markets, it's time to inventory and test four to five larger markets.

Third, at the end of the advertising schedule and several weeks of bleed, sales might be significantly below the advertising allowable. Under these conditions, there is very little that can be done to make the product profitable. However, never abandon any product without thoroughly re-evaluating the commercial, reexamining the media schedule, and, most important, analyzing the positioning of the product to see if it could meet the requirements of a different market. Losers have often been turned into highly profitable winners by merely finding a new positioning niche. On the other hand, it is rare when a change in creative can transform a big loser into a winner.

Remember that additional advertising will seldom achieve profitable results unless the product comes close to selling at the maximum advertising allowable in the test markets.

Although the original TSM test budgets were based on trial and error, test budgets for new products can be determined by estimating the number of units the consumers in the selected test market should be expected to buy. This number should be estimated based on demographics, market size, and the percentage of potential buyers you would need to sell in order to have a successful product. For example, let's say that statistical research indicates it would not be unreasonable to expect to sell 3,000 units of a product in the selected market over a 3-week period. After you determine that the product could afford $3 for advertising, $9,000 would be budgeted. It is now imperative that 4,500 units be put on the shelves of the retail outlet. The media is then purchased. Remember, TSM media buys should follow direct marketing concepts.

Maintaining Profitability

Once a product has proven to be profitable using the TSM concept, how can you extend or maintain the profitability of the product?

There is, of course, a distinct advantage to continuing with the TSM marketing technique. A limited number of retail outlets are getting the benefit of the total sales volume, and the product becomes more important to these selected outlets as sales increase. The marketer has an advantage in allowing only a 30 percent discount, which allows an additional 20–30 percent for advertising. The controlled distribution makes it easier for the marketer to reschedule advertising based on sales. Finally, in markets in which distribution is in a highly dominant chain, the distribution to additional outlets could result in lower profits for the marketer, because he or she might have to grant a larger discount, and the dominant chain might become less cooperative.

Many consumable products that have chosen to continue with TSM have maintained a highly profitable share of their markets despite the fact that their competition is often universally marketed.

Tarn-X, a silver cleaner, still limits its distribution to selected outlets, yet holds the top position in the metal cleaning market after nearly 16 years. Nu Vinyl and Nu Finish, two auto care products that use the TSM concept, have sustained a high level of sales, and many universally distributed products in the same categories have come and gone.

An example of what can happen to a product that moved from TSM to universal distribution occurred with Butcher's Floor Wax. Butcher's had a highly profitable position in the floor wax market using TSM and confining its sales to hardware stores. Because of Butcher's franchised distribution and because the hardware stores did not have to sell Butcher's at highly discounted prices to compete with supermarket, discount, and variety chains, the selected outlets found the wax's high profit an incentive to maintain substantial inventories and to provide Butcher's Wax prominent display space in their outlets.

As the sales of Butcher's continued to increase, however, the company's marketing strategy dictated that it take advantage of the added sales that universal distribution could provide. As soon as Butcher's gained distribution in the supermarkets and discount stores, many hardware outlets discontinued the product. Other hardware stores began to stock competitive, nationally distributed brands of floor wax they had not previously inventoried. In a short time, Butcher's became just another product in the hardware stores' inventory. It lost its advantage of preferred treatment. As it became just another product in a highly competitive but relatively slow-moving category of floor waxes, sales continued to weaken and Butcher's Wax never again achieved its former position in the market.

On the other hand, universal distribution is the ultimate goal for most, if not all, major nationally advertised products. A product that gains acceptance via trade support marketing can use the TSM introduction technique to easily gain universal distribution.

Products that have had the benefit of advertising exposure and consumer acceptance find buyers in all distribution categories eager for the opportunity to put the product on their shelves. Whenever successful TSM companies ask to make sales presentations to new outlets, the buyers that have not had an opportunity to buy the product greet the salesman with, "I've been waiting for you!"

One final observation should be made to tie direct marketing and TSM together. The law of product acceptability states that whenever an offer is profitable in direct marketing, it usually becomes even more profitable when converted to TSM.

Some marketers employ outside sales organizations familiar with TSM to implement the program, while others use their own sales facilities. Whoever presents the TSM program, it is important to remember the following points:

- Explain all the benefits of the product.
- Convince the buyer that the commercial for the product will stimulate immediate sales action.
- Explain the profit structure that allows a full 30 percent markup without the need to dilute the profit by closing out excess inventories.
- Emphasize that the terms of the sale are "return privilege" of all unsold merchandise.

Perhaps the strongest selling point for TSM is a 1982 EIOM study, which shows that consumers motivated to go to a designated outlet to buy a specific product spend an additional $14.67 on other merchandise. This consumer purchasing pattern is a highly important selling tool in obtaining initial distribution and maintaining the inventory levels necessary for a continuing, profitable TSM program. (The research conducted by EIOM Research Company shows consumer buying habits when entering a store for a TSM-promoted product.)

CHAPTER 8

Test Marketing

Direct marketing demands constant testing. Every day that a commercial runs—whether in a previously tested time period or a new one, on a new day of the week or the old one—every insertion or commercial becomes a new test. It is even a new test when it exactly duplicates previous exposures. There are a number of accepted testing procedures, but to begin any test, you must first have a product and a commercial.

DEVELOPING A COST-EFFECTIVE TESTING PROGRAM

If you are a direct marketer with a great deal of experience, or if you work with a highly experienced advertising agency, you should be able to initiate an easily interpreted test program for the cost of a commercial, plus about $15,000 for radio or $25,000 for television. The cost of a commercial depends a great deal on the product, but it should usually not exceed $25,000. Radio tests should not exceed $2,000. The total of the commercial plus the time should be the maximum capital risk you take. If properly supervised, this media budget will give you as accurate a readout as a $1 million test budget.

You will read throughout this book that tradition is a great deterrent to progress. For years, advertising agencies and research organizations have looked for the ideal test markets that should be as close to an average market as possible, with close-to-average demographics of ethnic and religious groups, an affluence level that resembles the national norm, an average age level, a division of blue-collar and white-collar workers that nearly resembles national averages, no unusual habits or likes and dislikes, and a geographic location that makes it as free as possible from outside influences. Sophisticated marketers believe these characteristics are necessary to give the tester the best basis to use for projections.

In direct marketing, we do not look for the average market to test. In direct marketing, it is essential to first find out if the offer can be profitable under the most ideal conditions. For this reason, test commercials should only be run in those markets that are known to be the most highly productive. It can, therefore, be assumed that if a product does not produce profitable results when given the best exposures . . . on the best stations . . . that are producing at the lowest possible cost, then it would be too costly and inefficient for the direct marketer to attempt to find those few areas and stations where the offer might work.

This method of testing requires that the direct marketer or agency has some successful campaigns on the air at the time of the new product test. The testing ideology is simple:

> If you can't make an offer work under the most ideal situation, then it's too costly to try to find areas where it will work.

When one is able to select the best spots on the best stations, the cost of a TV test program (based on 1993 prices) should not exceed $25,000 This should buy about ten, 120-second spots on four or five stations. If you wished to test two price levels or a slight offer variation, then the test budget should be increased by about 50 percent for each variation.

If you have had no experience in direct marketing and are unable to employ an agency with valid experience, there are several ways to gain enough information to conduct the test with less than hit-or-miss potential. To conduct the test, you will need an experienced phone service with adequate incoming 800 lines and operators to handle your traffic. Usually you can find these services by looking in the Yellow Pages of your phone book or calling a local radio or TV station. Keep in mind that these phone services are national, and therefore they are aware of the results being obtained by other direct marketing products. Although they keep client results completely confidential, they are able to tell you which stations seem to be favored by direct marketers and which seem to get the best results for direct marketing offers. Because phone services are interested in obtaining and building new clients, they will often work with new clients in helping them set up test programs.

A second source of information might be stations themselves, but remember that TV and radio stations are in the business of selling time, so they might exaggerate their potential. Often, however, if you work directly with the sales manager and reiterate the importance to the station of a successful test, he or she will give you sound advice and reasonable rates. It is always advisable, however, to meet with several stations before making a selection for testing.

Once the test program shows the potential of success, phone services are a sound source of information necessary for rolling out your campaign.

Testing direct marketing radio should not exceed $10,000. Although the (per) exposure rate for radio is usually less costly than for television, it is important that more saturation be used for direct marketers on radio. Keep in mind also that talk radio is far more effective for direct marketers than is music radio, unless the offer is the specific type of music the station programs.

Once the test marketing shows signs of success, the expansion into new markets should be conservative. The experienced direct marketing media buyer should work down from "the very best" to the "best" to the "good" to the "fair" until a level is reached at which the commercial ceases to produce. Some commercials are effective only on about 50 stations; others have been profitable on any station. (See Exhibit 8–1.)

The roll-out techniques usually used by sophisticated direct marketers require an appropriation of about $25,000 for a TV test. The successful test is followed by another $40,000 for the initial roll-out. If this second phase is successful, an open-ended budget should be appropriated that restricts new media purchases to a maximum of 1 week's exposure per station. The budget should allow minimum expenditures for a single unproven medium. As the offer proves its viability, the profitable stations are renewed and the unsuccessful stations are revised, cut back, or cancelled.

There are many factors that can affect a specific market on a day-to-day basis, including weather, local tragedy, and unusual events. If a station has been profitable for several schedules and it suddenly stops providing sales at a profitable level, the station should be renewed at least one more week to see if the failure was a fluke caused by some unusual event.

Normally, when the seasonal fall-off occurs (as set forth on the seasonal trend chart, Exhibit 8–2), nearly all stations react simultaneously. Usually it is beneficial to increase the intensity of the schedules on successful media, but such expansion faces the danger of oversaturation, where the additional spots bring the cost per unit sale above the Magic Number.

It is logical to assume that each additional commercial becomes less effective, as an experienced buyer will select best exposures first. Thus the 20th spot selected should be less effective than the first, and the 30th even less efficient.

Inexperienced direct marketers often make the costly mistake of expanding schedules based on averages, when the original schedule is pulling under the Magic Number and the added commercials bring the cost up to the Magic Number. The additional spots, in this case, are producing orders above the allowable and are decreasing the actual profits.

EXHIBIT 8-1
Radio Testing Report: 1st Quarter 1994

Station/Market Schedule Dates	Budget	Invoiced	Phone Leads	Mail	Total	CPL
WGNX Atlanta						
1/9–1/15	$ 930	$ 540	90	1	91	5.93
WATL Atlanta						
12/26–1/2	880	680	151	0	151	4.50
1/2–1/8	880	780	396	12	408	1.91
1/23–1/29	880	580	121	7	128	4.53
	2,640	2,040	668	19	687	2.97
WAGT Augusta						
12/26–1/2	400	0	6	0	6	—
1/2–1/8	400	160	115	2	117	1.37
1/9–1/15	400	280	162	6	168	1.67
1/16–1/22	400	40	10	0	10	4.00
1/30–2/5	400	0	6	0	6	—
	2,000	480	299	8	307	1.56
WQTV Boston						
1/2–1/8	750	675	590	29	619	1.09
3/5–3/11	750	750	505	18	523	1.43
	1,500	1,425	1,095	47	1,142	1.25
WSBK Boston						
2/6–2/12	1,700	1,700	310	11	321	5.30
2/13–2/19	1,700	1,280	265	35	300	4.27
	3,400	2,980	575	46	621	4.80
WCCB Charlotte						
12/26–1/2	1,210	710	120	6	126	5.63
WGN Chicago						
12/26–1/1	4,200	5,900	1,952	60	2,012	2.93
1/2–1/8	5,250	3,000	1,365	86	1,451	2.07
1/9–1/15	5,550	2,550	905	35	940	2.71
1/16–1/22	5,550	2,850	745	42	787	3.62
1/23–1/29	5,550	2,250	553	87	640	3.52
	26,100	16,550	5,520	310	5,830	2.84
WXIX Cincinnati						
1/2–1/8	1,240	150	84	1	85	1.79
1/9–1/15	1,240	465	96	10	106	4.39
	2,480	615	180	11	191	3.22

EXHIBIT 8-2
Seasonal Direct Return Curve

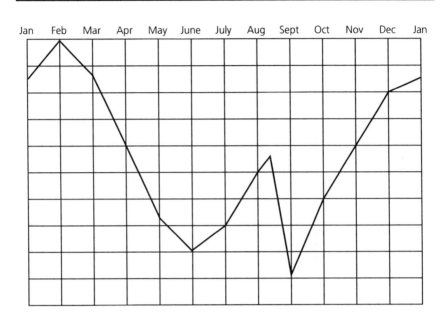

| Jan | Feb | Mar | Apr | May | June | July | Aug | Sept | Oct | Nov | Dec | Jan |

DRY TESTING

One advantage of direct marketing is its flexibility in allowing marketers to "dry test." Dry testing is a method of advertising a product that has not yet been produced. Its great benefits allow the direct marketer to test the potential of a product before sizable investments are made for tools, dies, importation, inventories, etc. For example, let's say you have a product that requires $250,000 in tooling costs, and you're not really sure how the consumer will react to it. Simply produce a prototype and use it to produce a commercial, then schedule in the normal test mode. A prototype, of course, isn't necessary for radio. Your test results will give you a reading on consumer reaction. If you receive orders within the parameters of the advertising allowable, you immediately refund all the money sent in and inform buyers that the product will not be available for several months.

After a successful test, however, you can proceed with the heavy expenditures with confidence that your product will be successful. If you receive fewer orders than necessary for success, you merely refund the money and inform the customers that due to production problems, the product is not available. This method of testing, although considered unethical by some direct marketers, is legal, providing all monies are returned within 30 days after receipt.

DEALING WITH BORDERLINE TEST RESULTS

In the preceding section, you were advised on what to do when your test was clearly a winner or loser. But how do you handle the borderline test? Suppose a product has a Magic Number of $4 and the test media produces orders at $4.15 to $4.50. Should you discard the offer? No! Not until every aspect of the program has been reevaluated. Profitable products are too hard to find to give up when tests show borderline results.

There are several aspects of your marketing program that should be considered:

1. **Consider the season.** Perhaps the test was done in July and under the normal seasonal variations. It is logical to assume that it will be highly profitable in January and February. Over the years, many products have established a track record of being only successful in the most productive months and failures the rest of the year.

2. **Reexamine the offer.** Perhaps a new premium could be added or the old one improved. Perhaps the price is too high or too low. Sometimes you can turn a loser into a winner by increasing the price, whereby the increased income more than compensates for the loss of unit sales.

3. **In the case of a series, reevaluate the initial offer.** Often in a book or collector's series, a stronger initial offer will be positive enough to turn the borderline case into a big profit maker.

4. **Reevaluate the commercial.** Remember, you only have to improve the commercial by 10–15 percent to improve the results enough to make the offer profitable.

5. **Reevaluate each media buy.** If you can lower the advertising cost 10–15 percent, you have turned a borderline product into a profitable product. If you can limit buys to more productive areas, you can bring the allowable down to a profitable level.

Success might not be limited to improving one area, but by improving each of several areas enough to cause the necessary sales swing to turn losses into profits.

There are also many bumps along the road to success. Often one encounters tests where the initial stages are highly productive but the roll-outs proved unprofitable. It is nearly impossible to arrive at the reason for roll-out failures after successful tests, and it is even more difficult when the second week fails to repeat the success of the first week. Despite the trials and tribulations of direct marketing testing, remember the following guidelines:

1. Compared to general marketing, tests are relatively inexpensive.
2. It is easy to interpret test results.
3. One can use the profits from a successful market to finance the expansion.

Keep in mind that direct marketing is one of the most inexpensive and expedient ways to become an entrepreneur. It involves a limited organization and minimum capital risk. I have actually seen investors start with less than $10,000 and make $1 million in less than one year. Direct marketing is an easy, fast, and inexpensive way to start down the road to success. (See sidebar.)

HOW TO MAKE A MILLION-DOLLAR IDEA WORTH A MILLION BUCKS

Before there was the plastic sandwich bag, the disposable razor, and the electric toothbrush, there were the ideas for all those products. And often the first people who had those ideas never acted on them. They let someone else come up with the idea and make a fortune from it. It's not unusual to be walking through a store or watching television and to see a new product that you invented in your mind years ago. You smack yourself on the head and ask, "Why didn't I do something about it?"

The answer is that you didn't know what to do. For the average person, the process of translating a product idea into reality seems to require a prohibitive amount of money, resources, and knowledge. When you first think of that wonderful product, you are too wrapped up in the power and glory of the *idea* to worry about actually making it work. You cloak the idea in the fabric of fantasy, imagining the fame and riches it will bring you. Instead of doing something about the idea, you think it to death. The product idea, once an indelible image in your mind, fades like an old photograph. The real problems of manufacturing, marketing, and advertising it keep the idea imprisoned in your head, and eventually it disappears. The next time you think of it is when you see your idea as somebody else's product.

I grimace every time somebody tells me a story like this, and, believe me, I've heard infinite variations on this same theme. To avoid hearing any more of those stories, I will now give you a do-it-yourself kit that contains instructions on how to build a successful product from scratch.

First, let us begin with the idea. You must objectively determine whether it is a viable one. I stress the word *objectively,* because you tend to fall in love with your idea to the exclusion of any rational analysis of it. To prevent this, here is a checklist to use in analyzing your idea.

Even to consider a direct marketing venture, some elements are essential. Other elements, although not totally essential, greatly increase the opportunities for success.

A reliable post office or private method of delivery is an absolute in considering a direct marketing venture. Many nations have unreliable mail services that often pilfer, lose, or do not deliver packages. Unless the direct marketer can rely on some type of delivery service, there is no way a direct marketing business can be successful.

For years, there were no toll-free (800) phone systems, and direct marketers relied solely on the mail for the delivery of orders. In the very early days of TV, local phone services were set up to receive orders within the area of dominant influence of the TV stations (usually a 50-mile radius). In the larger metropolitan areas, as many as seven local phone services were used in order to offer the listener a toll-free call. Because of the much broader coverage of radio, radio stations could not offer toll-free calls until the advent of the 800 service. Even with this service, however, both TV and radio continue to offer the mail-in option, which often includes a bonus for payment with order. Today, of course, credit cards are honored through the phone-in order.

Methods available to the direct marketer for collecting money also are critical to the success of the business. In countries that have a high circulation of credit cards among potential customers, this is an expedient method that can be used in collecting for both phone and mail orders. A reliable collect-on-delivery offer can greatly increase sales, particularly to skeptics who are not certain they will get what they order. Unfortunately, in the United States there are certain areas in which neither the post office nor the private services will face the perils of delivery. Thus, packages often are returned marked "no such address" or "refused" or "address cannot be located." Money orders and checks can also be used as methods of collection, but direct marketers should be careful not to ship merchandise paid for by check until they have notification of check clearance. ■

CHAPTER 9

After the Test Campaign

Handling Customer Response

AGENCY ORGANIZATION

The guiding principle behind any direct marketing organization is that every direct marketing exposure must provide sales within the limits of a predetermined allowable. A corollary to that principle is that an organization must be programmed to act—or react—as fast as possible to all variations of a direct marketing campaign.

To achieve the flexibility and reaction time required, you must streamline the chain of command. The media buyer must be able to react instantly to renewals and cancellations. This is particularly true where renewals and cancellations occur on a daily basis. Any organizational flow that slows this reaction process will result in lower profits or, even worse, greater losses for the direct marketer.

To reduce or eliminate any delays, the direct marketer must constantly communicate with both the creative and media staff. As the results come in, the media-buyer team must constantly communicate with creative so the latter group can immediately react to the results.

The media buyer, however, must take control of the campaign as soon as the commercial is completed. The media buyer is responsible for arranging a suitable phone-answering network so that the order-taking system is organized smoothly and efficiently. This means that the media buyer provides the answering service with all necessary product information, while obtaining the proper phone numbers for the creative department to integrate into the commercials or tag lines. The media buyer should also be given the responsibility for evaluating all aspects of the offer. The major function of the media buyer, however, is to immediately renew exposures that produce profitable results and cancel, revise, or negotiate new terms for unprofitable exposures. When organizational structures dictate that the media buyer must obtain approval for any reaction, the direct marketing project suffers.

Whenever a direct marketer works with an agency, he or she must give the agency a predetermined budget for each level of campaign roll-out. Normally, the first level of roll-out budget should be approximately four times as large as the initial test budget—assuming, of course, that the initial test was successful. If tests continue to be successful, successive levels of budget should be allocated contingent on the direct marketer's ability to deliver.

The direct marketer should limit media purchases by the buyer to a single week until that medium has proven successful. After that, all renewals (no matter how many weeks the schedule encompasses) should be cancellable on 1 week's notice. When an exposure is unsuccessful—and all renegotiations of schedule revisions that would change a loser into a winner have been exhausted—the buyer must have the authority to cancel.

On rare occasions, there is a need in direct marketing for the services of a trouble-shooter, or account manager. The account manager's role is to coordinate the creative and media teams so that they operate at peak performance. Please note that in the suggested organization chart (Exhibit 9–1), the account manager is over the creative and media people, but not necessarily in the direct line of communications.

EXHIBIT 9-1
Organization Chart

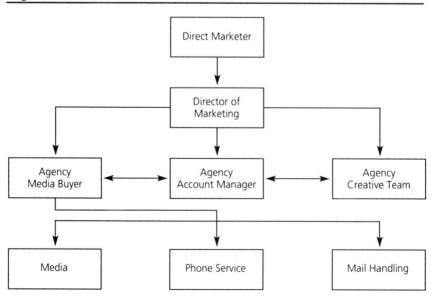

PHONE SERVICES

In order to understand how phone services fit into the direct response broadcast picture, it is important to understand the historical evolution of radio and TV order handling.

In the early days of radio, phones were not used, because of logistical problems. Radio stations covered as many as 30 states, and since there was no such thing as a national 800 phone number, it was impossible to find phone services that could handle the coverage areas.

In the late 1940s, 1950s, and 1960s, before the advent of cable systems and superstations, TV stations had a limited coverage area, often no more than 50 miles. As a result, most cities had local phone services that could handle the TV station's area of dominant influence (ADI). These services were often very small, with a maximum of 10 in-lines, and manned by as few as three operators. In New York City, because of the problem with toll-call zones and the relatively small local phone-answering services, it was necessary to use local phone services in Manhattan, Brooklyn, Westchester, Long Island, Staten Island, and New Jersey. Even more absurd—at least by present-day standards—the best results were obtained only when each phone number was mentioned two or three times. Consequently, 1 minute of a 5-minute commercial had to be devoted to phone numbers and mailing addresses. When stations began placing 120-second limits on commercials, it was often difficult to tell whether a direct marketer was selling a product or phone numbers. All types of incentives were given to viewers in an effort to convince them to buy only by mail, but mail-only offers were never successful. When the convenience of ordering by phone was eliminated, the response was insufficient to reach the advertising allowable, and the results did not warrant continued advertising expenditures.

Local phone services, however, offered three major benefits. First, the fact that they were local bridged a credibility gap. Viewers were sure they weren't being charged for the call, and a local number gave them better access to the advertiser if they were not satisfied. Second, local numbers made it easier to allocate the orders to the proper stations. And third, local phone services charged only 15–25¢ per call. These charges were confined only to actual orders received. This made the cost of taking orders by phone relatively insignificant. In addition, the small local phone charge made it possible to offer items for as little as $2.98. Thus, $2.98 became a significant TV and radio mail order price. And $4.98 became practically the upper price limit for volume response, because it was the highest price at which an item was successful.

In the mid-1960s, inflation increased local phone prices to 35¢. This pushed the minimum selling price of direct marketing offers to $3.98. By the early 1970s, the minimum offer had increased to $4.95, with the upper limit established at $14.95.

Cognizant of the increased number of stations carrying these offers, Western Union designed a telemarketing service to handle national calls. Western Union implemented a central, toll-free number, "Enterprise 25," that routed calls to the local Western Union office. In turn, that office took the orders and forwarded them to the direct marketer. But Western Union's service had its flaws. First, local Western Union offices weren't open between midnight and 7:00 A.M., a lucrative time for direct response offers. Second, the public didn't believe the calls were toll-free.

The 800 Series

In the early 1970s, AT&T offered a new 800 series for incoming calls, a procedure that would allow long-distance calls from any part of the United States to be directed into the subscribing phone service. Car rental companies, stockbrokers, and hotel reservations departments were among the first to see the great benefits of the national telemarketing concept. When the 800 number first appeared on TV commercials, however, the public was again skeptical. The early direct marketers who experimented with the 800 series found the local phone services more efficient and more profitable.

The 800 series was far more costly than local systems, increasing the cost of a phone order from 35¢ to almost 70¢. Because of the high cost of 800 lines and installations, the national phone services included charges for "nonorders," "false" orders, and "crank" calls (see sidebar)—as well as any inquiries relative to product, delivery, or complaints. In addition, orders from a wide variety of stations and offers often used a single phone number, which frequently made it difficult to credit the proper medium for the order. (Today costs can range from $1.25 to $2.50 per call.)

IN DEFENSE OF DIRECT MARKETING

"You crooks cashed my check and I never got my CDs. Either you send them today, or I'm reporting you to the post office, Better Business Bureau, and Consumer Fraud Department. . . . I'll sue your company for every cent you've got!" What direct marketer hasn't heard this? The irate phone call from a dissatisfied customer is as common to the business as toll-free numbers. Occasionally, the phone call is justified. However, often such calls come from consumers intent on getting something for nothing. And, most often, they get it.

One reason for this is the general perception of the direct marketing industry. It is watched more closely than the most dangerous criminal. Numerous federal and local agencies track the direct marketer's every step, ready to pounce at the slightest hint of any wrongdoing. So, when that caller complains, the direct marketer is as nervous as a long-tailed cat in a roomful of rocking chairs.

Perhaps the government's overzealous attitude is justified. The public should be protected from a handful of unscrupulous direct marketers. But who protects marketers from the unscrupulous public? Certainly not the government. By their seeming indifference to the problems direct marketers face, they give tacit approval to every budding con artist scheming to bilk a company out of a product or money.

Direct marketers lose an estimated $300 million each year because of these con artists. And for each con artist, there is a different con. Here are a few examples: (1) People who claim they sent in their money for a product and didn't receive it; (2) people who claim they never received a product when in fact they did; (3) those who send in phony orders as a joke, and when the product is delivered, do not accept it; (4) those who say they sent their product in for a refund and never received it; (5) the product is stolen by either a postal official or someone who sees it outside a door; (6) people who deliberately misuse a product and send it back, taking advantage of the money-back guarantee.

True case: A customer informs the company that he or she returned the product and never received a refund. It's possible the product was returned and not properly processed, or the customer's name was recorded wrong. It's usually less costly for the direct marketer to send out a refund then to spend hours checking the files. The customer receives the refund and sends a second letter with the same complaint, using a different first name. Another refund is sent. After the fourth refund, the clerk noticed the similarity of addresses and reported the incident to the post office. After all, customers are also subject to mail fraud laws.

Several weeks later, the post office returned a check for three of the four refunds, and my client thought the incident was ended. Unfortunately, the customer's name remained in the client's database. When a mailing was sent to all active customers, one was returned from the customer that had given the money back to the post office with the notation, "I wouldn't do business with you crooks. I sent back your product months ago and have never received my refund."

It was not unusual for me to receive calls from disgruntled customers who were deluged with deliveries of a particular product ordered by pranksters. This was particularly true of *Playboy* magazine subscriptions. Often students in a "square" professor's class would conspire to call in subscriptions, and the professor would receive as many as 20 magazines. The recipient of an unwanted subscription would often call, pointing out the pornographic story on page 8, the terrible nude pictures on page 15, 21, 26, and 30, and the vile jokes on page 46. The complainer would have obtained my name from the TV station, which, of course, was aware of the agency placing the campaign. I always had a stock answer for these complaints: "Had I known the magazine carried anything like you're telling me, I wouldn't have handled the account. As soon as I hang up, I'll call them and resign their business." I imagine, over 20 years, I resigned the account several dozen times.

Then there was the customer who was greatly concerned about the preservation of turtles. I was handling a turtle oil cosmetic, made, of course, of synthetic oil. This customer ranted and raged for 10 minutes about the beaches being cluttered with the shells of slaughtered tortoises. After she was finished with her tirade, I responded, "You shouldn't be calling me, you should be calling Johnson & Johnson."

"Why," she asked, "do they make turtle oil?"

"No," I replied, "they make baby oil."

What is so insidious about mail order con artists is that they're virtually foolproof. Direct marketers routinely send both money and product back to those who complain. They do so because the ominous threat of a lawsuit or FTC interference is behind every call. Because mistakes are made—letters lost, checks misplaced— the complaint might be legitimate, so a refund is the most economical solution to the problem. A small loss won't break any company, especially one that does a high volume business.

But these losses add up. And consumers, as well as the direct marketer, end up losers. Prices of items must be raised as much as 25 percent to compensate for pranksters and scams. I once wanted to find out how other companies handled this type of scam, so I wrote the same note to every mail order offer in one issue of *Esquire* magazine. I merely said, "I sent you my money and never received your product. Either you send me the product or refund my money or I'm reporting you to the post office." I received nearly every item. Only two asked for a copy of my check or money order.

Can anything be done? Well, the first and easiest thing to do is for direct marketers to conduct a public relations campaign, explaining to consumers the negative aspect of cheating a direct marketer. Too often, people view this cheating as harmless. Who does it hurt? These are mail-order kleptomaniacs, people who order something by mail and then ignore the bills that follow. These people have to be made aware that they are ultimately hurting themselves.

On another level, the government has to be made aware of the problems direct marketers face. An effective lobbying effort would be a good start to solve government apathy. This lobbying effort should act as a catalyst for the creation of an independent watchdog group that would ferret out those who attempt to defraud direct marketers. This would act as a central clearinghouse, supplying direct marketers with the names of repeat offenders. Such a list would cut fraud almost in half.

Finally, this whole situation is exacerbated by something neither consumers nor direct marketers can control. From reading a variety of studies, I would estimate that 20 percent of products ordered by people in inner-city areas are never delivered. The reason is that UPS and post office employees often refuse to venture into "bad" neighborhoods and attempt to collect COD. They are not entirely to blame, when you consider that police often are reluctant to enter public housing projects for any reason. The problem, however, is that these postal employees cover themselves by reporting that the customer wasn't at home. Hence the legitimate nondelivery complaints from inner-city dwellers. And so a hue and cry is raised, and direct marketers are its object. Yet they are powerless to stop this mail-order redlining.

Obviously, there is no easy answer to the problem. But the wrong answer is to say nothing can be done. That will only encourage those who cheat direct marketers to continue to do so. Since some of you reading this are experts in the art of selling, perhaps you could use your talents to sell both the public and government on the need for action. I'm sure you'll get an overwhelming response.

Source: Copyright © DM News Corporation, 1981, reprinted by special permission. ■

National 800 services still pose problems for direct marketers. Because these phone services handle numerous clients with numerous offers—some of which may be competitive—the individual direct marketer has little control over the number of operators working at a given time or the number of calls coming in at any given moment. Sophisticated direct marketers exert some control over the flow of orders generated by their own commercials (see Exhibit 9–2), but they have little control over crowded lines filled with calls generated by competitive commercials. For this reason, customers often have trouble connecting with an available operator to take an order.

EXHIBIT 9-2
Order Flow Chart

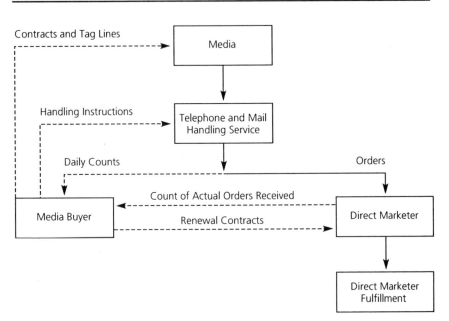

In addition, with a national phone service, there is always the risk of "weather blackout," or accidents that cause the communications lines to go down during a period when heavy schedules are running. This has occurred on occasion in the blizzard months of January and February and during the tornado months of April, May, and June. There are cases where clients have lost as much as $500,000 worth of orders because of these communication breakdowns. For example, when Elvis Presley died in 1977, a Presley record offer aired on Atlanta Superstation WTBS. The volume of calls generated by the Presley offer caused the entire 800 system in the Southeast to overload. The phone company demanded that the offer be taken off the air, because even emergency calls couldn't get through. Other direct marketers, of course, suffered from this overloading to the extent that they received practically no calls from their exposures because of the traffic jam.

Undoubtedly, satellite phone systems, coupled with fiber-optic distribution lines, will alleviate much of the phone system overloading and breakdown problems. Still, the logistics of scheduling and training telemarketing operators will always be a critical problem.

Although most direct marketers contract for outside telemarketing services, there are some direct marketers that are now installing their own 800 systems. This provides some insurance and protection against overloading, competitive conflict, and confusion. It also gives the direct marketer an opportunity to properly train operators to intelligently handle customers. Because of the inevitable logistics problems, however, the direct marketer-owned 800 system might prove to be less efficient and quite costly. Many direct marketers that have installed 800 systems have already found it more efficient to supplement their system with outside phone services.

Choosing a Phone Service

There are approximately 10–15 legitimate phone services from which a direct marketer (or its agency) can choose. Some are better than others. To make the right choice, a direct marketer should consider the following factors:

1. **How fast is the phone service?** This is a critical question, because every 24-hour delay in relaying leads to the direct marketer results in a significant loss of sales. Some services promise fast turnaround and don't deliver. You should contact other companies that have used services to determine how quick they really are.

2. **Does the service have a manual or computerized system?** If you're really concerned about speed, and if you have a compatible computer system, you'll opt for the computerized phone service.

3. **How big is the phone service?** How many lines does it have? The more lines it has, the more likely that callers won't encounter busy signals.

4. **Does it provide accurate sourcing?** It's essential that phone services tell direct marketers the source of each lead—the station that generated it and the time and day when the spot ran. This tells direct marketers which spots are most and least productive, giving them a barometer to measure a buy's effectiveness and to plan future buys. Some phone service firms are sloppy or inaccurate. Those services should always be avoided, no matter what other advantages they offer.

5. **What is the reputation of a phone service?** You want to find a service that will do what it says. You don't want a service that, for instance, accepts a telethon as a client without telling you far in advance. The telethon will invariably tie up all the lines, preventing callers responding to your offer from getting through.

6. **How good is the service with the nitty-gritty details?** Examine the procedures for and quality of scriptwriting, the general demeanor of operators, and credit card validation. Some services make a special point of training their operators to be helpful and courteous. Others don't care.

7. **What does the service charge?** Costs vary greatly, and comparative shopping is often a good idea until you've found a service with which you're comfortable. Don't always go to the lowest bidder, however. The service that charges a little more might offer much better service.

CHAPTER *10*

The Magic Number Concept

The Mathematics of Broadcast Direct Marketing

Direct response advertising, trade support marketing, and all types of support advertising differ from general advertising in that the results are instantly measurable, and, in most cases, the advertising is only effective when it returns an instant profit. (See sidebar.) The amount of money that can be spent to profitably move a product or sell a service is known as "allowable" or the "Magic Number."

Because the Magic Number is so critical to any direct marketing campaign, it is essential that it be ascertained, not only to evaluate the viability and potential of the offer, but also as the means of evaluating the success or failure of the initial tests and the subsequent roll-out of the campaign.

In the case of negative option, continuous shipment, club plans, two-step sales conversions, and catalog distribution, there are many unknowns that exist in the basic formula needed to arrive at the Magic Number. These unknowns include such questions as "How many will the buyer ultimately buy?" "What will be the size of the initial order" In the case of catalog distribution, "What is a customer worth?" Experienced direct marketers can provide an educated estimate about the answers to these unknowns, but often new entrepreneurs will have to guess the best they can until they have gained the necessary experience for an educated guess.

The following pages set forth the facts and solutions for many variations of direct marketing sales. To make these solutions simple, we consider the administrative overhead, insurance, production cost, distribution of film or tape, insurance, etc., as immediate write-offs. These costs are not contributing factors to the basic formulas. Administrative costs, for example, would depend on the number of offers within the business. Production and logistics costs can be allocated once the offer is a proven success, but these costs should not be considered in the initial Magic Number formula. If it is very successful, the cost of tools, dies, creative, etc., is usually irrelevant to the total profit picture.

CALCULATIONS FOR TRADE SUPPORT MARKETING

Direct response, implemented properly, is virtually a foolproof testing method for any product. It gives the product the benefit of the doubt: you must choose the best market, the best stations, and the best times to run the test. Thus, if the test doesn't work under these conditions, it will never work. If it does work, the test is expanded gradually to other markets, and expansion to new markets is actually financed by success in previous markets. Often, a successful direct response product can be channeled into trade support marketing and eventually into universal distribution.

From the discussion of trade support marketing (TSM) in Chapter 7, you should have a basic grasp of what it entails and how it is distinct from any other kind of retail advertising. But no matter how carefully I have explained TSM in theory, the story is not complete until I explain how it actually works in practice. So here is an example of the calculations necessary when you've brought your product idea to the threshold of success and decide to test the TSM waters.

Let's begin with a product that we will call TSM-1. The selling price of TSM-1 is pegged at $10. Of that, 30 percent, or $3, goes to the chain stores, leaving you with $7. Next, factor in the following expenses: $2 for actual cost of goods, 50¢ for freight, 42¢ (6 percent) for administration, and 70¢ (10 percent) for sales cost. Then you must determine the absolute minimum profit you would accept for your capital investment. You decide on $1 as that minimum profit. Deduct all the aforementioned numbers from $7, and you end up with $2.38. That $2.38 is what we call the Magic Number. If your advertising costs stay around that number, everything works like magic.

Next, choose two markets for test marketing. We have certain markets that we use almost exclusively for tests. They include

Albany, Toledo, Tampa, Sacramento, San Diego, Orlando, and Louisville. All these cities have certain things in common: excellent retail chains with which our agency has established a working relationship, TV stations where we can make excellent media buys and where there is a history of full cooperation.

In addition, all these markets rate 100 on the product marketing index (PMI). The PMI was developed years ago by our agency as a tool to differentiate one market from another. Of course, that violates the normal test procedures in advertising, which often select "average" markets for tests.

Individual markets vary just as individual people do. That is why the PMI came into existence. Some markets, such as Chicago and Detroit, have index numbers above 100, while others have numbers below 100. The index, however, uses 100 as a base number. It tells you that for X number of advertising dollars, you can move 100 units in a 100-indexed market. But if you spend the same amount in a 115-indexed market, you will move an additional 15 units. This index is based on a normal universal product and is accurate to plus or minus 5 percent. The PMI is of incalculable value in helping clients budget their advertising expenditures.

The PMI was developed by factoring in such things as the number of TV stations in a market, the rates of those stations, the strength of the key outlets, and the results of thousands of tests run in those markets. The only time the PMI has to be adjusted is for seasonally, geographically, or regionally oriented products. To use an extreme example, a snow shovel cannot be plugged into the PMI for New Orleans, because snowfall there is minimal.

Now, let us go back to TSM-1 and our Magic Number, which was $2.38. We decide to test it in Portland and Louisville, 100-indexed markets. We also decide to spend $4,500 in a 3-week campaign in each market. The next step is to take $2.38 and divide it into $4,500. The result is 1,890. Thus, we have to sell 1,890 units in each market in the 3-week test to reach the Magic Number. Of course, it is rare to hit the Magic Number on the nose. To cover ourselves in case we sell more than expected, we stock the stores with approximately one-and-a-half times what we need to reach the Magic Number. In this instance, that means 2,850 units per market. The commercial airs, and four things can happen:

1. We sell all 2,850 units in the markets, which means our advertising allowance (the Magic Number) is too high, and we must compensate by increasing the amount of product in the market. Because the test was successful, we then expand to five upgraded markets—markets with slightly higher PMI numbers. If those five markets continue to work for the product, we continue to expand, always limiting the expansion to five upgraded markets. We have found that five markets allows for a good profit while still ensuring that if the product doesn't sell in the new markets, the losses will be minimal.

2. We sell about 1,890 units, thus hitting the Magic Number. We reschedule advertising, resupply the market, and expand.

3. We sell about 1,600 units. If this occurs, we'll give the product the benefit of the doubt, because it has come reasonably close to the Magic Number. We'll allow the product to remain in the stores for several weeks to see if we move the necessary 1,890 units. Because we are so close to success, we reexamine our packaging, TV commercials, and media selection, hoping we can improve them to produce the needed additional sales.

4. The product bombs. This happens infrequently, but it does happen, and we try to defuse the bomb before it does any more damage. We'll give the client a choice: to let us reexamine the commercial and see whether we can improve it and run another test, or to take the losses and get out of the market. It is unprecedented for an agency to even suggest to a client that a product might be a failure, but that is what we do if the test doesn't work.

You might wonder why we chose a 100-PMI market when we could have chosen 115-PMI markets. The answer is that the higher PMI markets are far more costly. For example, it costs $4,500 to test a 100-PMI market but $20,000–40,000 to test New York City, Chicago, or Los Angeles. We test the less expensive markets to hold down the client's risk factor.

If you follow the steps outlined in this chapter, your chances for success are 90 percent. That has been our agency's success rate with new product introductions. Any agency worth its billings should be able to guarantee you a similar success rate if they are cognizant of the strategies I've discussed. ■

CASE A: STRAIGHT SALE WITH COD, 10 PERCENT BAD DEBT

Using the following facts, how much can you afford to spend with the media to sell one record set? (Or, what is the Magic Number for the known offer?) Note that the minimum acceptable profit number is decided by the direct marketer. In this case, if the offer doesn't return a minimum profit of $1.50 per unit, it is not worth the effort or capital risk to continue with the offer. The media facts are as follows:

- 85 percent of all orders will be by phone, to be shipped COD.
- 15 percent of all orders will be by mail, thus a check will come in with the order.
- 25 percent of all COD shipments will be refused, thus will be returned to sender.
- The price is too small for credit card companies to allow charges.

		Each Unit
Selling price		$10.00
Costs:		
Cost of goods	2.50	
Cost of packaging and label	.50	
Postage	1.00	
Phone service	1.00	
Administrative cost	.50	
Total cost	5.50	
Margin before bad debt		4.50
Bad debt—10% of orders		1.00
Balance available for profit and advertising		$ 3.50
Minimum acceptable profit		1.50
Balance allowable for advertising (the Magic Number)		_____

Solution to Case A

In order to arrive at the solution, you must separate CODs and prepaid orders. With 25 percent COD refusals, you get paid for 75 percent.

	10 CODs		**10 Prepaids**	
Sales	10 × 75% paid x $10	$75.00	10 @ $10 =	$100.00
Cost of goods	$2.50 × 10 × 75%	$18.75		$ 25.00
Packaging and label	50¢ × 10	$ 5.00		$ 5.00
Phones	$1.00 × 10	$10.00		—
Postage (charged to customers on COD(s)		—	10 × $1.00	$ 10.00
COD returns	2.5 × $3.00	$ 7.50	—	—
Repacking (returns)	2.5 × $1.00	$ 2.50	—	—
Administration expenses	10 × 50¢	$ 5.00	—	$ 5.00
Total costs		$48.75		$ 45.00
Balance available for profit and advertising		$26.25		$ 55.00
Minimum acceptable profit	$1.50 × 7.5 sales	$11.25	$1.50 × 10	$ 15.00
Balance available for advertising		$15.00		$ 40.00

Funds Available for Advertising:

10 CODs generate $15 × 8.5 orders = $12.75

10 prepaids generate $40 × 1.5 orders = $6.00

Funds available to produce 10 orders: $18.75

Magic Number = $1.88

CASE B: TWO-STEP CONVERSIONS

A direct marketer is offering an office machine for $100. The advertising asks for an inquiry. The client mails two brochures in response to each inquiry. The known facts are as follows:

Selling price of office machine		$100.00
Cost of goods delivered	$25.00	
Cost of phones	1.00	
Cost of each mailing piece	.50	
Cost of postage	.20	
Cost of administration	6.00	
Minimum acceptable profit per unit	10.00	

The media facts are 85 percent by phone, 15 percent by mail. Fifty percent will pay for unit with credit card, at a cost of 5 percent. What is the Magic Number with 5 percent conversion? What is the Magic Number with 10 percent conversion?

Solution to Case B

5% Conversion

Sales (5 × $100)		$500.00
Cost of goods (5 × 25)	$125.00	
Cost of phones	85.00	
Cost of mailing pieces	100.00	
Postage (200 × .20)	40.00	
Administration per unit	30.00	
Credit card	12.50	
Minimum profit acceptable	50.00	
	442.50	
Total advertising allowable	$57.50	
	.58	(Magic Number)

10% Conversion

Sales (10 × $100)		$1,000.00
Cost of goods (10 × 25)	$250.00	
Cost of phones	85.00	
Cost of mailing pieces	100.00	
Postage	40.00	
Administration per unit	60.00	
Credit card	25.00	
Minimum profit	100.00	
	660.00	
Total advertising allowable	$340.00	
	$3.40	(Magic Number)

CASE C: CLUB OFFER

This is a book club offer. The direct marketer offers any four books for $1, with a commitment to buy four books at regular price in the course of the year. How much per order can the client pay for advertising if he or she wishes to break even after one year and make a profit on the 30 percent who buy four books the second year? The known facts follow:

Average sale price/book		$10.00
Average cost/book	$3.35	
Phones	1.00	
Package and label	.50	
Postage (4 books)	2.00	

The media facts are 85 percent phone orders, 15 percent mail orders. Fifty percent will pay by credit card at a cost of 5 percent. The direct marketer has had the following shipping experience:

20 percent buy 8 books
40 percent buy 4 books
10 percent buy 3 books
10 percent buy 2 books
10 percent buy 1 book
10 percent buy 0 books
30 percent buy 4 books second year

Solution to Case C

	Sales + Cost	Gross Profit
20% buy 8 books		
Sales (8 × $10 × 2)	$160.00	
Cost of books	$53.60	
Package and label	8.00	
Postage	8.00	
Credit card cost (.025 × $160)	4.00	
Total cost	73.60	
		$86.40

		Sales + Cost	**Gross Profit**
40% buy 4 books			
Sales (4 × 10 × 4)		$160.00	
Cost of books	$53.60		
Package and label	8.00		
Postage	8.00		
Credit card cost (.025 × $160)	4.00		
Total Cost		73.60	
			86.40
10% buy 3 books			
Sales (3 × $10 × 1)		$30.00	
Cost of books	$10.05		
Package and label	1.50		
Postage	1.50		
Credit card cost (.025 × $30)	.75		
Total cost		13.80	
			16.20
10% buy 2 books			
Sales (2 × $10 × 1)		$20.00	
Cost of books	$6.70		
Package and label	1.00		
Postage	1.00		
Credit card cost (.025 × $20)	.50		
Total cost		9.20	
			10.80

		Sales + Cost	Gross Profit
10% buy 1 book			
Sales (1 × $10 × 1)		$10.00	
Cost of book	$3.35		
Package and label	.50		
Postage	.50		
Credit card cost	.25		
Total cost		4.60	
Total gross profit			5.40
			205.20
Cost of initial offer		$10.00	
Cost of sales (40 × $3.35)	$134.00		
Phones (8.5 @ $1.00)	8.50		
Package and label (50¢)	20.00		
Postage (10 sets of 4 books @ $2.00 per set)	20.00		
Credit card	0.25		
Total cost		182.75	172.75
Balance available for advertising			32.45
			$ 3.25

(Magic Number)

CASE D: SUBSCRIPTION OFFER

A magazine publisher needs subscriptions to meet its advertising guarantee. This is an offer of a subscription to the magazine, plus a new world almanac, for $18.50 per year. The first magazine is mailed with an invoice for the year's subscription to those who do not pay in advance. The magazine is mailed for 3 months. How much can the publisher afford to pay for advertising per subscription to break even at the end of one year? The known facts follow:

Cost of magazine to publish	$ .50
Postage for each issue	.11
Cost of putting label into computer	.50
Cost of phones	1.00
Cost of almanac premium	1.00

The media facts are as follows:

- 90 percent of orders will be by phone
- 10 percent of orders will be by mail with full payment.
- 33 percent of phone orders will charge the subscription to a credit card at a cost of 5 percent.
- 33⅓ percent of all orders not paid for immediately will never pay.

Solution to Case D

Subscription Sales

Via mail (1 × $18.50)	$ 18.50
Via phone (3 paid by credit card)	55.50
Via phone (6 remaining, 4 will pay)	74.00
Gross sales from 10 subscription orders	$148.00

Costs

Cost of magazines (8 × 12) + (2 × 3) @ .50 × 102	$51.00	
Postage (102 × .11)	11.22	
Label cost (10 × .50)	5.00	
Phones (9 × $1)	9.00	
Premiums (10 × $1)	10.00	
		86.22
Advertising allowable for 10 subscriptions		$ 61.78
		$ 6.18

(Magic Number)

CASE E: BUSINESS-TO-BUSINESS/ DOOR-TO-DOOR SALES

The offer is a business machine for $3,000. What can an advertiser pay per lead to make a minimum profit of $450 net per unit sale the first year? The known facts follow:

Cost of producing machine	$900.00
Cost of shipping and installing	120.00
Cost of phones	1.00
Cost of first 90 days' servicing	60.00
Administrative cost	24.00
Sales commission per unit	600.00
Markup on accessories 3 to 1 ($60, cost $20)	66⅔%
Commission on accessory sales	30%

The media facts are that salespeople close 20 percent of all calls, customers buy an average of $500 worth of accessories in the first year, and 100 percent of inquiries are by phone.

Solution to Case E

Sales on 10 inquiries (2 × $3,000)	$6,000.00	
Accessory sales on 2 units	1,000.00	
Total Gross Sales per 10 inquiries		$7,000.00
Costs:		
Cost of machines ($900 × 2)	$1,800.00	
Cost of shipping and installing (2 × $120)	240.00	
Cost of phone inquiries	10.00	
Cost of 90 days' service	120.00	
Administrative cost	48.00	
Sales of commissions (2 × $600)	1,200.00	
Cost of accessories	333.33	
Commission on accessories	300.00	
Minimum acceptable profit (2 × $450)	900.00	
Cost and profit		4,951.33
Advertising allowable on 10 inquiries		$2,048.67
(Magic Number)		$ 204.87

CASE F: TRADE SUPPORT MARKETING

An air mattress is being offered through retail chains for $60. The air mattress is a one-time sale, with little chance for repeat business. It is sold to the chains with "return privilege" (guaranteed sales), which means that they can return anything that they do not sell. If the campaign is successful, excess merchandise will NOT be returned, but new inventory will be shipped to supplement inventory still on hand. The chain stores receive a 30 percent discount.

Each market must make a profit at the end of the 3-week campaign (allowing for 3 weeks of "bleed,"* if necessary). The client anticipates an 80 percent sell-through of merchandise. Test Market A cost $6,000 for a 3-week campaign. Test Market B cost $10,000 for a 3-week campaign. Initial distribution should be 1⅓ the amount necessary for minimum profit return. The client won't continue with the product without a minimum of $5 per unit net profit. How much can the client afford to spend to sell a unit? How many units should be stocked in the two selected test markets? The costs are as follows:

Wholesale selling price (70% x $60)		$42.00
Cost of air mattress	$14.50	
Cost of freight each way	1.00	
Cost of repacking returns	2.00	
Sales commission (10%)	4.20	

---

* "Bleed" (or "drag") is additional sales after the advertising ends.

Solution to Case F

Sales: 10 units × 80 percent sell-through × $42 ($60 × .70) = $336.00

Costs:

Cost of goods ($14.50 × 8)	$116.00
Freight (8 @ $1, 2 @ $2)	12.00
Sales commission (10%)	33.60
Administration (6%)	20.16
Repacking	4.00
Total costs	<u>185.76</u>
Balance available for profit and advertising	150.24
Minimum acceptable profit ($5)	40.00
Balance available for advertising	110.24
	$110.24 ÷ 8 = $13.78

Test Market A—Cost $6,000

$6,000 ÷ 13.78 = 435 units to reach sales goal + 25% for returns = 109

Units needed in Market A = 544

Test Market B—Cost $10,000

$10,000 ÷ 13.78 = 762 units to reach sales goal + 25% for returns = 191

Units needed in Market B = 953

CASE G: PROMOTION SUPPORT ADVERTISING

You are running a coupon advertisement for a grocery product in a free-standing insert (FSI) in Sunday newspapers. The coupon is good for 15¢ off at the store on a purchase of one package. The average user uses 3.5 packages per year, and 25 percent of coupon redeemers become product users. Given the following facts, how long will it take to break even on your investment? You decide to spend $150,000 on TV support for this coupon. To what level must you increase redemption to pay out on your investment in TV in one year? The known facts are as follows:

Media costs, FSI	$285,000.00
Redemption costs per coupon (15¢ + 8¢ handling fee to retailer)	.23
Gross profit per package	45.4¢
Circulation	44,000,000
Estimated redemption (based on prior experience)	4%

Solution to Case G

Solution #1:

Costs:

Space	$285,000.00
Redemption (4% of 44,000,000 = 1,760,000 × 23¢)	404,800.00
Total Cost	689,800.00

Revenue:

25% of redeemers become users	(440,000 users)	
440,000 × 3.5 packages per year	(1,540,000 packages)	
Gross profit (45.4¢ × 1,540,000)		$699,160.00

1-year pay-out on FSI alone.

Solution #2

To pay out $150,000 TV cost in 1 year:
(1 user buys 3.5 packages per year
at 45.4¢ gross profit) $1.59 profit per user per year

Less redemption costs (to get 1 user,
you need 4 redeemers, with redemption
cost at .23¢ each)   .92

Profit per user after redemption costs $.67

At $.67 profit per user, you need 223,880 users.

If 25% of redeemers become users, you need 895,520 redeemers.

Added costs:

TV cost	$150,000.00
895,520 redeemers at 23¢ each	205,970.00
Total cost	$ 355,970.00

Added revenue:

25% of 895,520 redeemers = 223,880 users

223,880 users × 3.5 packages per year = 783,580 packages

783,580 packages @ $.454 gross profit = $355,745

Estimated redeemers on FSI alone = 1,760,000

Additional redeemers needed to pay out TV investment	895,520
Total redeemers needed	2,655,520

2,655,520 redeemers on 44,000,000 circulation = 6.04%

CASE H: PROMOTION SUPPORT ADVERTISING

You are selling a book through direct mail for $10. Your allowable is $2.50. You have conducted a test of TV support advertising. Media costs and orders in a group of test and control markets follow. Is it worthwhile to expand the support program? Would it be worth expanding if total orders in the test markets were 3,875?

Control Markets (no TV support):

	Last Year			This Year		
	Media Costs, Direct Mail	No. of Orders	CPO	Media Costs, Direct Mail	No. of Orders	CPO
Market 1:	$1,000	410	2.44	$1,100	490	2.24
Market 2:	2,500	1,060	2.36	2,750	1,250	2.20
Market 3:	1,300	530	2.45	1,350	625	2.16
	4,800	2,000	2.40	5,200	2,365	2.20

Test Markets (TV support):

	Last Year		
	Media Costs, Direct Mail	No. of Orders	CPO
Market 1:	$3,000	1,270	2.36
Market 2:	1,800	725	2.48
Market 3:	1,200	505	2.38
	6,000	2,500	2.40

This Year

	Media Costs, Direct Mail	TV Costs	Total Media Costs	No. of Orders	CPO
Market 1:	$3,200	$1,100	$4,300	2,050	2.10
Market 2:	2,000	750	2,750	1,275	2.16
Market 3:	1,300	450	1,750	825	2.12
	6,500	2,300	8,800	4,150	2.12

Solution to Case H

Comparative results in the control and test markets over the two years were as follows:

| | **Last Year** | | | **This Year** | | |
	Media Costs	No. of Orders	CPO	Media Costs	No. of Orders	CPO
Control Markets:	$4,800	2,000	2.40	$5,200	2,365	2.20
Test Markets:	6,000	2,500	2.40	8,800	4,150	2.12

It clearly is worth expanding the TV support. The overall CPO improved more versus last year in the test markets than in the control markets. In addition to a CPO well below the allowable, volume in the test markets increased far more than in the control markets (+66% vs. +18% in the control markets). The increase in the test markets is very consistent from market to market, which adds important support to the overall results.

TV support still would be worth expanding, if total orders in the test markets were 3,875. Notice that 3,875 orders at a cost of $8,800 comes to $2.27 per order, which is well below the allowable and better than last year. Direct mail alone costs $6,500. Assume that without support it would have produced a $2.20 CPO, the same as in the control markets, or 2,955 orders. TV cost $2,300. If there had been 3,875 total orders, and direct mail alone should have produced 2,955, then TV would have produced an additional 920 orders (3,875 – 2,955). Notice that 920 orders at a cost of $2,300 comes to $2.50 per order. Thus, even if there had been 275 fewer orders than were actually received, and the entire reduction were "charged" to TV, it still would have produced orders at the allowable and increased volume significantly.

CASE I: CONTINUOUS SHIPMENT

A direct marketer is offering a set of 30 books on a continuous shipment. That is, after you buy the first book, about every 30 days you are sent another book in the series. You may examine the book and return it, or keep it and pay for it. Keep in mind that it is better NOT to number the volumes in an offer of this kind. This allows you to vary the lead (first) book offered. It's also important to recognize that often there are about 5 to 8 books in the offer that stimulate high interest. As you continue to ship, the value of the product declines.

This offer states that you get the first book on a 10-day free trial. If you like it, you pay $10, and each month you receive another book in the series. If you don't like the book, you may return it and pay nothing, in which case your name will be purged. The same offer holds true with each subsequent book. Following are the known facts:

Selling price of each book		$10.00
Cost of book in package (Invoice enclosed with book)	$2.00	
Postage for book	.50	
Processing and labeling	.50	
Repacking returned books	1.00	
Phone cost	1.00	

All purchasers of the first book will get one more book before their names are purged for not paying. About 20 percent in each category will not keep the book, and 30 percent of those won't pay for it. What can your client pay for advertising per order if he or she wants to break even after the third shipment?

Solution to Case I

Profits in this type of offer come from subsequent sales. Your client is looking to pay out (break even) after three shipments. There are also other costs involved, such as the value of money over a 3-month period, amortization of commercials, etc. These have been deleted for simplicity reasons.

Sales of first book

Books shipped	1,000	
Less books returned	200	
	800	
Books not paid for	240	
Books sold	560	5,600
Cost of books 800 × $2		
(20 will be returned to be used later)	$1,600	
Postage	1,000	
Phones	850	
Processing returns @ .50	500	
Repackaging 200 × $1	200	
Total Cost	4,150	
Gross profit on first shipment		1,450

Sales of second book

Books shipped (of which 240 are to non-payers on first book)	800	
Therefore, "live" prospects receiving second book	560	
Less books returned	112	
Less books not paid for	134	
Books sold	314	3,140
Cost of books	1,376	
Postage	800	
Phones	—	
Processing	400	
Repackaging	112	
Total cost	2,688	
Gross profit on second shipment		$452

Sales of third book

Books shipped (of which 240 are to non-payers on first book and 134 are to non-payers of second book)	688	
Therefore, "live" prospects receiving third book	314	
Less books returned	63	
Less books not paid for	75	
Books sold	176	1,760
Cost of books	896	
Postage	448	
Phones	—	
Processing	224	
Repackaging	63	
Total cost	1,631	
Gross profit on third shipment		$129

Gross profit on first three shipments:	
First shipment	1,450
Second shipment	452
Third shipment	129
	2,031

Funds available for advertising ($2,031 ÷ 1,000 orders) = $2.03
(Magic Number)

CHAPTER 11

Record Keeping

In the previous chapter, we demonstrated various methods of arriving at the Magic Number for specific types of offers. Because direct marketing is a numbers game, and the Magic Number is crucial to the success or failure of any direct marketing venture, accuracy of the records is absolutely essential.

THE IMPORTANCE OF ACCURACY

To emphasize the consequences of even the smallest error in record keeping, let's look at what happens when one misreads a station's call letters. If you have schedules running on KOMO in Seattle, Washington, and KOMU in Columbus, Missouri, and you credit KOMO with KOMU's orders, you might later decide to renew KOMO and not renew KOMU. You would have rescheduled an unprofitable station and failed to renew one that was profitable. This example clearly indicates how easy it is to turn a small error into a financial fiasco.

This type of record-keeping error also applies to direct mail. One simple mistake could result in the continued purchase of names from a nonproductive list or in the repurchase of unprofitable print exposures. When purchasing broadcast or print schedules, everything starts with a contract. These contracts can be individually typed (see Exhibit 11–1) or can be created using a computer (see Exhibit 11–2). Basically, radio and TV contracts use the same forms. The form should be designed so that it clearly shows the day and time periods that are being purchased, the starting and ending date of the contract, and the cost of each individual commercial exposure.

When run of station (ROS) schedules are purchased for a package rate, the individual commercial costs should be allocated to the commercials based on the various ratios of costs to the exposure time. That is, if late night costs 30 percent as much as early access, then that cost relationship should be used in pricing each exposure in the package.

EXHIBIT 11-1
Broadcast Contract

A. Eicoff & Company A DIVISION OF OGILVY & MATHER
520 NORTH MICHIGAN AVENUE · CHICAGO, ILLINOIS 60611 · (312) 944-2300
676 THIRD AVENUE, SUITE 2400 · NEW YORK, NEW YORK, 10017 · (212) 883-9500

AGENCY-1

BROADCAST ORDER

No. 82122

STATION:
AFFILIATE: REPRESENTATIVE:
CITY: STATE:
DATE: 3/25/85

Please furnish Broadcasting Facilities to: Acting as Agent for:
ADDRESS: CITY: STATE:
PRODUCT: CODE:

CLIENT No. ___ STATION ___

JAN.	A	MAY	E	SEPT.	I
FEB.	B	JUNE	F	OCT.	J
MAR.	C	JULY	G	NOV.	K
APR.	D	AUG.	H	DEC.	L

LENGTH	DAY	TIME	TIMES PER WEEK	PROGRAM	COST PER SPOT
BDCT.	M-F	8 - 9P	5X		600.00

SCHEDULE DATES
1/28 - 2/3/85

NO. OF WEEKS 1 FOR 5 SHOWS PER WEEK $ 3000 /WK TOTAL FOR 1 WEEKS $ 3000.00

Per _____ A. EICOFF & COMPANY

INSTRUCTIONS:

FORM 4 3/82 2.5M

EXHIBIT 11-2
Computer-Generated Broadcast Contract

A. Eicoff & Company A DIVISION OF OGILVY & MATHER
401 N. MICHIGAN AVE. CHICAGO, IL 60611
PHONE: 312-527-7100

TIMEBKS

BROADCAST ORDER

WPWR-TV
50 IND 196

	Contract Number	Date
PRODUCT	3-0219-227-5	2/23/
CLIENT TIME-LIFE BOOKS	TPEE0152	
777 DUKE STREET		
ALEXANDRIA VA 22314	2/01/ THRU 2/28/	

STATION   W P W R -TV
MARKET   CHICAGO
FIRM   W P W R - T V
REP   KIM MC LOUGHLIN
BUYER   JULIE WHITEHOUSE

REF. NO.	COMM. LENGTH	DAYS MTWTFSS	TIMES START	END	PROGRAM	SPOT COST	* * * * * WEEK OF * * * * * *				
							FEB 1	FEB 8	FEB 15	FEB 22	
1.	120	MTWTF	6A	9A		$175.00	4	4	4	4	
2.	120	MTWTF	2P	430P		$240.00	3	3	3	3	
3.	120	SU 6A	11A			$550.00	1	1	1	1	

ORIGINAL CONTRACT TOTALS   AMOUNT $7,880.00   SPOTS   32 **

FEBRUARY $7,880.00	FEB 1	$1,970.00
	FEB 8	$1,970.00
	FEB 15	$1,970.00
	FEB 22	$1,970.00

After the broadcast contract is written, it must be properly recorded in the space provided on the record keeping form. (See Exhibit 11–3.) The specific days of the schedule should then be indicated in the proper monthly column. As the count reports come in from the phone answering services and you receive confirmation reports from the client, they should be immediately entered in the space provided. (See Exhibits 11–4, 11–5 and 11–6.)

STREAMLINING THE RECORD-KEEPING PROCESS

The report form used in this chapter was designed by A. Eicoff & Company and has been accepted as the standard for the industry. In order to minimize errors, each product is kept in a separate loose-leaf binder, and each has its own individual colored sheet. Although count entries could be made by computer, the entries from the phone answering service and client are entered by hand by each media buyer. This forces the buyer to track the results of every commercial on every station.

The counts from the answering service and the client are entered individually so that the agency can compare the phone service counts with the physical counts received by the client. Reporting errors will be caught, and the client will receive all reported orders.

Because the Magic Number determines the fate of a schedule, it is important that all direct marketing broadcast schedules be bought on a week-to-week basis. If multiple-week schedules are purchased to ensure time reservations, it is important that the contract have a 1-week cancellation clause. Otherwise, the purchaser must be prepared to replace the offer with another direct marketing offer as soon as it stops producing at a profitable level.

Computerized phone answering services are now able to provide direct marketers with direct feed into their computers. This interfacing is becoming more and more popular, because it saves the expense of retyping shipping labels and eliminates the need for the advertising agency to reenter counts from client reports.

When the process is computerized, the media contracts and exposure mail counts can be instantly compared. The computer can be programmed to "red flag" any media cost that exceeds the Magic Number. With this instant information, the media buyer can continuously monitor the relationship between days of the week, times of day, and rating levels as they affect order production. The computer has made great strides in giving the media buyer more time to negotiate with stations for spot times.

EXHIBIT 11-3
Schedule Record-Keeping Form

STATION *KBMY* CITY *Omaha* STATE *Nebraska* REP *Blair*
CLIENT *Beer Club* REP. FIRM _____
MAIL _____ PRODUCT *Membership*
PHONE *237-1444* TAPE CODE *BC1-20*

	DAYS	TIME	COST	DAYS	TIME	COST	DAYS	TIME	COST	
1	M-Su	6-9A	2 x 120	M-Su	9A-12N	5-120				1
2	1/18-1/25	9A-12N	2 x 330	2/15-2/22	12N-6P	2-330				2
3	$2860	12N-6P	2 x 330	$4380	6P-12M	4-330				3
4		6P-12	2 x 400		12M-6A	3-400				4
5		12M-6A	5 x 60		6A-9A	10-60				5
6	M-Su	6-9A	2 x 120							6
7	1/26-1/31	9A-MN	2 x 330							7
8	$2860	6P-12M	2 x 330							8
9		12M-6A	2 x 60							9
10		6-9A	2 x 120							10
11	M-Su	6-9A	2 x 120							11
12	2/1-2/7	9A-12N	2 x 330							12
13	$2860	12N-6P	3 x 330							13
14		6P-12M	3 x 400							14
15		12M-6A	5 x 60							15
16		6A-9A	3 x 120							16

	JAN PHONE	JAN MAIL	FEB PHONE	FEB MAIL	MAR PHONE	MAR MAIL	APR PHONE	APR MAIL	MAY PHONE	MAY MAIL	JUNE PHONE	JUNE MAIL	
1													1
2			36/17										2
3			88/31										3
4			41/27										4
5			17/6										5
6			104/52										6
7			95/49										7
8			30/8										8
9			33/16										9
10			38/14										10
11			41/15										11
12	17/9		53/32										12
13	15/8		17/8										13
14	12/9		78/32										14
15	3/3		123/38										15
16			61/40										16
17	36/10		63/31										17
18	3/2		71/22										18
19			58/33										19
20	28/15		249/150										20
21	12/10		128/78										21
22	15/8		91/39										22
23	15/6		55/42										23
24	12/7		40/10										24
25			12/10										25
26	15/9		3/7										26
27	2/11		1/1										27
28	19/4												28
29	26/4		1/1										29
30	3/12												30
31	2/10												31
T													T
TT													TT

EXHIBIT 11-4
Phone Service Report

TMS-902 SOURCE REPORT		WATS MARKETING OF AMERICA, INC.					RUN DATE		PAGE

BATCH DATE

CLIENT - 10029 EICOFF
PRODUCT - MENS2 REPORT VERSION NUMBER - 0
ATTN -

ORDER DATE 07/31/93

MARKET	SOURCE	ORDERS	CCRD	NONCRD	UPS 1	UPS 2	SHIPTO	KEY CODE	NUMBER	ST	CO.
CABLE	MISC	4		4				T750166	555-2744		USA
SOUTH BEND-ELKHART	WSJV	1		1				T7S0099	228-5010	IN	USA
WACO-TEMPLE	KWKT	1		1				T7S0100	228-5010	IN	USA
TOTAL		6		6							USA

ORDER DATE 08/01/93

MARKET	SOURCE	ORDERS	CCRD	NONCRD	UPS 1	UPS 2	SHIPTO	KEY CODE	NUMBER	ST	CO.
ANCHORAGE	KTVA	2		2				T7S0062	228-3399	AK	USA
ATLANTA	WAGA	31	5	26	1			T7S0001	228-2343	GA	USA
BATON ROUGE	WAFB	13	2	11	3			T7S0039	228-3111	LA	USA
	WGHB	1		1				T7S0003	228-2343	LA	USA
CABLE	AMOR	1	1					T7Y0001	228-2299		USA
	CMTV	125	29	96	14			T7C0002	228-1500		USA
	CMTV	22	9	13	3			T7C0002	228-1500		CAN
	CNN	266	73	193	23			T7C0003	228-1688		CAN
	CNN	11	3	8				T7C0003	228-1688		CAN
	CNN	2	1	1				T7C0032	228-5020		USA
	CNNH	1	1					T7C0004	228-1800		USA
	COME	23	3	20	1			T7C0005	228-1881		USA
	DISC	469	166	303	45			T7C0006	228-1990		USA
	LIFE	206	46	160	25			T7C0008	228-2101		USA
	PREV	27	6	21	4			T7C0010	228-2110		USA
	STUN	21	5	16	3			T7Y0012	234-9080		USA
	SUPE	81	13	68	7			T7C0013	228-2210		USA
	SUPE	1		1	1			T7C0013	228-2210		CAN
	TLC	17	6	11	2			T7C0007	228-1999		USA
	TLC	5		5	1			T7C0007	228-1999		CAN
	TWC	48	21	27	5			T7C0016	228-2225		USA
	VIDE	4		4	2			T7S0034	824-1800		USA
CHARLOTTE	WSOC	4	1	3	2			T7S0005	228-2343		
NC											USA
CHICAGO	WGBO	1		1				T7S0066	228-3399		
IL											USA
CLEVELAND	WOIO	9	1	8				T7S0008	228-2343	OH	USA
COLUMBIA, SC	WLTX	1		1				T7S0012	228-3111	SC	USA
EUREKA	KVIQ	1	1					T7S0081	228-2343	CA	USA
GREENWOOD-GREENVILLE	WXVT	9		9				T7S0044	228-3111	MS	USA
HONOLULU	KGMB	11	3	8	2			T7S0084	228-2343	HI	USA
	KHNL	1		1	1			T7S0045	228-3111	HI	USA
LAS VEGAS	KFBT	11	1	10	1			T7S0049	228-3111	NV	USA
LINCOLN-HASTINGS-											
KEARNEY	KHGI	1	1					T7S0050	228-3111	NE	USA
MANKATO	KEYC	1	1					T7S0051	228-3111	MN	USA
NEW YORK	WPIX	1		1				T7S0086	228-2343	NY	USA
OCALA	WOGX	3		3				T7S0083	228-2343	FL	USA
PHILADELPHIA	WCAU	91	18	73	15			T7S0070	228-3399	PA	USA
RALEIGH-DURHAM	WYED	15	2	13	1			T7S0094	752-7900	NC	USA
WACO-TEMPLE	KWKT	1		1				T7S0100	228-5010	TX	USA
WICHITA FALLS-LAWTON	KJTL	7	2	5				T7S0076	228-3399	TX	USA
WILKES BARRE-SCRANTON	WOLF	3		3				T7S0095	752-7900	PA	USA
TOTAL		1509	408	1101	157						USA
		39	12	27	5						CAN

BATCH DATE 08/01/93

PRODUCT	—TOTALS—	ORDERS	CCRD	NONCRD	UPS 1	UPS 2	SHIPTO
MENS2	GRAND TOTALS	1554	420	1134	162		
	(USA)	1515	408	1107	157		
	(CAN)	39	12	27	5		

EXHIBIT 11-5
Phone Service Report by Hour

TMD-022   SOURCE SUMMARY REPORT   WATS MARKETING OF AMERICA, INC.   RUN DATE   PAGE

CLIENT - 10029 EICOFF   BATCH DATE
PRODUCT - MENS2

SOURCE ST CODE	NUMBER DIALED	ORDERS	LIT REQ	CUST SERV	INCOMPLETE	RESP1	RESP2	RESP3	RESP4	SHIP 1	SHIP 2	SHIP 3	NO. OF CR CARDS	IT?	Q?
COMEDY	800-228-1881	23	0	3	4	1	0	0	0	0	0	0	3		3?
DISC	800-228-1990	469	0	20	25	45	0	0	0	0	0	0	166		4?
LIFE	800-228-2101	206	0	7	9	25	0	0	0	0	0	0	46		2?
MISC	800-555-2744	4	0	0	0	0	0	0	0	0	0	0	0		?
PREVUE	800-228-2110	27	0	4	1	4	0	0	0	0	0	0	6		2?
STUNTS	800-234-9080	21	0	1	2	3	0	0	0	0	0	0	5		2?
SUPER	800-228-2210	82	0	4	4	8	0	0	0	0	0	0	13		8?
(USA)		81	0	4	4	7	0	0	0	0	0	0	13		8?
(CANADA)		1	0	0	0	1	0	0	0	0	0	0	0		?
TLC	800-228-1999	22	0	3	2	3	0	0	0	0	0	0	6		2?
(USA)		17	0	3	2	2	0	0	0	0	0	0	6		1?
(CANADA)		5	0	0	0	1	0	0	0	0	0	0	0		?
TWC	800-228-2225	48	0	1	5	5	0	0	0	0	0	0	21		4?
VIDEO SPOT	800-824-1800	4	0	0	0	2	0	0	0	0	0	0	0		?
SOURCE TYPE CABLE TV / MISC.		1334	0	71	74	136	0	0	0	0	0	0	383		133?
(USA)		1295	0	70	72	131	0	0	0	0	0	0	371		129?
(CANADA)		39	0	1	2	5	0	0	0	0	0	0	12		3?
ZZZZ	800-752-7900	0	0	0	1	0	0	0	0	0	0	0	0		?
ZZZZ	800-228-2343	0	0	0	0	0	0	0	0	0	0	0	0		?
ZZZZ	800-228-3399	0	0	0	2	0	0	0	0	0	0	0	0		?
SOURCE TYPE UNKNOWN SOURCE		0	0	0	4	0	0	0	0	0	0	0	0		?
PRODUCT CODE MENS2 TOTALS		1554	0	81	88	162	0	0	0	0	0	0	420		155?
(USA)		1515	0	80	86	157	0	0	0	0	0	0	408		151?
(CANADA)		39	0	1	2	5	0	0	0	0	0	0	12		3?

REPORT VERSION NUMBER—

NUMBER OF CALLS — RESPONSES — NUMBER OF SHIP-TOS

EXHIBIT 11-6
Phone Service Report by Phone Number

TMD-024   COMBINED SOURCING REPORT   WATS MARKETING OF AMERICA, INC.   RUN DATE   PAGE

CLIENT - 10029 EICOFF   BATCH DATE

PRODUCT -   ENTRY DATE 08/01/93   REPORT VERSION NUMBER - 02

SOURCE — SUMMARY BY HOUR

ST CODE	0000	0100	0200	0300	0400	0500	0600	0700	0800	0900	1000	1100	1200	1300	1400	1500	1600	1700	1800	1900	2000	2100	2200	2300
ORDERS	82	36	12	80	3	0	5	13	12	46	32	8	64	189	287	94	48	25	43	20	308	46	22	73
(USA)	82	33	11	79	3	0	5	11	12	41	32	8	60	188	276	86	47	24	43	19	308	46	22	73
(CANADA)	0	3	1	1	0	0	0	2	0	5	0	0	4	1	11	8	1	1	0	1	0	0	0	0
CUST SRVC	2	7	0	3	0	0	0	2	1	2	1	1	1	6	15	7	1	7	2	0	17	3	0	3
INCOMPLETE	5	7	4	5	0	0	0	1	1	1	3	1	2	11	11	5	2	1	4	2	16	4	0	2

ENTRY DATE 08/01/93

NO. OF ORDER CALLS	1548
NO. OF CREDIT CARDS	420
NO. OF NON-CRED CARDS	1128
RESPONSE#1	162
CREDIT CARDS WITH RESPONSE#1	29
NON-CRED CARDS WITH RESPONSE#1	133
ITEM QUANTITY	1548
NO. OF CUSTOMER SERVICE	81
NO. OF INCOMPLETE CALLS	88
TOTAL NO. OF CALLS	1717

PROD MENS2

	0000	0100	0200	0300	0400	0500	0600	0700	0800	0900	1000	1100	1200	1300	1400	1500	1600	1700	1800	1900	2000	2100	2200	2300
ORDERS	82	36	12	80	3	0	5	13	12	46	32	8	64	191	288	96	48	25	43	20	308	46	22	74
(USA)	82	33	11	79	3	0	5	11	12	41	32	8	60	190	277	88	47	24	43	19	308	46	22	74
(CANADA)	0	3	1	1	0	0	0	2	0	5	0	0	4	1	11	8	1	1	0	1	0	0	0	0
CUST SRVC	2	7	0	3	0	0	0	2	1	2	1	1	1	6	15	7	1	7	2	0	17	3	0	3
INCOMPLETE	5	7	4	5	0	0	0	1	1	1	3	1	2	11	11	5	2	1	4	2	16	4	0	2

PROD CODE MENS2

NO. OF ORDER CALLS	1554
NO. OF CREDIT CARDS	420
NO. OF NON-CRED CARDS	1134
RESPONSE#1	162
CREDIT CARDS WITH RESPONSE#1	29
NON-CRED CARDS WITH RESPONSE#1	133
ITEM QUANTITY	1554
NO. OF LITERATURE REQUESTS	0
NO. OF CUSTOMER SERVICE	81
NO. OF INCOMPLETE CALLS	88
TOTAL NO. OF CALLS	1723

The computer's ability to produce an instantaneous spot-by-spot, station-by-station activity report is, however, the computer's greatest benefit. Reports of total advertising expenditures, total orders, and the cost per order on a day-by-day, week-by-week, month-by-month, campaign-by-campaign basis allow the direct marketer to evaluate profits and losses at any instant and allow for immediate adjustments that can maximize profits.

Afterword

This book has covered a great deal of territory, ranging from the pitchman's past to cable's future. Despite the diversity of style and substance within this book, there is an underlying theme that pertains to everything I've written and to everyone reading this. Whether you are an advertising agency executive or a *Fortune* 500 company president or an industrial manufacturer or a chain-store operator or an inventor or a consumer, there is one message I wish to convey above all else: Tradition is one of the greatest deterrents to progress.

In the world of advertising and marketing, reliance on traditional methods is ultimately fatal—fatal to a business career, a product, or even an entire company. Those who rely on tradition will continually avoid innovation, modernization, and growth. They will not be able to change with the changing times.

Therefore, I am dismayed when I see agencies and advertisers making the same mistakes day in and day out simply because they did it that way yesterday or because they tried a new approach two years ago and it didn't work, so they refuse to try again. Too many advertisers and agencies create unmotivating advertising because they are bound to the tradition of awards, theoretical research, prime-time buys, and bureaucratic hierarchies. And they are horrified by such nontraditional approaches as the theory of sales resistance, the isolation factor, and key outlet marketing.

The problem in many agencies and companies is that the entrepreneur is no longer the policy maker. I am talking about the entrepreneur who started the company, who had that spark of intuition that often took precedence over logic. In many cases, the entrepreneur has been replaced by the MBA, whose business decisions are governed only by tradition and logic. This "logic" prevents the MBA from understanding why ratings or cost per thousand, for example, should not be the only criteria in buying TV time.

At this point, I should clarify the difference between tradition and experience. Tradition means doing something today because that is the way it has always been done. Experience is the realization that it doesn't work that way any more. Unfortunately, the new generation of management is often short on experience and long on tradition. They use tradition as a crutch, leaning too heavily on it for support. It's safe to justify one's actions by saying, "Well, that's the way it's always been done." Although this approach might provide someone with an excuse when things don't work, it doesn't provide the motivation to take risks that are necessary for progress.

In the near future, the business world will undergo numerous, significant changes. And the more things change, the more unfeasible traditional methods become. For instance, one significant change that is taking place is the installation of sophisticated computer systems in virtually every mass-merchandising operation in the country. These computers feed a central computer with day-to-day movement reports for the advertisers, and each store is given an ethnic and affluence factor breakdown.

For the first time, advertisers have a foolproof method of measuring how their advertising affects sales. Once a campaign breaks, they can look at daily computer printouts and determine whether that campaign is affecting sales positively or negatively. Agencies no longer have the luxury of such traditional practices as running long, unproductive advertising schedules and relying on awards, high recall scores, or brand awareness as the criteria for measuring success. When the printout gives a market-by-market, store-by-store, hour-by-hour breakdown of a product's sales, none of the traditional barometers of advertising's effectiveness will mean anything, except the NCR (National Cash Register) report.

As this widespread system of computers expands, agencies and advertisers will be forced to restructure their advertising, marketing, and merchandising strategies. Those strategies will be forced to become more flexible and innovative, adaptable to a sudden change in sales results. Agencies will have to be able to write and produce a new commercial at the drop of a hat . . . or the drop of sales. Advertisers will have to have a first-person direct line with the agency media buyers who place their advertising. How else can they react to the fluctuating sales in each market?

With all due modesty, I would like to think that I have laid the groundwork for some of the nontraditional approaches that will be used in the future. The "alternative" media buying, marketing, and creative techniques I have discussed in this book are designed solely to maximize sales. In the computerized, high-definition, interactive future, that will be an advertiser's only consideration.

In fact, I can see a day in the future when these nontraditional approaches become (dare I use the word) "traditional." When that happens, I hope a new generation of entrepreneurs will challenge the status quo. I hope that there will always be some brazen young entrepreneur who has the courage to make such a nontraditional statement as "Satisfaction Guaranteed or Your Money Back."

1993 World Direct Marketing Broadcast Summary

The following information was received from Ogilvy offices worldwide relative to the use of broadcast direct marketing in their various countries. In many cases, the rates indicated for the various media are estimated rates subject to negotiation. Where rates are omitted, either the media refused to quote any rate or the variations of rates are too numerous to list.

AUSTRIA (VIENNA)

Both radio and television are Austrian owned. Cable is owned by German companies.

Radio:	60 and 120 seconds accepted
TV:	60 and 120 seconds accepted
Cable:	60, 120, and infomercials

RADIO	60	120
Prime	$6,000	$10,000
Access	2,500	5,000
Fringe	2,000	4,000

TV	60	120
Prime	$50,000	$100,000
Access	30,000	60,000
Fringe	20,000	40,000

CABLE		

See Germany

AUSTRALIA (MAINLAND)

Both radio and television are privately owned. As of 1993, there is no cable. Direct marketers are using both radio and television.

Radio: 60 and 120 seconds accepted
TV: 60 and 120 seconds accepted

RADIO	60	120
Prime	$2,840	$5,680
Access	2,090	4,180
Fringe	1,440	2,880

TV		
Prime	$27,550	$55,100
Access	19,280	38,560
Fringe	11,250	22,500

Australia (Tasmania)

RADIO	60	120
Prime	$70	$130
Fringe	40	60

TV		
Prime	$180	$280
Fringe	90	140

BELGIUM

Belgian communications are divided into north and south areas, with radio, TV, and cable stations both government and publicly owned.

Radio: Up to 60 seconds acceptable
TV: 60 seconds and up to 60 minutes, infomercials
Cable: Up to 60 seconds acceptable

RADIO	60	120
Prime	$1,546	N.A.
Access	1,215	N.A.
Fringe	450	N.A.

TV NORTH		
Prime	$24,000	$30,700
Fringe	22,000	Sat. 11–12 A.M. only

TV SOUTH		
Prime	$12,000	$21,500
Fringe	11,000	Sat. 10–11 A.M. only

CABLE		
Prime	$1,200	N.A.
Access	400	N.A.
Fringe	600	N.A.

BRAZIL

Port Alegre

Brazilian radio and television are both government and publicly owned. Delivery service has improved over the past few years, but Brazil is still having phone problems in handling high volume. Also, all direct marketers on the networks use the same phone number. Port Alegre radio and television accept 60- and 120-second commercials, but the Port Alegre network does not take direct marketing commercials as yet.

São Paulo

See Port Alegre for post office and phone details. São Paulo does accept direct marketers.

RADIO	60	120	INFOMERCIALS
	OK	OK	OK

Rates were not available at publication, but some regional networks are accepting 20 percent per order contracts. The larger markets are accepting direct marketers, but rates vary.

CANADA

Radio and television are both privately and publicly owned in Canada. Both public and private radio and TV stations accept direct marketing, which can be purchased on networks or on a spot basis. Radio, TV, and cable stations all accept 60s, 120s, and infomercials, and all markets are subject to package negotiations.

Toronto

RADIO	60	120	INFOMERCIALS
Prime	N.A.	N.A.	N.A.
Access	N.A.	N.A.	N.A.
Fringe	$150	$225	$1,500

TELEVISION	60	120	INFOMERCIALS
Prime			(Globe) $18,000
Access			3,500
Fringe			1,500
ROS	90	165	

Montreal

RADIO	60	120	INFOMERCIALS
Prime	N.A.	N.A.	N.A.
Access	N.A.	N.A.	N.A.
Fringe	$120	$190	$1,250

TELEVISION	60	120	INFOMERCIALS
Prime			$6,000
Access			4,500
Fringe			3,000
ROS	50	85	

Vancouver

RADIO	60	120	INFOMERCIALS
Prime	N.A.	N.A.	N.A.
Access	N.A.	N.A.	N.A.
Fringe	$135	$200	$1,350

TELEVISION	60	120	INFOMERCIALS
Prime			N.A.
Access			$6,000
Fringe			4,500
ROS	110	200	

CHINA

Beijing

Radio, television, and cable are all government owned. Government stations solicit commercial advertising and allow up to 120-second commercials, which direct marketers are presently using. Infomercials are now allowed as of July 1, 1993.

RADIO	60	120
Prime only	$500	$1,000

TV		
	$7,600	$15,200

CABLE		
	$4,200	$8,400

Shanghai

All radio and TV stations in mainland China are government owned. As of July 1, 1993, they accept no direct marketing commercials and limit commercial length in all media to 60 seconds.

RADIO	
Cost of 30-second prime commercial	$120

TV	
Cost of 30-second prime commercial	$900

ECUADOR

Radio, television, and cable are privately owned. There has been no attempt to purchase infomercial time on any of the media as of 1993, so no rates are available.

RADIO	60	120	INFOMERCIALS
Prime	$10	Various	Negotiable
Access	10	Various	Negotiable
Fringe	10	Various	Negotiable

TV	60	120	INFOMERCIALS
Prime	$825	Negotiable	Negotiable
Access	380	Negotiable	Negotiable
Fringe	255	Negotiable	Negotiable

CABLE			
Prime	$123	Negotiable	Negotiable
Access	65	Negotiable	Negotiable
Fringe	45	Negotiable	Negotiable

FINLAND (HELSINKI)

There are both government and privately owned radio and TV stations, but the publicly owned stations are noncommercial.

RADIO	60	120	INFOMERCIALS
Prime	$2,100	$2,900	N.A.

TV	60	120	INFOMERCIALS
Prime	$5,000	$26,000	$21,000

CABLE	60	120	INFOMERCIALS
Prime	$1,900	$3,500	Various

FRANCE (PARIS)

Radio and television in France are both government and privately owned. Cable is privately owned. All media accept direct marketing commercials. Cable still has minimal penetration as of July 1, 1993, and has not proven to be an effective direct marketing medium. Because of the high cost of both prime and prime access, only fringe time has proven to be profitable for direct marketers.

RADIO	60	120	INFOMERCIALS
Prime	$10,000	$20,000	N.A.
Access	4,000	8,000	N.A.
Fringe	N.A.	N.A.	N.A.

TV			
Prime	$55,000	N.A.	N.A.
Access	40,000	$70,000	N.A.
Fringe	Negotiable	Negotiable	N.A.

CABLE			
Prime	$3,000	$5,000	Negotiable
Access	2,000	3,500	Negotiable
Fringe	Negotiable	Negotiable	Negotiable

GREECE (ATHENS)

Radio and television are both publicly and privately owned. Greece has no cable as of July 31, 1993. Both radio and TV commercials are limited to 60 seconds. Neither radio nor television has accepted broadcast direct marketing commercials.

RADIO	60	120	INFOMERCIALS
Prime	$696	N.A.	N.A.
Access	394	N.A.	N.A.
Fringe	240	N.A.	N.A.

TV			
Prime	$7,057	N.A.	N.A.
Access	3,068	N.A.	N.A.
Fringe	2,148	N.A.	N.A.

HUNGARY (BUDAPEST)

All radio and TV stations are government owned. There are no direct marketing offers on the air as of July 1, 1993. Radio, television, and cable do accept 120-second commercials.

RADIO	60	120	INFOMERCIALS
Prime	$1,500	Negotiable	N.A.

TV			
Prime	$11,000	$22,000	N.A.

CABLE			
Prime	$6,000	Negotiable	N.A.

HONG KONG

All radio and TV stations are privately owned. Cable will be initiated in 1994. Infomercials are available on radio and television, but as of July 1, 1993, there are no direct marketing commercials using either radio or television.

RADIO	60	120	INFOMERCIALS
Prime	$650	$1,300	Negotiable
Access	600	1,200	Negotiable
Fringe	500	1,000	Negotiable

TV			
Prime	$13,000	$26,000	Negotiable
Access	8,000	16,000	Negotiable
Fringe	3,000	6,000	Negotiable

CABLE			

Not available until 1994

INDIA

Bombay

Radio, TV, and cable stations are government owned. There are presently direct marketing commercials running on television, cable, and from the satellite.

RADIO	60	120	INFOMERCIALS
Prime	$1,253	$2,400	Negotiable
Fringe	361	700	Negotiable

TV			
Prime	$17,142	$34,284	Negotiable
Fringe	8,571	17,162	Negotiable

CABLE			
Prime	$20,571	$41,192	Negotiable

Calcutta

All radio, TV, and cable stations in India are government owned. Although they have no restrictions relative to direct marketers and allow 120-second commercials on television, there are no direct marketers using any broadcast media. As of July 1, 1993, cable was still disorganized and had no rate card.

RADIO
30-second maximum time allowed

TV	60	120	INFOMERCIALS
Prime	$23,226	$46,451	N.A.
Fringe	2,903	5,806	N.A.

New Delhi

Radio, TV, and cable stations in India are all owned by the government. Direct marketers are using all media.

RADIO	60	120	INFOMERCIALS
Prime	$80	Negotiable	Negotiable
TV			
Prime	$23,226	$46,451.61	Negotiable
CABLE			
Prime	$241	$483.86	Negotiable

INDONESIA (JAKARTA)

Radio and television are both government and privately owned. There is no cable as of July 1, 1993. Although both radio and television accept commercials up to 30 minutes in length, there are no direct marketers presently using broadcast.

RADIO	60	120	INFOMERCIALS
Prime	$65	$125	Negotiable
Fringe	48	95	Negotiable
TV			
Prime	$14,000	$28,000	N.A.
Fringe	4,000	8,000	Negotiable

KENYA (NAIROBI)

Radio is government owned, and television is both government and privately owned. As of July 1, 1993, there is no cable in Kenya. Although both radio and television will accept direct marketing commercials, there are none scheduled as of July 1, 1993.

RADIO	60	120	INFOMERCIALS
Prime	$228	$456	$562
Access	162	325	562
Fringe	143	285	502

TV			
Prime	$280	$560	$675
Access	200	400	675
Fringe	132	264	469

KOREA (SEOUL)

Radio and television are both government and privately owned. As of July 1, 1993, there is no cable in Korea, nor is there any broadcast direct marketing. Stations do sell 15-minute infomercial segments in all time categories.

RADIO	60	120	INFOMERCIALS[1]
Prime	$625	$1,250	$625
Access	250	500	250
Fringe	125	250	125

TV			
Prime	$25,000		$5,625
Access	5,000		5,000
Fringe	1,250		1,250

NETHERLANDS (AMSTERDAM)

Radio and television in the Netherlands are both privately and government owned. Cable is XTEL+IP+STERX, originating over Europe but distributed by language. Direct marketing offers are running in all media.

RADIO	60	120	INFOMERCIALS
Prime	$4,975	$10,275	N.A.
Access	2,591	4,922	N.A.
Fringe	2,591	4,922	N.A.

RADIO WABEL			
Prime	$1,865	$3,730	N.A.
Access	1,399	2,798	N.A.
Fringe	1,399	2,798	N.A.

XTEL+IP+STERX			
Prime	$16,781	$33,575	N.A.
Access	7,461	14,922	N.A.
Fringe	6,520	13,040	N.A.

NORWAY (OSLO)

Radio and television are both government and privately owned. There is one state-owned TV channel and two radio channels. There are three privately owned TV stations and hundreds of privately owned radio stations. All media accept direct marketing commercials, including infomercials.

RADIO	60	120	INFOMERCIALS
Prime	$5,000	$10,000	Negotiable
Access	3,000	5,000	Negotiable

TV	60	120	INFOMERCIALS
Prime	$20,000	$35,000	Negotiable
Access	10,000	15,000	Negotiable

CABLE			
Prime	$20,000	$35,000	Negotiable
Access	10,000	15,000	Negotiable

NEW ZEALAND (AUCKLAND)

Radio and television are both publicly and privately owned in New Zealand. There are two VHF commercial government channels, one private commercial VHF, and two private UHF channels. There are three subscriber channels: CNN, ESPN, and HBO. Radio and television accept direct marketing commercials. Radio prices include commercials on 76 stations. The TV rate is for one spot on the leading channel.

RADIO	60	120	INFOMERCIALS
Prime	$4,500	$6,800	N.A.
Access	3,200	4,800	N.A.

TV			
Prime	$11,000	$17,200	N.A.
Access	880	1,500	$16,000

PARAGUAY (ASUNCION)

Radio, television, and cable stations are all privately owned. As of July 1, 1993, there were no direct marketers using any broadcast media, although they will accept all lengths of commercials, including infomercials.

RADIO	60	120	INFOMERCIALS
Prime	$11.50	$22.90	$747
Access	6.80	13.70	747
Fringe	6.80	13.70	747

TV			
Prime	$2,069	$1,207	N.A.
Access	1,207	2,414	N.A.
Fringe	233	465	N.A.

CABLE			
Prime	$260	$520	$3,905
Access	98	195	1,464

SOUTH AFRICA (JOHANNESBURG)

Radio and TV stations are both government and privately owned. There is one independent TV station, one government-owned TV station, one independent radio station, and 23 government-owned radio stations. As of July 1, 1993, cable is available only via encoded pay TV. Both radio and TV accept direct marketing commercials. M-NET is a station-emanated encoded signal that has a great penetration level and has been highly effective for direct marketers.

RADIO	60	120	INFOMERCIALS
Prime	$295	$591	N.A.
Fringe	62	125	N.A.

TV			
Prime	$11,179	$22,358	N.A.
Fringe	7,447	14,895	N.A.

M-NET (Pay TV)[2]			
Prime	$6,622	$13,243	N.A.
Fringe	3,310	6,622	N.A.

SPAIN (BARCELONA)

Radio and TV stations are both government and privately owned. As of July 1, 1993, there is no cable in Spain. There are presently direct marketing commercials on all media, with a maximum of 3 minutes of commercial time. Spain has developed an interactive TV system that is rapidly expanding. The costs quoted are for network radio and an average price for the three TV networks.

RADIO	60	120	180
Prime	$5,400		$5,520
Access	4,400		5,520
Fringe	3,000		5,520

TV			
Prime	$129,000	$280,000	$416,000
Access	43,000	62,400	93,600
Fringe	16,000	35,000	43,000

TAIWAN (TAIPEI)

Radio, TV, and cable stations are all government owned in Taiwan. All media accept direct marketing commercials. Radio and television limit the time segments to 120 seconds, while cable accepts infomercials.

RADIO	60	120	INFOMERCIALS
Prime	$1,230	$2,460	N.A.
Fringe	680	1,360	

TV			
Prime	$6,900	$13,800	N.A.
Fringe	2,770	5,540	

CABLE			
All time	Negotiable	Negotiable	Negotiable

THAILAND (BANGKOK)

Radio is both government and privately owned. Television is government owned, as is cable. As of July 1, 1993, there are no direct marketers using broadcast in Thailand, although they allow 120-second commercials on television and sponsorship of 30-minute shows on both television and cable. The contents of the 30-minute sponsored shows have not been defined.

RADIO	60	120	30-min. sponsorship
Prime	$120	N.A.	$3,200
Fringe	64	N.A.	2,400

TV	60	120	30-min. sponsorship
Prime	$5,540	$11,080	N.A.
Fringe	3,160	6,320	N.A.

CABLE	60	120	30-min. sponsorship
Prime	N.A.	N.A.	$600
Fringe	N.A.	N.A.	480

UNITED KINGDOM

London, England

Radio, TV, and cable commercial stations are all privately owned. Cable is defined as comprising both cable and satellite channels. Costs for all media are for one transmission across the entire United Kingdom.

RADIO	60	120	INFOMERCIAL 3.5 min.
Prime	$7,500	$15,000	$17,250
Access	4,500	9,000	10,350
Fringe	1,500	3,000	3,450

TV	60	120	INFOMERCIAL 3.5 min.
Prime	$172,953	$345,906	N.A.
Access	69,624	139,248	N.A.
Fringe	18,531	37,072	N.A.

CABLE			
Prime	$3,750	$7,500	N.A.
Access	2,550	5,100	N.A.
Fringe	1,050	2,100	N.A.

England (London Only)

RADIO	60	120	INFOMERCIALS
Prime	$1,500	$3,000	N.A.
Fringe	1,000	2,000	N.A.

TV			
Prime	$96,000	$192,000	N.A.
Fringe	6,000	12,000	N.A.

CABLE (European)			
Prime	$4,000	$8,000	N.A.
Fringe	500	1,000	N.A.

URUGUAY (MONTEVIDEO)

Radio and TV stations in Uruguay are both privately and government owned. As of July 1, 1993, cable does not exist. Direct marketers are using television only, with 120-second limitations on time. There are no infomercials using broadcast.

RADIO	60	120
Prime	$77	$155
Access	66	132

TV		
Prime	$1,253	$2,505
Access	660	1,320

VENEZUELA (CARACAS)

Radio and television are both government and privately owned. Cable is privately owned. As of July 1, 1993, there were no direct marketers using broadcast, although all media accept 120-second commercials. There are also no designated time segments in any media.

RADIO	60	120
All time	$35	$70

TV		
All time	$5,000	$10,000

CABLE		
All time	$240	$480

---

1. In quoting infomercial rates, the stations quoting rates did not seem to understand the meaning of the request.
2. Offers 60 percent off quoted rates to direct marketers on an ROS or unsold inventory basis.

Index